Escape from Canada!

ESCAPE FROM CANADA!

The Untold Story of German POWs in Canada 1939-1945

JOHN MELADY

Macmillan of Canada
A Division of Gage Publishing Limited
Toronto, Ontario

Canadian Cataloguing in Publication Data

Melady, John.
    Escape from Canada!

Bibliography: p.
ISBN 0-7715-9537-9

1. World War, 1939-1945 — Prisoners and prisons, Canadian.
2. Prisoners of war — Germany.   3. Prisoners of war — Canada.   I. Title.

D805.C2M45   940.54′72′71   C81-094890-7

Design: Maher & Murtagh

Macmillan of Canada
A Division of Gage Publishing Limited

Printed in Canada

Contents

Acknowledgements

Photograph of Franz von Werra from *The One That Got Away* by Kendal Burt and James Leasor is reproduced by kind permission of William Collins Sons & Co. Ltd.

Excerpts from *Deemed Suspect* © 1980, published by Methuen Publications, reprinted by permission of the author.

Excerpts from *Six War Years* by Barry Broadfoot © 1974, published by Doubleday Canada Ltd., reproduced by permission.

Excerpt from *The Faustball Tunnel* by John Hammond Moore © 1978, published by Random House Inc., reproduced with permission.

In memory of my brother John

KILLED NOVEMBER 27, 1980

Preface

Several years ago I was driving west along the Trans-Canada Highway in Northern Ontario. Not far from the town of Marathon, I pulled over to take a picture of the Lake Superior shoreline. A few yards from where I stood, a highway maintenance man was painting guardrail posts. After I put my camera away, he walked over and asked if I knew what I was photographing. I told him I was impressed with the view.

"I didn't think you knew," he muttered.

Then he went on to tell me that I had just taken a picture of what used to be a German prisoner-of-war camp. He also said that beside the highway a short distance from where we talked, Canadian guards once killed a couple of prisoners who had escaped. "The whole thing seemed to be hushed up at the time," he added.

That brief conversation sparked my curiosity and ultimately led to the decision to write this book. The decision was not made overnight, of course, but came after a great deal of letter-writing, travel in Canada and in Europe, and interviews with ex-POWs and their guards. It was only then that I realized that the stories I was being told were part of the history of this country — a part of Canada's past that relatively few people knew about. I felt that unless the stories were soon written down, they would be lost forever. Already, most of the men who guarded the camps were dead and the prisoners they once guarded were scattered across the world.

And both prisoners and guards had stories to tell.

Initially, most told me that the events of their war took place too long ago to be remembered. Little by little, however, they recalled more and more details of the time — until I was finally able to piece together a reasonably comprehensive account of what it was like to become a prisoner of war, what it was like to guard men who were your enemy, and, ultimately, what the experience of incarceration meant to those who endured it.

This book is that story.

As with any book of this scope, many individuals and groups gave of their time and expertise. In addition to those who are actually named in the text, I would like to thank those who assisted in other ways. These include: Dick Allan, Jerry Anglin, Bill Barnicke, Hildegard Becker, Bob Blakey, Barry Broadfoot, Philip Chaplin, Jack Chapple, C. L. Carbert, Ruth Fenaughty, Cy Gary, Gordon Gayford, Doug Gibson, G. P. de T. Glazebrook, John Grenville, Mary Hoskin, Roy Ingram, John Kelly, John Koegler, Bill Lesniak, Bill Mathieson, John Muller, Stan Obodiac, Dieter Rolf, Jack Sisson, Lt.-Col. E. M. Watts, and Clayton Wise.

In addition, my sincere thanks to Anne Holloway for her editing skills, Esther Parry for her typing, and my wife Mary for her patience.

John Melady
June, 1981

ONE

Capture

The road to Caen is quiet now. The hedgerows are lush green; the wheat and barley fields stretch golden to the horizon. Summer in northwest France is peaceful, save for the hum of farm machinery and the whine of tires on blacktop. To the visitor, this land called Normandy is undoubtedly beautiful: cliffs of chalk like Dover; rolling farmland like Ontario or Iowa; ancient towns like those in Ireland or Italy.

Arrow-straight rows of trees complement the orderly landscape. The villages that dot the plain are just as tidy. Yet their names — Argentan, Nécy, Falaise and the others — remind us of something else, of battles now buried forever in our war-shattered past. These were the places where armies clashed and brave men died in that summer so long ago.

And today, though the road is quiet — quiet all the way to Caen and the Channel — one wonders what it must have been like that summer in 1944.

"It was noise, dust, sweat and the smell of death," recalls Howard McDonald. "I was with the Fifteenth Field Artillery of the Canadian Fourth Division, and it was the first time that I ever felt sorry for Jerry. We laid down a barrage one night that I'll never forget. It scared the hell out of me, and I was *behind* the guns. I don't know how anyone in front of us survived. You can only find so much cover.

"The next day we advanced in that goddamned heat. Dead horses and cattle were all over the place. So were dead Germans

— lots of them, bloated and stinking. Flies buzzed around their rotting flesh.

"Someone beside me stumbled over a body behind a hedgerow. A wallet lay nearby. I remember a photo in it of a blonde woman and a pretty little girl, about three. Her German father had had his throat torn out and I cried. We were winning and I cried. I was glad the little girl would never know what her father looked like as he lay there."

At about the same time, in the heat and noise and surrounded by tangible death, German Red Cross Corporal Leo Hoecker ran and ran and ran. He carried one man to the rear as the next screamed at the front. There was little time for tears.

"We were so busy," he says now. "And I was so scared. We all were. Terribly scared. We knew it was only a matter of time. Many of my friends had been hit. I found myself running almost blindly. The earth was ripped up by every shell that came in. There were explosions and curses and then everything would be quiet for a time. But the Canadians and British were right opposite us and coming closer. Their shooting became more accurate, so finally we just dug in.

"A small woods was a few metres to the right. Somebody thought we had a chance in it but there wasn't time. A few minutes and the trees were blown away. Twenty-one of us saw that happen. The little woods just disappeared.

"Then soldiers were running. The next thing I knew, the line was *behind* us. The battle had passed, and in the Canadian advance we were not even seen. We all wondered what in hell to do next. That's when the war ended for me.

"The man who ordered me to stand sounded Scottish. I don't know. Maybe he wasn't. At any rate, he noticed that I was Red Cross and probably assumed I was harmless. Then he saw my gun. That's when I thought I was a dead man.

"For two years I had been on the eastern front. We always wore a gun there because everyone knew stories of Russian prisons. Most of us intended to shoot ourselves rather than be captured and sent to Leningrad or somewhere. So when they sent me to Normandy, I kept the gun though I'd never used it.

"This officer grabbed my rifle and saw that it was empty. He even smelled the barrel. Because it was clean, I'm alive today.

"Then they lined us up and sent us to the rear."

Howard McDonald described the scene: "By this time we were getting a bit more experience. We moved forward and set our guns. After a while we moved on a bit farther. Several times German prisoners walked down the same road toward us, asking where they were to go. We just waved them in the general direction we had come from. I remember one guy grinning as though he'd just won a million bucks. His hands were up over his helmet all right, but they were clasped together like a prizefighter who's just been declared champ. I guess he didn't mind leaving the front."

"I know we walked a long way," Leo Hoecker remembers. "Finally we got to a wire cage somewhere. They kept us there for four weeks and then took us to England. A few weeks later I was in a place in Canada called Medicine Hat."

When he was fifteen, George Fehn went away to sea. It was 1935, and to the youngster from northern Germany, determined to make the merchant navy a career, fifteen was not too young. In those days you had to first spend two years on a sailing ship anyway, so the younger you could get this training over with, the better. Fehn spent these years on a coastal craft that was actually half motor, half sail. "We still had the storms, the seasickness, the loneliness, though," he recalls, "but I was at least started on the life I wanted."

Finally, a few weeks after his seventeenth birthday, he *really* started to have a look at the world. As the rawest recruit on a large merchant vessel, Fehn remembers the trip southward, then Gibraltar, the coastline of North Africa and the culture shock of Port Said, Ismailia and Suez, China and Japan. To a boy his age, this was the best of jobs. In all, the trip encompassed half a world and lasted four months.

Other journeys followed: New York, Panama and the California littoral. Back to the Orient. Then in May of 1939, he was on board the cargo ship *Weser* en route to San Francisco with, among other things, all the worldly possessions of Jews who had fled the barbarism of Hitler's regime.

"Of course, I didn't know it at the time," Fehn reminisces now, "but it would be almost eight years before I would see Germany again. We had just cleared the Panama Canal when war broke out back home. We were expecting war, of course, but the news was still a shock when it came.

"We were ordered to go to a neutral port, pending further directives. We tied up in Punta Arenas in Costa Rica with the intention of being there a few days or a week at most. Five months later we hadn't moved, but by this time we had unloaded the freight onto smaller vessels, which took it on up to San Francisco.

"I can still remember that cargo. There was everything you'd ever imagine. Huge packing cases, as large or larger than the big shipping containers around today. Personal items, books, china, glass and even an entire set of furnishings for a dentist's office — chair, drills, surgical equipment, the works."

At almost ten thousand tonnes, the *Weser* was small in the supertanker world of today. Nevertheless, she was too valuable a commodity to leave tied up in a remote Latin American backwater when almost anything that would float was involved in the Axis war effort.

Another signal came through. This time the ship was ordered to proceed northward along the Central American coast to the Mexican port of Manzanillo. The *Weser* had now been designated as a supply ship for German submarines in the Pacific.

"We got to Manzanillo okay," says Fehn. "But that's as far as we got. We took on enough oil and supplies to last for weeks but went nowhere. We were tied up there for another half a year. The weather was good and the beaches and scenery out of this world, but the boredom drove us crazy. We read everything we could find, sunbathed until we were black, and walked that beach so many times we knew every grain of sand."

Mexico was still friendly with Germany, but there were Allied spies in the town who observed every movement in or out of the harbour. They had a short-wave transmission tower on a promontory on the coast, so if any ship in the vicinity moved, its progress could be monitored and reported. Eventually the *Weser* decided to make a run for it. Anything was better than the inactivity.

"Departure time was set for five minutes after midnight," Fehn continued. "There was no moon and low cloud blotted out the stars. You could sense the tension in everyone on board. We cast off without a sound. Nobody even coughed. I could hear my heart beating.

"A couple of minutes later, I had just climbed up the mast with the short-wave antenna when the most godawful hulla-balloo broke out. For a minute I thought we were tangled up in a fisherman's net that was somehow attached to lights. Everything lit up bright as day. The trouble was, we were so blinded by the lights, we couldn't see a damned thing.

"Then there's this booming loudspeaker ordering us to stop

our engines. Hell, we had hardly got them started. We were still well within the two-mile limit — far inside the limit.

"We stopped. Another ship pulled alongside, trained guns on us, and boarded us. The whole thing happened so fast it was unbelievable. They had been ready for us all along, so we never really had a chance. They were very business-like, so we didn't do much arguing."

The ship that made the seizure was a Canadian armed merchant vessel called the *Prince Robert*. She was old and slow, but the *Weser* learned this too late. Fehn and a skeleton crew were left on board the German ship, which was escorted to Victoria, British Columbia. By December 1940, the *Weser* crew were singing Christmas songs as they boarded the train that took them to their first prisoner-of-war enclosure at Seebe, Alberta. Snow was falling.

In the late 1930s, at the same time Winston Churchill's warnings regarding the resurgence of Germany were being ignored in the British House of Commons, Hitler Youth member Hans Peter Krug was learning to fly. The first aircraft he flew were gliders. However, by 1938 the planes had motors, and the man who flew them was one of many highly trained pilots in the German Luftwaffe.

"I *joined* the air force," he recalls now. "I was not drafted. I did all my basic on smaller aircraft and then after a year and a half switched to larger ones. A lot of the flying was near Berlin, although we were based in several places.

"I was young and flying was exciting. We lived well and we liked the glamour. I still love to fly. There is a certain freedom in it that you can't find anywhere else. We all liked the uniform, and most of us never got tired of the girls who flocked around because of who we were."

Krug was an officer before the war started. Hermann Goering himself not only signed the young man's commission certificate, but shook Krug's hand and presented the paper in person.

"We were his special charges, I suppose," says Krug in recalling the ceremony, "and for this reason I guess he wanted to show his interest in us. I was not overawed by him, though. He was still a human being just like the rest of us. He wasn't a god. Of course, before he became hooked on drugs, Goering was a damned good pilot. We knew that."

Soon the months and years of training were being put to use.

The Battle of Britain started and in no time Krug had flown a dozen missions over England, all as aircraft commander.

Wednesday, August 28, 1940, was a sunny day in Western Europe. The clouds of summer were high and cumulous as Krug taxied the Dornier 17 to the end of the strip for his thirteenth mission. Though neither he nor the three crew members with him were especially superstitious, they looked upon this trip as the one that would bring them luck.

The first leg of the flight was uneventful. Then as the coast of France disappeared behind them, puffs of black smoke dotted the skyline ahead. They were over the Thames when the flak hit.

"At first I thought we had a chance," says Krug. "I swung the ship around and figured I could get her back to France. Luckily, there was no fire. Then one of the men noticed a Spitfire and two Hurricanes on our tail. I dropped down and tried to roll to one side, but I couldn't manoeuvre very quickly."

Within seconds it was all over. The British planes went after the stricken Dornier and finished it off.

"I was hit myself," remembers Krug, "but at least I was conscious. The other guys were also injured, but we stayed in our seats, hoping like hell that the fuel would not go up. Somehow, I managed to get her down. We hit the water hard and were thrown around a bit. I remember that the sea was warm, twenty degrees or so, I suppose. As soon as we stopped we all piled out on the wings before she sank. There was a film of oil over everything and we slithered around, trying to keep our footing. Somehow we held on.

"In no time at all a small motorboat was beside us. They helped us get on board and treated us like gentlemen. At that time, the war was fought fairly."

The English brought their charges on shore at Margate and took them for immediate medical attention. Then, after their release from hospital, Krug and his crew began their enforced sojourn behind barbed wire.

Peter Krug was not the only man shot down over England that week in 1940. Three days later fighter pilot Horst Liebeck met the same fate. With more or less the same training behind him as Krug — gliders, small trainers and finally Messerschmitts — Liebeck was as enamoured of the air force as Krug had ever been.

"There was a lot of fun in it then. We were young and thought we were terribly important. The uniform was part of the image. It was also a form of escape, I suppose," says Liebeck. "Still, it was better than sitting in a foxhole with water in your boots. That didn't particularly appeal to me.

"We flew so many missions I started to lose track of the number. Today I have no recollection of some of them, but everyone recalls his last."

That day the twenty-year-old flyer had completed his fourth sortie within a few hours, when he had a premonition of danger. He grabbed a few minutes as his ME-109 was being refuelled, packed all his belongings, and wrote a quick note to his parents. Then he found someone who would mail the letter and dispose of the gear, should the need arise.

He was flying in those days with Adolf Galland, the great German ace. They were using a second-rate strip on the Cotentin peninsula but prided themselves in their ability to jump into their planes and get in the air and up to the Channel within half an hour. The routine was gruelling, tough on both men and equipment. Nevertheless, they flew.

"I was sitting in the runway line-up, starting my run-up, when I noticed that my cockpit cover wouldn't close. I pulled, pushed and smashed at the damned thing with my fist. It would only come so far. That's when I was sure. I remember saying to myself: 'That's it. I'll never come back.'

"We took off okay, and climbed to about nine thousand metres, using oxygen. We crossed the Channel and headed north in the general direction of London. The bombers we escorted were well below. At first nothing happened. Pretty soon, though, we were busy."

At first, Liebeck held his own with a single Spitfire directly in front of him. But as he manoeuvred himself for a good shot at it, a second British fighter came in from behind. As the bullets hit, the ME-109 vibrated but plodded on.

Then, without warning, glycol started streaming from the engine. The motor sputtered for a minute or so and finally seized completely. The next second it caught fire. Flames engulfed the ship as acrid smoke poured into the cockpit. The plane shuddered wildly and lost altitude.

Liebeck remembers the front of his jacket burning, the flames searing his face and cutting off his vision. Then he passed out and the plane blew up.

"The explosion saved my life, no doubt about it," Liebeck says now. "I don't remember much of what happened. I fell over and

over and over, and the cold air did two things: it put out the fire
and it brought me around. The next thing I knew, my chute was
open and I was hanging there. I wasn't really sure if I was alive
or dead. My face was raw, and when I touched the side of my
jaw, burnt flesh came away on my glove. I almost vomited.

"Two Spitfires followed me quite a way down. They never shot
at me, just saluted and flew away. I was damned lucky, but at that
point didn't really care too much what happened to me. The pain
was too terrible."

Liebeck came down a short distance from a British ambulance
camp. Because he was picked up as soon as he fell and given
treatment for second- and third-degree facial burns, he survived
his ordeal. He was blind for three months because of the fumes
from the burning lead-based gasoline.

Following his recovery, Liebeck was placed in a British POW
camp for a short time. Then he was sent to Canada — for a
long time.

It was during a bitter midnight storm that they sailed out of the
harbour at Bremerhaven. A gale blew from the southwest, and
within hours the German ships bound for the ice-fringed Norwegian
port of Narvik had to fight to stay in formation. With each passing
minute, the weather worsened. Mountains of water threw the craft
around, heaving the sterns and leaving their screws whining in
the air. Then the next wave would crash across the bow, causing
each vessel to wallow in the trough between the combers.

Below decks, where they had been ordered to stay, landlubbing
soldiers retched and cursed their fate. When they tried to lie down,
they were tossed around like dice in a cup. When they stood, they
lost their balance and fell slithering across vomit-sloshed steel.
Hour after hour without respite. Several men suffered broken
bones after being smashed against bulkheads. The heat, confinement and stench were unbearable. A few, fearing they would die
where they were, disobeyed orders and forced their way out into
the open air. Almost all were immediately washed overboard. Ten
men drowned that wild night.

In this way, two thousand German mountain troops made that
dreadful journey to Narvik in early April 1940. One of them was
Max Schoellnhammer.

"I had always loved the mountains, so when I went into the army
I was able to do some training on skis. As it turned out, I never
had much chance to use the training, though," Schoellnhammer
says now.

"When we left Bremerhaven on April 6, we had no idea where we were going. Hell, many of the men had never been near a large river, let alone the ocean. A lot had never seen a ship. We all thought the trip would be a great adventure!

"They packed us below decks and ordered us to stay there. A lot of top-secret stuff or something. When we left Germany we were really excited. The whole thing was so new to us."

The flotilla steamed steadily past Stavanger, Bergen and Trondheim toward the Arctic Circle. Finally, in the predawn darkness of April 9, ten destroyers arrived at Narvik. Their purpose was to secure a winter port for iron ore from Sweden.

The long, deep, forked fiord that leads inland toward the town was ice-free, but in the grey bleakness of a spring storm, the dividing line between water and sky was scarcely visible. A metre of snow covered the land right down to the water's edge. Each time the snow stopped falling, sheets of fog drifted across the fiord, obscuring alternately the land and the other ships.

Norwegian resistance to the German landings was short-lived. Brief skirmishes took place but were soon quelled. Two old Norwegian warships put up a measure of defence, but both were sunk.

As they swept inland, the Germans overran the town and commandeered all of its facilities. The local post office, the police station and assorted municipal buildings soon fell. A hospital on the shore was taken in the early stages of the invasion; later, German wounded were placed in it. One of these was Schoellnhammer, who had sustained a serious leg wound.

Two great battles were fought in the Narvik fiord between the Germans, who had taken the port, and the British, who were trying to win it back. Following the second round, the British held the town and the German troops retreated inland — those who *could* retreat, that is. Max Schoellnhammer was still lying in his hospital bed when he became a prisoner of war. He had no chance to run.

By the time he became a prisoner of war, Unteroffizier Walter Woehr had been in the German army and out of it again. He had been drafted in 1936, had served his two years and had returned to civilian life. With the outbreak of the Second World War, he had found himself back in uniform. He had fought on the snows of Russia and on the sands of Africa. He had been transferred often, half frozen twice and shot once. To this day he bears the scars of the bullets.

In the early winter of 1943, he was part of General Erwin Rommel's army in North Africa. That army was surrounded but still weeks away from capitulation. In February they had pushed the U.S. Second Corps to the Kasserine Pass and beyond. Though the advance was short-lived, Rommel lashed out again, this time at Mareth on the Gulf of Gabés. All of his remaining tanks were used here, even the new Mark VIs. Yet the results were not what Rommel had hoped. In all, he lost fifty-two tanks at the hands of the well-equipped and experienced U.S. Eighth Army. The Germans had to withdraw.

By now Walter Woehr and the thousands like him who did the actual footslogging knew the seriousness of the situation. Their leader certainly knew. Rommel flew to Berlin to confer with Hitler and to propose that all of the Axis forces should be withdrawn from North Africa. If not, he reasoned, thousands of young Germans would die without cause. Hitler exploded in fury, called his general a coward, and ordered him to remain in Germany.

With the Desert Fox gone, General von Arnim took command. His tenure was not a happy one. Despite days of bitter and bloody fighting, the Allied advance was determined. By the end of March, the Germans were in full retreat.

Unteroffizier Woehr remembers being pushed northward in an ever-diminishing area. The Axis forces were in the predicament of a man who paints himself into the corner of a room, as they gradually lost their toehold in Africa.

"We were surrounded, of course, and we were running out of food," Woehr recalls now. "We were also homesick, disoriented and terribly tired. Then, when things looked completely hopeless, our commander came and talked to us. He asked us who we wanted to surrender to, the Americans, the British, or the French. We talked about it and decided on the British. Almost everyone agreed. We thought that we would be treated fairest by them. I surrendered at Tunis on May 5, 1943."

A week later the war ended in North Africa with the surrender of thousands of Germans and Italians, who had been driven out onto Cape Bon peninsula, a promontory jutting into the Mediterranean a hundred and fifty kilometres southwest of Sicily.

The hordes of new prisoners of war were corralled into large enclosures in Bizerte and Tunis. These first stockades were rather makeshift affairs, because the Allies had neither the time nor the facilities to construct anything resembling the prisoner-of-war camps in which these men would later be housed. Basically, these first compounds were little more than large fenced tracts of land, exposed to the flies and to the full glare of the Mediterranean sun. They were not pleasant places.

Walter Woehr remained at Tunis for a few weeks before they transferred him to Algiers. Later he spent four and a half months in Oldham, England, before coming to Canada. He was twenty-nine years old.

In December 1940, soon after he finished his basic military training, Horst Braun joined the crew of submarine U-11 in the Baltic. This small, rather ancient vessel was a training ship, but to Braun it was still a submarine, and he was thrilled to be aboard it.

As a wireless operator, he felt he had a greater understanding of what the ship did and where it went than most of the crew. He knew, for instance, that data of ship performance, weather and so forth collated by U-11 were sent to the Atlantic to be used by other, larger U-boats that actually engaged the enemy. Cruising up and down the Baltic might have been far out of torpedo range, but to Braun, the job was still important. Then in October 1941, U-11 made a brief trip westward, north along the Jutland peninsula and into the Oslo fiord in Norway.

"While we were there," Braun recalls, "a much larger U-boat pulled alongside. The radio man was ill and I was told to transfer to the other ship. The order came so quickly, I barely had time to grab my kit."

The new fifty-two-man submarine was larger, faster and more appealing to him than U-11. As well, the prospect of danger, probable enemy engagement and even further travel appealed to him. He welcomed the transfer.

U-434 departed Oslo a day or so later, sailed out into the North Sea, passed Scotland, and prowled the shipping lines west of Ireland toward North America. Insofar as enemy contact was concerned, the trip was uneventful. To Braun, the highlight of the voyage was something totally unexpected, but something he now says he will never forget.

"I saw Canada for the first time," he recalls. "We had not had much excitement on the crossing, so we decided to sail through Cabot Strait into the Gulf of St. Lawrence. Somewhere near Gaspé, I looked through the periscope and saw the land that today I call home. But at that time I never dreamed I would one day live in this country. About all I can remember is the coastline, a lot of rocks and trees on the highlands above the water. I am not sure of the exact spot.

"Then we made our way back across the Atlantic for more

supplies. We went into the port of Vigo, Spain — underwater, of course, because British and American destroyers were patrolling the coast. There was a large supply ship there, and I remember going aboard her for my first shower in about six weeks. Today, that shower is almost as memorable as my first look at Canada. Then, as soon as we had taken on supplies, we submerged and left port at night. That was exciting because we were not sure we could get out."

Three days later they found the enemy.

"On December 18 we were engaged in a battle with one American and three British destroyers. Our captain thought we had a pretty good chance of getting one before we had to run. We were just below the surface but the skipper was using the horizontal periscope rather than the vertical one. That was our downfall. There was a plane up above us, but we didn't realize it.

"We turned toward one of the ships and fired our first torpedo. I'll never forget that. It was my job to do the timing so we'd know if we had hit anything or not. When we fired, I checked my watch. At fifty-four seconds we thought we had scored a hit. Everybody started to cheer — but not for long.

"In fact, the detonation we felt was a bomb hitting us. The plane up above had seen us and had dropped three bombs. One of them landed up ahead, one behind, and the third hit us dead on. It destroyed all our oxygen supplies and blew a hole in the top. We started to sink.

"We went down and down and down. The engineers tried to do everything they could, but we just dropped farther. Everyone became quiet, listening. The last recorded depth reading I was given was 307 metres, or close to a thousand feet underwater. That was unheard of at that time. Then we were standing in water to our knees and the boat started to list. We grabbed supports and watched the gauges. Water sloshed over everything. I never thought we would get out of there. The air was so foul we could hardly breathe, and the lights got dimmer and dimmer. Acid fumes filled the place. A lot of us prayed.

"Then somehow, even though the batteries were actually under water, she started to come up — but very slowly. It seemed an hour until we surfaced. When we did, there was a mad scramble overboard. Guys were laughing, crying, shouting all at the same time. I don't think we were in the water for a minute when the sub went straight back down. Every one of us got out, though, but even then, the suction caused by the ship's sinking almost dragged us under.

"One of the British destroyers pulled over to us and took us on board. We were pretty scared and really miserable. Though they treated us well, I was now a prisoner of war. Still, I was alive. . . ."

TWO

Arrival in Canada

For the most part, prisoner-of-war compounds are not pleasant places. Even when they are well staffed, reasonably comfortable and miles from the war zone, they are — essentially and always — prisons. They restrict freedom. They prevent the inhabitant from coming and going as he wishes, from acting according to his own free will, and from enjoying normal relationships with human beings of both sexes. Unless faced with the threat of imminent bodily harm or death, few men voluntarily become prisoners of war. However grim the situation on a battlefield may be, it is almost always preferable to life in an enemy stockade. During the Second World War, this fact was one of the first and harshest realities encountered by captured members of most armed forces. It was certainly true for German POWs in North Africa.

The heat, primitive sanitation, lack of food and severe overcrowding of North African camps made incarceration barely endurable. Most of those who were herded into cages in places like Alexandria, Tunis and Bizerte still recall the experience with loathing. Boredom, filth, flies and the stench of sweat and excrement were all part of the memory. In Alexandria, two doctors were given the impossible task of ministering to the medical needs of thousands of fellow prisoners. The two did their best but fought a losing battle.

Fortunately, conditions elsewhere were, if not ideal, immeasurably better. This was particularly true in England, where a great number of POWs who later were brought to Canada began their imprisonment. Those who had been in North African camps found the English camps such an improvement that they later admitted to having been overly enthusiastic about how humane prisons in England were. Others spent periods of incarceration in local jails, interrogation centres and transit camps. In jail, the POWs were forced to live on minimum rations and sleep on straw mattresses like common criminals — an association they immediately and rightfully disdained. Nevertheless, an English jail was a world away from the stinking cages of Africa.

In general, the interrogation centres varied more in their amenities than the local jails or the transit camps. While all jails had much in common and the transit camps had a certain fluid, cosmopolitan element, the interrogation centres were different from place to place, as were the experiences of the men in them.

Many officers taken prisoner in the early stages of the war spent a few weeks or more in perhaps the best-known prison in the western world, the Tower of London. Here, in the same infamous confines where Anne Boleyn, Lady Jane Grey and Robert Devereux languished and died, twenty-year-old military men from a foreign land were counted, questioned and contained, while their brothers in arms across the Channel tried to destroy this landmark and all it represented. Germans who were held there watched the skies and hoped the waves of Heinkels and Dorniers over London would drop their bombs somewhere else. "When I was there," one prisoner told the author years later, "I really feared the sight of our planes overhead."

Anyone visiting the Tower today comes face to face with the artifacts of history. From Traitors' Gate to the ruins of the old Roman wall, the place tells the story of ages past. Unfortunately, the casual tourist is shown the cell where William Howard was held, but not the area where Rudolf Hess spent his time. He sees where Elizabeth I walked, but not where the captured cream of Hitler's Luftwaffe marched. Unless asked about the POWs who were in the Tower, the Yeomen Warder guides prefer to talk of earlier, and perhaps, for them, more romantic times. Even the official Tower guidebook seems to play down the prisoner-of-war episode. While everything from black ravens to wall etchings is described in detail, the more recent and surely more interesting POW inhabitants merit scarcely a line. And that is too bad because the men themselves and their memories are worth recalling.

Gerhard Rickertsen and Siegfried Bruse are two of the few men alive who can boast of having been tenants of the Tower of London. While neither was there for long, both mention their time there with a tinge of what might be called pride. Bruse was a twenty-two-year-old officer aboard U-35 when his ship was depth-charged by two destroyers in the North Atlantic. That was another experience he would never forget: the dull thud of explosives against the hull. The sub's massive death shudder, followed by the agonizingly slow rise to the surface. The mad scramble overboard into the slimy, choppy and terribly cold water. Finally, mercifully, the rescue by the enemy and the journey to the Tower.

Gerhard Rickertsen had been a commercial pilot before the war; with the outbreak of hostilities, he found himself in the Luftwaffe. On November 22, 1939, he was a commander of a long-range reconnaissance plane that was taking pictures of ship movements from the south of England. On that Wednesday, he had completed the assigned photo run and decided to take some pictures of the barrage balloons over London on the return flight home. British fighters saw him and made the hit. After drifting on a rubber raft in the Channel for several hours, he was taken ashore and sent to the Tower for interrogation.

Both men were rather unnerved by the glaring lights, disembodied voices, inconsistent scheduling and wily games of the inquisitors. However, they prided themselves that they withstood the ordeal and said little. Inconsequential memories come back even today: "There were things about life in the Tower that were either annoying or amusing, depending on your point of view," says Rickertsen. "I was air force, and I guess we were held to be on some kind of plane above the ordinary man. For example, Luftwaffe guys were served their meals on china plates. The plates for the other services were made of tin. That always seemed rather comical to me."

The great German U-boat commander Otto Kretschmer, who would later spend many months in Canadian camps, was treated with unusual deference after his U-99 had been sunk. Naturally enough, this man, who was responsible for the loss of three hundred thousand tonnes of Allied shipping, was not only somewhat of a curiosity to his captors, but was also looked upon as a very valuable source of information about his successful U-boat tactics. Though the crew of U-99 were taken ashore at Liverpool, Kretschmer would not spend long there. Within hours of his arrival, he was rushed by train to London for questioning. It was here that his interrogation was, to say the least, rather unique. Captain (later Admiral) George Creasy, British director of anti-submarine warfare, not only participated in the interrogation, but even did some of it in his own home. The U-boat ace was taken to Creasy's flat in Buckingham Gate, and while Mrs. Creasy remained in an adjoining bedroom, the two enemies drank port and talked about the war. Years later, Creasy recalled that afternoon.

> I saw him because I was anxious to judge for myself what manner of man a successful U-boat captain might be; to see for myself, if I could, the state of his nerves; to measure his judgment; gauge his reactions to his seniors and to his juniors, the expected and the unexpected. In simple words, to "size him up."
>
> It may be of interest to record the impression he made on me. I saw a young and obviously self-confident naval commander who bore himself, in the difficult conditions of recent captivity, with self-respect, modesty and courtesy. His record stamped him as brave and quick-witted; his appearance and manners were those of an officer and a gentleman. When he left me I sincerely hoped that there were not too many like him.[1]

Shortly after U-434 was destroyed, radio operator Horst Braun was taken to Gibraltar for two weeks of questioning. There, in a prison high on the Rock, he was subjected to countless queries about his former duties. This was in December 1941. Later that winter he was lodged in a huge London mansion off Hyde Park. "I still remember the place," he says now. "There were dozens of rooms, and each accommodated one or two POWs. We were interrogated much more severely there than in any previous camp. Certain methods were used that we considered at the time to be unethical. They got us up at two in the morning and placed us in a dark room. Then a powerful searchlight came on, and we sat right in front of it. Because of the brightness, we were not able to see behind the light where a voice or voices questioned us. The whole psychological effect of this kind of thing was trying. Of course, as a radio operator, I had had access to our naval codes, so I can't really blame the British for wanting information along this line."

After his capture at Margate, Peter Krug was shuttled around to a number of camps in Britain. Eventually he arrived in the north of England, where he was locked up in an ancient mansion called Grizedale Hall. At any other time the beauty of the area, in

Wordsworth's Lake District near the shore of Lake Windermere, would have been appealing. However, sightseeing through barbed wire left a lot to be desired. The house itself was set on a hillside, and the prisoners who lived in the upper rooms were able to see the craggy peaks of the Cumbrian Mountains.

At this time, however, Krug and others with him were more interested in getting out of the place than admiring the landscape from inside. Escape was uppermost in the minds of many, but to none more than Krug and another flyer he met while there, Franz von Werra, a German aristocrat given to braggadocio whenever his own or his country's exploits needed embellishment. Nevertheless, the friendship prospered during the long hours of confinement and the endless discussions of escape techniques. Neither man was to consider his time in Grizedale Hall a waste.

In the spring of 1940, what historians have called the "Phony War" ended. Across Western Europe, the Blitzkrieg struck. Germany invaded Norway in April and the Low Countries in mid-May, and four weeks later German troops were marching into Paris. By June 23, the date the Franco-German armistice was signed in the railway carriage at Compiègne, fears that German troops might soon be moving up from the beaches at Southend, Folkestone and Brighton were very real in England. At the same time, in POW compounds throughout the island, highly trained and battle-toughened German soldiers, sailors and airmen were confident that these fears would indeed come true. When Germany invaded England, these prisoners expected to be released to join the ranks of the invaders. The British government was acutely aware of the problem, of course, and made agreements with Canada and other Commonwealth countries to accommodate these prisoners for the duration of hostilities.

The POWs were brought to North America by ship. They sailed from Liverpool, the Clyde, Southampton and elsewhere on a variety of ships: *Île de France, Queen Mary, Duchess of York* — and the *Arandora Star*. The latter, a fifteen-thousand-tonne former luxury cruise ship, steamed out of Liverpool on the first of July, 1940. By six the next morning, she was almost 160 kilometres west of Ireland, her sixteen hundred prisoners jammed together, some below, and others on deck behind strands of heavy barbed wire and two hundred armed guards. Because of her speed, she was unescorted. That was her undoing.

The torpedo fired from U-47 hit the British vessel on the

starboard side, penetrated her engine room and exploded. More than half the prisoners died instantly, drowned when the ship sank, or died of exposure before they could be hauled out of the sea. A man who was there described the ordeal:

On July 2 at six in the morning (most of us were still asleep) a hollow explosion was heard in the engine room. I tried to switch the light on — in vain. I thought we had run upon a mine. Cries, steps and running started in the corridors. I dressed scantily and went on with a lifebelt. I wanted to go to the lifeboats. The armed guard prevented me from doing so. I went to the other side to a small half-open deck. There many men were already busy throwing pieces of wood into the water. I could not see any officer nor any sailor; nobody could give any advice. Most of the rafts were left on board and were tied down with wire, which could not be loosened in the hurry without implements. Many could not believe that the ship was sinking. Some became hysterical. I saw lifeboats and wanted to go on deck again, where the boats were. Suddenly, two shots were fired. Later on I heard that internees were shot at; they had wanted to go to the lifeboats, which were reserved for English soldiers only. But as the soldiers were no seamen, they cut the ropes with an axe when the boat was only halfway down to the water and were drowned.

The Nazis went at once on deck in files of two under the leadership of Captain Burfend; they had access to the lifeboats. They had many seamen and brought down about seven lifeboats. Captain Burfend stayed on board (eight lifeboats were in the water altogether) and was drowned. I came to the upper deck; no lifeboats were left. Scenes of distress. A man hanged himself; a sixty-two-year-old Jew sat in despair on his suitcase and could not be persuaded to put on his lifebelt. The old and ill people in the decks below had no chance. Among them there was the seventy-five-year-old Julius Weiss, who had been in England for fifty years.

I advised two soldiers who were still standing guard with drawn bayonets to throw away their bayonets and spring into the water. They said they were not allowed to because they had not had an order, but I persuaded them. I did not see an officer, military officer or sailor, who would have helped us or the privates. As the boat keeled over I climbed down a rope ladder with a plank in my hand into the water. The decision to do so was very difficult for me. I swam away from the ship and saw it sink.

. . . It took thirty-five minutes from the explosion to the sinking of the ship. The water was full of oil; hundreds of planks and pieces of wood with barbed wire threatened us. The first hours in the Atlantic Ocean were dreadful. The water was terribly cold, with fog and slight rain. Cries, praying, shouts of "Mother!" by old and young in every language (Italian, German, English, Hebrew) depressed us terribly. Old people got heart attacks and died. Bodies swollen by water floated beside me.

After about three hours a coastal airplane sighted us. It cruised about for hours over our heads, as if it wanted to tell us that rescue was coming. We took fresh heart. After six and a half hours I sighted one of our lifeboats. I swam to it. An English sailor (first mate) was at the helm. I spoke to him in English, told him that I was quite exhausted, and asked him to take me into the boat.[2]

The next day, survivors were put ashore in Scotland to await another ship. Fortunately, other voyages were made without such disastrous results, although on the *Duchess of York*, a man was shot. Sixteen-year-old Karl Kruger, a civilian internee being transported to Canada, was on board. His description of the shooting is as follows:

The killing occurred not long after we left port. By then we had got used to the procedure that at dusk we had to go below deck. On this occasion, the interpreter, Captain Savage, was on the upper deck, above where I was standing. He got rather excited about getting everybody to go down below. One of the prisoners of war turned around and touched his temple with his finger, suggesting that the captain was an idiot. The next thing I knew was that the prisoner was lying dead on deck. I never found out what exactly happened. Probably one of the guards from above had shot him — clean through the temple. He was dead immediately. Someone said that the guard was going to shoot above everybody's head, and that the captain had pushed the rifle down. Whoever did it was either a very good shot, or it was an accident.

There was tremendous panic. Everybody rushed frantically down the gangways, which were very narrow. Captain Savage lost his head, and was standing at the top of the gangway with a machine gun. The prisoner of war was buried at sea with full military honours.[3]

A. E. "Tony" Kleimaker was one of those brought to Canada at this time. He had been shot down near the Frisian island of Texel while on a patrol over the Channel and had spent time in various camps, the last of which was also Grizedale Hall. Today the former Luftwaffe officer can still recall the trip to Canada.

"We were packed together," he says now. "They had barbed wire around the decks and the outside guards were armed. Nevertheless, we planned to take over the ship and if possible divert it to a United States port just before landing. But then the guards did an interesting thing.

"They started a rumour that German troops had actually landed in England and were advancing on London. Gradually, most of us came to believe the story, to the point that we called off our takeover plans because we felt that if England fell, it would be only a matter of time before the ship would be ours anyway. We felt that there was no point in risking lives needlessly. However, when we landed in Quebec City, I spoke to a guard and asked him how far the Germans had advanced in England. I still remember his answer: 'There are *no* German troops in England.' I had to tell the boys we had been fooled."

Most of the POWs who came to Canada were more closely guarded on board ship than they had been or would be on land. While the ratio of guards to prisoners was not significantly higher than on land, in the minds of the guards, the ever-present possibility of being overpowered was greater at sea.

In 1943, Canadian historian Reginald Roy did guard duty on one of these prison ships. His comments on the experience are both interesting and amusing:

We boarded the ship, which was carrying back at least seven hundred prisoners . . . Afrika Korps, Luftwaffe, merchant navy — you name it. They were a very well disciplined group, and the rank they held prior to being captured carried all the authority inside the prison cages. I suppose I was a bit surprised at their appearance. The propaganda posters had depicted the Germans as grim-visaged, square-jawed, nasty people but we found that they were very much like ourselves. Their organization impressed me. We would bring in great platters of food at mealtimes and they would have everything carved up, measured out and properly served in no time at all. As a warder I was inside the cage. They occupied one entire deck and any exit from that deck had barbed wire strung between the floor and ceiling to keep them in. We went in amongst them unarmed, naturally. On the other side of the barbed wire there were always two men, one of whom had a Bren gun.

When we reached Halifax we turned them over to the Veterans' group and away they went. They were *very* surprised to have reached Halifax at all as they had understood that the Atlantic was dominated by their U-boats.[4]

The same regard for the invincibility of the U-boat was common among the German troops. The Toronto *Globe and Mail* quoted other guards as saying that when the prison ships moved into open water, many of the POWs became visibly afraid. They were convinced that no Allied vessel would be able to cross the Atlantic without being torpedoed. The article also indicated that the guards seemed surprised at the *esprit de corps* displayed by the POWs. "Whatever else they may think of the German soldier," reported the *Globe*, "Canadians haven't been able to uncover any signs of wavering morale since they took over guarding . . . across the Atlantic in prisoner-of-war ships. With few exceptions, returning Canadian troops have discovered German prisoners . . . still convinced of their nation's invulnerability. Their individual capture, to them, is just another of war's vagaries."[5]

Most of the ships came to Halifax, with fewer arriving in Quebec City. In addition, some tied up in New York, where groups of prisoners entrained for Canada.

For the most part, disembarkation was a reasonably orderly process. Armed guards lined the dock as the POWs came ashore, and they were often jostled by bystanders eager for a glimpse of the German soldiers they had seen portrayed in propaganda as bloodthirsty, villainous Huns. The propaganda German was invariably a grotesque monster with blood dripping from the corners of his mouth, in one hand a gun, in the other a dead baby. Often he stood on a map of Western Europe, glaring lasciviously westward toward Britain and across the Atlantic to Canada. Three words — WHO IS NEXT? — let the reader know that as soon as the Nazis finished their unspeakable deeds in France or Holland, they would be raping the women of Rimouski, Brandon and Kamloops. No wonder curious people crowded the quays for each arrival!

The news media covered these landings, but were unable to report specific details that might have been of use to the enemy. At times these stories were censored to a point that we find laughable today. The name of the port, the name of the ship, the number of POWs and their final destination were rarely given.

Instead, the public was told such things as: "A large ship carrying several hundred prisoners of war docked recently at an Eastern Canadian port. The POWs were shipped to various locations across the country."

The Germans were satisfied with the way they were handled aboard ship. None of them expected or received luxury accommodation, regardless of rank. Yet every attempt was made to ensure that these voyages were carried out as efficiently and as correctly as possible. In this regard, a German colonel sent the following message to the officers who had been his guards: "I confirm that the treatment of the officers and NCO men during transport has been irreproachable. British officers leading the transport took care of granting requests submitted by the German Command. Food was sufficient and good. The quarters on the ship were satisfactory."[6]

Some tried to escape as they were taken from the ship. During one landing, two young air force fellows got away from their captors. Military, railroad and local police cordoned off the dock area and stopped all traffic moving inland. Freight cars, trucks and city buses were checked with particular care. By the time the two — wearing civilian overcoats with large circular patches sewn on the back to mark them as prisoners of war — had been apprehended, their escapade had taught the guards a lesson. Security was immediately tightened and ship-to-train transfers were slowed down.

Railroad security was also increased. Here, specific orders from Internment officials left little to chance. Three men were designated for guard duty in each coach — one to remain at either end and the third to move back and forth in order to watch for breaches in regulations. These men carried whistles and small leather billies. They were ordered never to fraternize with their charges.

Guards were warned not to tolerate *any* deviations from the norm. Any suspicious act, movement or conversation was to be looked into immediately. Even periods of unexplained silence were to be regarded with caution. Frequent counts of prisoners were required, particularly before and after stops were made. Counts were also mandatory immediately before and after the guard changed. During the night, the faces of all the prisoners were to be uncovered so that faces and not forms could be checked. Except for the distribution of meals, not more than one prisoner at a time was allowed to leave his seat. Even when prisoners used the washroom, they were kept under observation. The lavatories had no doors.

Train windows could be opened in those days, and it was decided that, for ventilation purposes, prisoners would be permitted to open windows to a maximum of four inches. Prisoners were also forbidden to obstruct windows in any way with clothing or blankets.

As might be expected, firearms were not permitted inside any coach carrying POWs. However, security officers elsewhere on the train were armed. They also had access to a reserved supply of ammunition and several pairs of handcuffs. In addition, a buzzer alarm system had been installed in each car.

Any time the train stopped, vigilance increased. Each end-of-coach guard was detailed to secure the exit closest to him. A second guard took up a position on the passageway between coaches, and other soldiers stood on the station platform outside. These men were arranged six to a coach, three to a side, facing the train. All carried rifles with fixed bayonets. Civilians were kept well back.

What was it like to be a POW on one of these trains? The experience seems to have left a lasting impression on most prisoners. Almost all recall their trip to camp, but not necessarily for the same reasons or with the same degree of detail. To virtually every one of them, though, the quantity and quality of Canadian food came as a shock.

"On the train to camp the food was great, and from then on it was, too," says Siegfried Bruse, the young officer from U-35. "On the train the guards passed out brown paper bags full of food — meat sandwiches, apples, bananas and so forth. At first we were so distrusting. We thought the food we got was to last the entire journey, so we ate very carefully, just a little at a time to make it last. Then the guards came through and collected all the brown paper bags and threw them out the window. We got more at the next meal. We couldn't believe the waste!"

Many prisoners were in for another shock before they had travelled very far in Canada. From the train window they saw not only the geography of the land, but some of its inhabitants as well. Bruse continues: "I saw young men and women my age, on the streets, at train stations and once or twice at railway crossings in cars. They all looked so happy and carefree — totally unlike anything I'd been used to, with the military training and background I'd had. I suppose it was the amount of food and the freedom that started changing my views about Canada."

After being imprisoned at Tunis and later Oldham, England, Walter Woehr and two thousand others like him came to Canada on one ship. They were put on a train in Halifax. "At the time, I didn't know much about Canada," he recalls now. "I couldn't speak English and most of the place names and other signs meant very little to me. There were no boards or bars over the train windows, so we could see where we were going. We went on and on and on — through forests, along rivers, across the prairie to Medicine Hat. I just couldn't believe the immensity of the country. It was so much bigger than Germany."

For Horst Liebeck, the train journey meant something entirely different. Following his fortunate escape from the flaming Messerschmitt over southern England, his burns healed and he came to Canada determined to escape prison camp.

"I had always been an active person and very conscious of my freedom," he explained years later. "That was why I was one of those who started planning escapes as soon as we boarded the train in Halifax. We exchanged souvenirs with guards and other train personnel. One of our group even got a railroad map. We knew where we were. We made notes, kept track of time and distance and the places we passed through. Some of our men had been in Canada before, so their knowledge of the country was helpful to us."

So it was for Liebeck, Woehr, Bruse and thousands of others who rode prison trains to POW camps strung across the country from the Maritimes to the Rocky Mountains. These men were well disciplined, well fed and well trained. They were young and, with the exception of combat wounds, healthy and active. And even though the country where they were caged was remote from any fighting, their homeland was still at war. Germany needed them and they knew it. So during the months and years of captivity that lay ahead, several tried — and one even succeeded — to return home to fight again.

THREE

The Canadian Internment Operation

As is often the case during wartime, the Canadian internment operation was organized in haste. From the day war was declared, some kind of facility was necessary to house, feed and clothe captured enemy soldiers as well as troublesome and outspoken civilians. And while both the Department of National Defence and the Department of the Secretary of State became involved, the entire organization was generally referred to simply as Internment Operations.

Its first director was Edouard de Panet, a staff officer with the First Canadian Division during the First World War, who had received the Légion d'Honneur in 1918. Brigadier-General (later Major-General) de Panet was appointed to the office on September 4, 1939. The same day, Lieutenant-Colonel Hubert Stethem was made assistant director. Both men were conscientious about their jobs. Both had wide military experience. De Panet was respected by those above and below him in rank, and he had the reputation of being fair. A likable, friendly man, he had been active in cultural and community life in his home city of Montreal, particularly assisting paraplegics and the Rehabilitation Institute of Montreal. From 1921 until 1925, he was comptroller of the Quebec Liquor Commission, then headed the Canadian Pacific Railway investigation department. He left this job to take on the Internment Operations responsibility.

Stethem was a good assistant and later a good director, but he apparently angered some of those closest to him. According to Eric Koch, author of a book on wartime civilian internees in

Canada, Stethem "was so disliked by his own staff officers, and all the clerks and typists who worked for him, that his headquarters office in Ottawa was not a very cheerful place."[1]Apparently this view was not shared by everyone. In researching this book, I was told by people who knew Stethem that he was "a leader" and a "stickler for detail," but no one admitted disliking him. Koch does mention how conscientious Stethem was:

. . . On one occasion, while on an inspection tour to a northern prisoner-of-war camp, he personally participated in the pursuit of two escaped prisoners of war. Inadequately dressed for an outdoor chase in the Canadian winter, clad only in light shoes and slacks and a raincoat, he did not give up. Although he fell several times in the deep snow, he persevered until the prisoners were caught. Back in his office in Ottawa, he was on the verge of pneumonia, but he had done his duty.[2]

Fifty-one years old in 1939, Stethem was a professional soldier; the military way was his way and he never apologized for it. A native of Kingston, Ontario, he had spent most of his adult life in the army, particularly in Saint John, Toronto and Kingston and, during the First World War, in Belgium, France and Siberia. When the First War ended, he joined the staff of the Royal Military College in Kingston and was elected to the local city council. He was still on the council when Internment Operations was formed.

On September 5, three nondescript, rather drab offices in the West Block of the Parliament Buildings in Ottawa became Operations headquarters. What rooms 283, 285 and 285A lacked in elegance, they made up in location. The headquarters was on the Hill, at the seat of power. This fact in itself gave added credibility to the organization. The next day, while de Panet and Stethem were still scrambling to obtain a couple of desks for themselves, the first internees were being rounded up in various centres across the country. The RCMP made arrests on each of the following days as well; by the eleventh of the month, 246 persons had been apprehended.

The Internment service was actually responsible for four different groups of prisoners: Canadian citizens or landed immigrants whose loyalties were suspect; German nationals who were removed from ships when the war broke out, or who happened to be in Canada at the start of hostilities; enemy aliens who were living in Britain when the war began and who were sent to

Canada; and German military personnel who had been captured.

In many cases, the same camp was used for more than one group — although if different kinds of prisoners were in residence, the various types were separated. Often, however, one class of prisoner was moved out and another brought in. There were also, of course, many people of other nationalities — Italian and Japanese, to name two — who spent long periods of time in various camps.

The first two camps were open and in operation before the end of September 1939. One was in Petawawa, Ontario; the other was at Kananaskis, in Alberta. Both were used initially for civilian internees. The former was considered especially secure because it was surrounded by bush, easily guarded and not easy to get out of. Access was difficult for the public. As was the case with many other camps, it was slated for expansion from the day it opened. The camp at Kananaskis was composed of a series of huts on a flat stretch of land at the foot of the Rocky Mountains, an hour's drive from Calgary. The area is a natural beauty spot, and men who were there were impressed with the magnificent scenery. This camp, too, would later expand.

In all, there were twenty-six main internment centres, most in Quebec, Ontario and Alberta. In addition, there were numerous smaller work camps, holding a few dozen to a few hundred inhabitants. Some of the camps have long since disappeared; at other locations the barbed wire and guard towers are gone, but the buildings and grounds are essentially the same as they were then.

The greatest transformation has undoubtedly been at Camp 43 in Montreal. Here, on Île Ste-Hélène, where three hundred internees were housed for more than three years, millions of unknowing visitors walked during Expo, the World's Fair of 1967. Granted, the island itself had been enlarged, yet one wonders how many people at Expo (and later, at Man and His World) ever knew they were on the grounds of a former wartime prison. Likewise, few campers at Neys Provincial Park near Marathon, on the north shore of Lake Superior, know that some of Hitler's most fanatical Nazis lived there forty-odd years ago. At other sites such as Lethbridge, Alberta, and Gravenhurst, Ontario, traces of the camps are also gone.

In other locations, however, little has changed. In Kingston, Fort Henry is essentially the Fort Henry of 1939. The guards may be ornamental now, but the wall paintings in a room on the lower level of the fort are the original artwork of a German prisoner who was held there. The colours have faded somewhat, but the cheerful flamboyance of the jousting and drinking scenes is obvious still. At Bowmanville, Ontario, the officers' camp was a boys' training school before the war and continued to be a boys' training school for years afterward. The little log cabin built by the Germans for their pets still stands.

Some of the civilian internees were housed in temporary quarters such as Fort Henry. Here, where some of their fathers had been held in an earlier war, naturalized German-Canadians whose allegiance to Canada was questionable were locked up. From all parts of central Canada they came — Montreal, Toronto, Kitchener and dozens of towns in between. There were men of all ages, occupations and social classes. Some came with a suitcase or two, as if they had anticipated arrest. Others had nothing but the clothes they wore. A few who had been arrested at night arrived in pajamas. Several were openly cocky, publicly chanting propagandistic diatribes written in Berlin. Others were defiant and accused the police and military authorities of harassment. Most were scared. Some were innocent.

In Kingston one of the men who guarded internees was Graham Thompson, a pleasant, gregarious member of the local militia. He was one of four officers and seventy men originally sent to the fort to guard ammunition stored there. With the arrival of the internees, however, the ammunition was removed and Thompson and his men stayed on to guard the prisoners.

While their job was not terribly difficult in itself, living conditions and clothing allowances, even for the guards, were barely adequate. They were issued old, threadbare uniforms and told to guard not only the fort itself and the people in it, but also the various approaches. Men on outside duty almost froze; the fort is located on a slope above the shore where Lake Ontario and the St. Lawrence River meet. Anyone who has visited there in winter knows the howling winds, which sweep unabated across the frozen river and shriek around the casement walls. Because of the cold, the outside guards had to be rotated frequently.

The first internees were lodged in what is called the upper battery, in a series of rooms opening onto a large central courtyard. Here, above the same square where university students play soldier for the tourists today, came the bedraggled misfits of Canada's fifth column. Graham Thompson described how they were brought there: "It was a sad affair," he says. "Membership lists from the German clubs in places like Montreal, Toronto and

Ottawa were used. Without warning, the RCMP found these people, loaded them on trucks, and shipped them to Kingston." The same type of thing happened in Britain to enemy aliens, even though some of those in question were actually Jews, students and priests who had fled the onslaught of Hitler's barbarism.

Such treatment may seem unduly harsh to us today, but when one considers the mood of the time, the procedure was not exceptional. In the years after Hitler's ascendency in Germany, pro-Nazi organizations sprang up in many places in Canada. The most notable of these groups was based in Quebec and led by a gaunt, brilliant, bug-eyed malcontent named Adrien Arcand. Arcand and his followers enjoyed a measure of support up to the outbreak of the war, but by that time, as Lita-Rose Betcherman recounts in *The Swastika and the Maple Leaf,* "public opinion and the press . . . reflected greatly increased hostility toward homegrown Nazis."[3]

There was no time to screen properly the people on the lists. As far as the authorities were concerned, those who were brought in were only names. In the urgency of the moment, it did not matter whether the internees had families, jobs or other responsibilities. Some spoke little English and didn't know or pretended they didn't know why they were seized. Others did know and denounced the RCMP for the action.

Within a few weeks, most of the sorting had been done. People believed by senior internment officials to be innocent were released, often during the night and always quietly. Neither the other prisoners nor the majority of the guards knew why. Other internees who outwardly impressed the guards with their innocence were not let go.

At this time, internees were allowed brief visits once a month. A guard had to be present during the visit, so these meetings were never very private. Most of the guards hated being present at these meetings as much as the prisoners resented their intrusion.

"We had to remain nearby during these visits," recalls Graham Thompson. "Most of the time I only wanted to be somewhere else. The poor wives would arrive, often in a terrible state, most of them crying. A lot were obviously poor. Some were on welfare. Most of them were young. Often they were amorous. Some had kids. They'd carry one or two and one would tag along, holding onto the mother's skirts or coat. Then at the end of the visit there were always a lot more tears. At times the women would become hysterical. I tell you, I hated being there.

"I used to feel sorry for the older men. Quite often they spoke very little English and I'm sure that for them the German club had only been a place to go in order to be able to talk to someone else in their own language. I doubt very much if these fellows would have had much effect on the war effort of any country. When we got them in camp, they were upset and confused and worried because their wives never visited. I imagine that was because the wives were simply too old to make the trip in the first place."

Letters mailed into and out of the camp were censored. Prisoners had to write in English only, and if they could not write in English, another internee had to write letters for them. Obviously, such a set-up was far from private.

Graham Thompson remembers what it was like to read someone's mail: "Most of it was straightforward," he recalls. "Yet at times there were letters that stood out. I was put in charge of a particular group of prisoners, among whom was a camp spokesman. This fellow was quite a character. He was a natural athlete, tall, blond, a good singer and a real leader. He spoke German to the people in the compound and, if he felt like it, perfect English to us. He organized the prisoners and seemed to be their champion in all kinds of causes. In no time he seemed to know every internee there.

"But his letters to his wife! They were all long, filled with quotations from the Bible and dozens and dozens of questions about some kind of business they had shared. Then she would write back and tell him how terrible things were at home, how the children were sick and that because no money was coming in, relief seemed to be the only solution. If he did not get a letter, he'd berate me in front of the other inmates and accuse me of keeping his mail. The internees all supported him.

"Then one day he got a letter saying his wife was coming for a visit. The whole camp soon knew and we wondered what to expect. I suppose if the guy had not been so obnoxious, we wouldn't have cared.

"Anyway, this terribly poor-looking young woman showed up and said she had walked all the way from the train station in Kingston, which was about three kilometres away. It was a cold winter day, and she wore these long grey woollen pants with holes in them. When she got to the gate she was crying and in a real mess. Then she collapsed. We brought her around and they had their visit. They did a lot of hugging and crying and praying. Then she left. The husband, of course, got all kinds of sympathy from the prisoners, because they could see what was happening to the wife and how cruel it was to have him in prison.

"Eventually, the internees were moved to another camp and this joker was released! It was only then that I learned there had been no kids and no wife. The whole thing had been an act. I couldn't believe it at first. I hated that fellow so much, but he sure did his job. He was an undercover RCMP officer. He was responsible for making the decision as to who was released and who was held. He gained the confidence of the prisoners and through conversations with them was able to judge who was pro-Nazi and who was not."

In the months immediately following the outbreak of the war, the guard duty at POW camps was performed by the regular army or by units of the local militia. This procedure had been the one used in the First World War camps here. On May 24, 1940, however, a new organization was created to do the job. Because its members were predominantly First World War survivors who were now too old to be sent overseas, the new service was named the Veterans Guard of Canada. From a small nucleus, the Guard increased in strength until June 1943, when it comprised a total of 10,257 officers and men. Maximum age for entry was set at fifty, but as usual with military enlistment, some of the recruits were not the age they claimed to be. Many were years older.

There were units of the Guard formed in several areas or military districts across Canada, and all were under the authority of the Minister of National Defence in Ottawa.

As soon as a decision had been made to establish a particular unit, local military authorities would be deluged with men eager to sign up. Initially, at least, no recruitment drives were needed; in fact, quite the reverse was generally true. Each centre had far more men than could be accepted.

In Military District 2 in Toronto, for instance, so great was the lure of being back in uniform that hundreds of veterans lined up at the Fort York Armouries the day recruiting opened in June 1940. The first Veterans Guard commanding officer there, Major Charles B. Lindsey, told the crowd that most of them would be disappointed because only 160 men would be accepted from the entire city; however, very few were deterred.

Most of the men were there because their country needed them and they wanted to help. Others came because they had been cajoled, shamed or dared to come by the beer-parlour crowd the night before. Some arrived because life at home was monotonous, and they treasured all the good things about their imagined glory days in the Great War. Many came because they needed a job. The words of an internal Guard journal described them:

> These were not young, tough, trained-to-a-hair troop troops. They were "Vets," fathers of families, many with sons overseas, and their ages were from mere youngsters of forty-five to more mature men of sixty-five. It's true that their army papers didn't show their real ages, nor did those who were entitled to them wear their South African ribbons. Some of them had to be sent to the doctor . . . but these "old Vets" never faltered.

They were sent out to police not only the many POW compounds that sprang up across the country but also some of the more obvious military targets in the event of enemy bombing: dams, power plants, government installations and the like. One company did guard duty in Britain at the Canadian Army headquarters there, while other units were sent to Newfoundland, at the time not yet part of Canada, and to British Guiana and the Bahamas. When they are remembered today, however, it is the POW job that arouses the most interest. It was also the toughest.

These "elder citizens" were ideally suited for the job. They knew army life and its demands. They knew its pain, frustration, loneliness and utter boredom. They also knew its highs, its joys and its rewards. But perhaps more important than any other single factor, they knew the mind of the prisoner of war, because some of them had once been POWs themselves. They knew what it was like to live behind barbed wire; to be unable to leave; to have to obey the commands of a jailer; to dream twenty-four-hour dreams of being free.

Those who were accepted into the Guard came from such a variety of backgrounds that their First World War experience often seemed to be the only thing they had in common. Major Charles Lindsey had joined the army as a bugle boy of fourteen in Kootenay, British Columbia. By the end of the first war he had fought with each of Canada's four divisions and had won the Distinguished Service Order in the process.

Fred Chapple, like Lindsey, was one of the first officers in the Veterans Guard. English born, Chapple had served in Gibraltar, France and Germany. He was awarded the Distinguished Conduct Medal in March 1918 and seven months later won the Military Cross at Le Cateau. In peacetime he worked for a hydro company.

Ed House, a grizzled, tough-talking, no-nonsense sergeant-major who lived for many years at Trent River, Ontario, fought "all over hell" in Europe from 1914 to 1918. This man, who had once scooped up the unmarked body of his own captain from a street in Amiens, realizing too late that the man had been killed by concussion and that every bone in his body was broken, now offered his services once again.

From western Canada, Jim Grieve joined the Veterans Guard in Winnipeg. The forty-seven-year-old NCO had fought for fifteen months in France before being shot at the Somme. His injuries long forgotten, he welcomed the return to life in uniform.

Bill Kennedy of Kincardine, Ontario, came down to Bowmanville to enlist in the Guard. At the POW camp there he rubbed shoulders with hundreds of German officers, the same breed he had fought overseas when he first left Canada as a sixteen-year-old private in the First World War.

In all, there were 35,046 prisoners of war and internees incarcerated in Canada during the Second World War. They were housed in the twenty-six main compounds, although there were dozens of smaller camps for logging, farming and manufacturing endeavours. No POW in Canada was ever employed making munitions. Internment records for the major camps give dates of opening and closing, capacity and types of prisoners held. Records detailing the various farming, logging and industrial operations are not as easy to locate, in part because some of these moved to where the work had to be done. Major camp capacities ranged from 300 at Île Ste-Hélène, Montreal, to 900 at Fredericton, to the massive 12,500 at Lethbridge. The last camp to close — at Monteith, Ontario — operated until December 1946.

There was very little difference between the compounds that housed internees and those that held military personnel. Veteran guards policed both. Infractions of the rules resulted in periods of detention apart from the camp population in all kinds of camps. Food was ample and good. All camps were out of bounds to the general public, although internees were allowed occasional visits from family members. As a general rule, military POWs were not permitted visitors. Educational, recreational and cultural pursuits were encouraged in all camps. No POW or internee was allowed the use of a telephone.

Because the camp, regardless of its size, was a closed society, day-to-day events that were in any way unusual or unexpected were soon known to all. Stories about camp life were told and retold so often that today there is a certain folklore about many of them.

Ed Billet, a gentle, unassuming former sergeant in the German army, was one of about forty "other ranks" personnel at Gravenhurst. Because Gravenhurst was primarily an officers' camp, the OR complement used to complain that they spent half their day working and the other half saluting.

"I had a certain number of duties each day," recalls Billet. "As a batman, I had to help clean the officers' rooms, polish their shoes, do laundry and so forth. All the work could be done in three or four hours. Then we used to play sports, read, walk around the perimeter of the camp, that sort of thing. But we had to be sure to salute any officers we met. Because there were so few of us and over three hundred of them, we seemed to be saluting all the time, like puppets or toy soldiers with movable parts. We would be involved in some game and an officer would come by. We'd all salute and return to the game. Then there would be another and another. It was crazy. Later the rule was changed so we had to salute the first time we saw them each day. Still, many hollered if you didn't salute them each time. They probably forgot you had saluted so you had to keep running around saluting all over the place. When I look back now, the whole thing was so ridiculous."

What kind of a reception were the German POWs given in Canada? The answer to that question was and is rather varied. The answer also changed as the years of the war passed. At the outset, most Canadians were not pleased to have Germans here. The propaganda of the day had taught them to hate Germans, and so they did. They also feared the "supermen" who had crushed so much of Europe so quickly. Then, when the war started to go against Hitler and his thugs, fears in Canada eased. It seemed that the Axis powers were beatable, although no one was under the delusion that victory would be easy.

By 1944, when more and more POWs were in Canadian work camps and on farms, anti-German feeling was much less evident. Because we found that we needed the POW labour to harvest wheat, build roads and cut logs, we decided that the Germans who were already here were not a bad lot. But then Canadians started to hear about places such as Dachau, Buchenwald and Belsen. They were shocked by the news of these horrors, and for a time, anti-German feeling ran high. It gradually dissipated, however, to the point that many Canadians actually hoped, and even petitioned Members of Parliament, to allow POWs to remain here.

It is doubtful that such a change in public opinion could have been imagined in 1939 and 1940. This was particularly true of the public that had to live near the camps. Almost without exception, people who learned that a POW camp was to be established near them reacted negatively. Most were afraid: afraid for themselves and their property, but especially for their wives and mothers and daughters. After all, because the Allied propaganda pictured Germans as a bloodthirsty, barely civilized, rapacious people, it might be fine to bring them to Canada, as long as no one had to live near them. What would happen if they escaped?

There were probably as many individual reactions to the Germans as there were POWs in Canada. A woman in Fingal, Ontario, told the author that she begged her husband to sell their farm and move when they learned that a camp would be established nearby. Another, not far from Bowmanville, still remembers being so terrified of the prisoners that she drove some distance to another town rather than do her shopping locally. Because her husband worked a night shift at the time, she was careful to lock the house and put knives into door jambs so that no door could be opened from outside. When she slept late one morning, her husband almost had to kick the place down in order to get in. Occasionally roads that ran past some of the camps were closed and traffic was rerouted. While this in itself was a nuisance to those who lived there, it had little effect outside the immediate area.

Sometimes the methods used to establish some of the camps caused friction. Jim Thompson, a staff member at the boys' training school at Bowmanville before the place was taken over for the POWs, remembers the disruption the conversion caused: "We were given exactly twenty-four hours from the time word came down from Ottawa to the time when we had to have all of the boys out of the place. It was not easy to do. There was one hell of a lot of scrambling, I know that. Finally we found a big house not too far away and stayed there for a while before moving into town. Then as soon as possible after the war ended and the POWs were out, our boys were brought back."

Thompson also remembers his feelings as the first contingent of Germans arrived: "A short while before any of their officers were brought here, several men from the other ranks came to get the place ready. The kitchen, dormitories and washroom facilities had to be altered a bit." In short, the place that had been built for boys suddenly had to be ready for men. "It was quite a shock to me when I first saw the new arrivals. Each of us had seen pictures of German troops, of course, but seeing them in the flesh was a different matter. The day the first ones arrived I was working in one of our buildings when the door opened and a guard and four or five tall, blond soldiers in field grey uniforms walked in. I just stood and stared. Later on, when I flew Spitfires against them, I thought of that moment. But by that time I knew they were not supermen. Today they're our friends."

And so it went in camp after camp. In cases where adequate facilities for POWs already existed, any civilians who were there were issued eviction notices and the POWs were brought in. Little if any advance warning was given, not only because the operation had to be done in haste, but also because the Canadian government had no desire to communicate its every move to the Axis powers. There was always the chance that advance notice of camp openings and locations would be reported by the media, the War Measures Act notwithstanding. While the press and radio of the day generally avoided naming the specific town where a POW camp was located, their euphemisms for the various places were fairly well known to Canadians. The "Muskoka Officers' Camp" was Gravenhurst. The "Lake Ontario Officers' Camp" was Bowmanville, a "Mountain Camp" was Kananaskis, Alberta, and "the Fort" was Fort Henry at Kingston.

The media did not hesitate to tell Canadians about the POWs themselves, however. Newspapers, magazines and motion picture newsreels supported the Allied cause and swayed public opinion toward that cause. The unpatriotic and Axis-loving civilians who had been rounded up just after war broke out were blamed for all sorts of evils, from unemployment to sabotage. But with the arrival of the first enemy military personnel, Canadian newspapers and magazines found the scapegoats they really needed.

An editorial in the Toronto *Globe and Mail* on September 2, 1940, is more or less typical of the period. While the paper urged that POWs be treated with humanity and fairness, it also pointed out that Canadians in German camps were living under decidedly more adverse circumstances. The paper went on to state that the Germans in Canada should be granted only those amenities called for under international law. After all, the editorial continued, "these prisoners . . . have been taught to believe they belong to the 'master race' and . . . those who would impede them are to be beaten and trampled underfoot." The writer told his readers as well that Germans were "dangerous," "fanatical," "potential murderers" and "monsters." In other words, these were the kinds of nasty persons who were now settling into various POW camps across the land. Obviously, such men would bear careful watching.

The media also reflected the aversion of many Canadians to the prisoners being here at all. A writer named W. A. Higgins expressed this point of view in an article entitled "Prisoners of War, Canada's Unwelcome Guests." He said, in part:

> Canada has become the somewhat harried host to German prisoners
> of war whose rights, privileges and prerogatives as guests have been
> carefully defined by international convention. If the escape of an
> occasional prisoner makes it appear that we are too bountiful in our
> hospitality and are merely operating exclusive clubs for the benefit of
> captured forces, appearances may not be wrong. . . . Leniency is
> now the order of the day.[5]

In an article at a much later date, November 12, 1945, the Medicine Hat internment camp paper *P.O.W. WOW,* published by the Veterans Guard, defended the treatment of prisoners:

> A good deal of criticism has at one time or another been levelled
> against the treatment accorded German prisoners of war in Canada.
> It is said that the guards are too lenient, the POWs are housed and
> fed too well. Why pamper them when our own boys in Germany got
> hell and a starvation diet? Generally speaking, those who so freely
> voice their opinion are people who know nothing of internment
> camp work, either in Canada or Germany, and only enlarge on little
> snatches of information and hearsay.
>
> The facts are, of course, that the German POWs in Canada were
> never pampered but treated as soldiers — just as we hoped our own
> boys in Germany would be treated. It would not improve the
> situation if the Canadians imitated the degrading example of the
> Germans throughout Europe. Two wrongs do not make a right.
> These critics do not seem to understand that an internment camp is
> not a place for punishment or retaliation. The Vets did their guard
> duty, unmoved by either sympathy or hatred, even though some of
> them had tasted the miseries of German prison camps. It is
> important that this correct attitude continue.

Beating and starving German prisoners is not the way to teach them democracy. We believe in right and wrong in this world and the only way to demonstrate it is by example. The policy regarding prisoners of war in Canada has paid and is continuing to pay dividends.

The writer of a letter to the *Globe and Mail* on July 8, 1943, would not have agreed. "We are giving our German prisoners of war better food than the average Canadian taxpayer can afford to buy," complained a woman in Niagara Falls, Ontario. "In return for this," the letter continued, "we are receiving only contemptuous insults from these self-styled 'superior' people."

Another citizen complained about POWs to Ernest Lapointe, the federal minister of justice. In a letter dated July 10, 1940, a Winnipeg woman maintained that no POWs should be brought to Canada; instead they should be placed "somewhere where there will be no possibility of them causing trouble. . . . Such ideal locations could be found on some of the rock grit uninhabited islands of the South Pacific. If there should happen to be any natives on the islands selected," the letter continued, "the British Government could quite easily remove them to other islands some distance away." The writer went on to say that the POWs should be given medicine, food for four or five months, and "enough seed grain and vegetable seeds" to maintain themselves for the remainder of the war. She also suggested that "the waters surrounding the islands be mined in order to prevent any outside sympathizers from coming too close."

From time to time, selected members of the press, Canadian servicemen and, now and then, a politician or two visited the camps. In many cases, the politician was the local MP who, after he had seen inside for himself, was able to reassure his constituents with the information that no inmate would escape *this* enclosure, and that even if one did, the POWs here were all anti-Nazi boys who would harm no one. And, for the most part, he was right. Considering the number of prisoners who were brought to Canada, very little injury was done by them to Canadian persons or property. Now and then an escapee broke into a deserted house or cabin for supplies and on at least one occasion, a pair of escapees stole a car. Apart from their role in such isolated incidents, the vast majority of POWs behaved themselves.

These men behind the wire were not criminals in the sense that an inmate of a jail is a criminal. The German POWs were typical of the young men in any armed service anywhere, and they had been captured while doing their job. Most Canadians knew this and reacted accordingly. Most Canadians differentiated between the German soldier in the field and his corrupt and debauched leaders in Berlin. For their part, most German soldiers deliberately dissociated themselves from the Himmlers, the Keitels and even the Goerings. Peter Krug once spoke with Goering, and when asked years later for his reaction to the Luftwaffe commander, said, "I was not impressed." Those words said it all.

But not only reporters and politicians wanted to visit POW camps. Internment headquarters in Ottawa received hundreds of requests from private citizens who wanted to see what was behind the wire. Some of these entreaties were legitimate — where a friend, relative or acquaintance was one of the prisoners. Others who asked to visit did so for humanitarian reasons. They wanted to learn for themselves whether indeed the POWs *were* well looked after. As might be expected, a few sought to be admitted for less praiseworthy motives. Such people were sympathetic to the Axis cause, and would have delivered maps, names and addresses of contact persons or whatever else could have been smuggled inside.

Then, of course, there were some who wanted to see and perhaps get to know some of the prisoners. At Gravenhurst, teenaged girls often used rowboats to approach the enclosure on Lake Muskoka. An unidentified woman mentions the episodes in the book *Six War Years*.

> Our girls' camp, the usual kind of summer camp, was on the other side of the lake, and although we weren't supposed to, at night, before it got dark, we'd row in our rowboats across this lake. There'd be three or four girls in each boat and we'd stop about twenty feet from the shore and talk to the German prisoners. A lot of them were young boys, maybe twenty or so, and we were all about sixteen or seventeen, and things went along okay because some of them talked English and quite a few girls spoke German. They spoke it at home. I spoke Hungarian with my parents; even that helped me because a couple of the Germans were Hungarians, and we'd have quite a conversation. In fact, you could easily say we did quite a lot of flirting.
>
> Nothing ever came of it, of course. It was only in the summer, in the camp season about six weeks, and they were still prisoners, although they were just like boys from the towns, but more polite.[6]

At Espanola, a few girls found themselves in trouble when it was learned they had been putting messages into snowballs and throwing them over the fence to the POWs. At the Petawawa camp, a female newspaper reporter was reprimanded for coming too close to the wire. And so it went in camp after camp. At Bowmanville, however, a boy actually got into the enclosure for a couple of hours. The youngster was one visitor no prisoner ever forgot.

The ten-year-old son of a guard had travelled from western Canada in December 1944 to spend Christmas in Ontario. One day when the father came to work, he brought the youngster with him. This visit turned out to be a very happy time for the boy, and an unexpectedly emotional one for the prisoners. For the child, the guard towers, barbed wire and strange uniforms were all exciting, the fabric of dreams. The fact that these men were actually U-boat commanders, bomber pilots or German commandoes was heady stuff for a kid from the Canadian prairies. To the boy, the experience was better than any book or movie. These strange men talked to him, carried him around, and fell over one another in their eagerness to be near him.

For the POWs, the visit was emotionally charged. Some of them had not even seen, let alone talked to or touched, a child in years. Those who spoke English fawned over the boy, showed him around, and played with him. Those who knew little or no English approached him, smiled, rumpled his hair and, for a few brief seconds, imagined themselves in a world where children existed, where there was no barbed wire and no war. Some of the most hard-bitten fighters from Rommel's desert army looked at the boy and dissolved in tears. Then they remembered that it was Christmas. Prisoners of all ranks showered gifts on the child.

"That little fellow got such good treatment," recalls Siegfried Bruse, the U-35 officer who had been in Bowmanville for some time. "You see, we hadn't seen a child for such a long time, and this was Christmas. We had Christmas trees made up, decorated with tin cans, and some of them were beautiful. But this was a child! The guys each wanted to give him a gift. When he left he had all kinds of wall plaques, carvings, paintings, chocolates, everything we could think of giving him. It took about ten guards to carry all the stuff out. But for us it was a tremendous thing."

Luftwaffe officer Tony Kleimaker still regards the visit of that boy as a highlight of his prison years. "We heard later that the guard had been demoted for what he had done, though,"

Kleimaker remembers. "Still, we were happy he brought that little boy inside. I'll never forget it."

Occasionally POWs were seen outside the wire. When this happened, they generally made quite an impression on Canadians. Jim Thompson told the author about watching a group of German officers marching under guard from the railway station to the camp at Bowmanville. "They came right down the middle of the street," he recalls. "Traffic stopped and everybody came out to gawk. I have to admit that those guys really looked impressive. They were all in uniform and in perfect formation."

Another Canadian who was impressed by the POWs saw them out of uniform. Barry Broadfoot relates the story in *Six War Years.*

> We were travelling east, heading overseas, a boiling hot summer day and I can't remember why we weren't in our summer issue, but there we were in our heavy battle dress. A wonder some jerk didn't make us wear overcoats. To top it off, there were about 120 or so in one of those 1908 immigrant cars, the kind with the cooking stove at each end, and there were probably seats for eighty or so guys. A real madhouse, and we'd come all that way from Calgary like that. What a scruffy lot.
>
> The train stopped at one of those places on the top of Lake Superior, Marathon or some place like it, and we all got out to breathe some air and scratch.
>
> Now here's what happened. All of a sudden, out of the bush, down a trail, comes this bunch of guys. About forty of them, I'd say, and every bloody one was a giant, six-foot-two, six-foot-four. You never saw such a bunch. All fair-haired, blue-eyed, thighs like hams and tanned like Charles Atlas, Mr. World, and we thought, "Christ, who *are* these guys?"
>
> We caught on quick because a couple of ginky little Veteran Guards, about sixty, were herding them along. Better still, they were just following. They had rifles, sure, but they probably hadn't fired one at anyone since 1918. We caught on quick because of the guards, but also because of those hats these guys were wearing, the kind German troopers wore. We'd seen them a hundred times in newsreels, you know, and here they were, going down to the lake for a swim. Well, Jesus Christ!
>
> We asked one of the guards who these guys were, and he said they were of the Eighth Army, Rommel's supermen, Hitler's elite, and they'd been captured in North Africa. The desert war was winding up then. Here were these supermen, and I do mean supermen, and

they looked at us as if we were common clay. The way we looked, I guess we were. A pretty scruffy lot.

Then the whistle tooted and we piled back on, into our sweatbox, and we sat around quiet for a while and then somebody said what we were all thinking. He said, "God, do we have to fight guys like that?" It kept us thinking for a while.

That's not the end of the story, though. In Normandy when we were taking hundreds of prisoners at a crack, just digging them out of culverts and nunneries and old stables, I thought of that bunch of supermen. The men we were herding into compounds weren't the same breed. They never are. Bullets flying around, body lice, no food for a day or two and that cheap brandy everybody was drinking, and the smoke and the stink, our stink and theirs — it takes just about every bit of parade square out of a man. Most of the German boys we picked up were about as scruffy a lot as you could find, and I don't think I saw one superman in all that time. I guess maybe we got them all in North Africa. Just as well anyway. They wouldn't have liked it around Falaise.[7]

From time to time, Canadians had chance encounters with escaped prisoners of war. In most cases, the police were called, a manhunt was organized, and the fugitive soon recaptured. Things didn't always go according to plan, however.

A couple of days after an escape from Gravenhurst, for instance, Norman Phillips, a reporter for a Toronto newspaper, was driving along a highway near the town of Huntsville when he noticed a man walking beside the road. Thinking the stranger might be one of the missing POWs, Phillips stopped the car and asked the man for his wartime registration card. In his story about the incident, published in the Toronto *Star* on September 3, 1940, Phillips said the stranger looked somewhat confused and was unable to produce the card. Instead, he said in a heavy German accent that he was going to Ottawa. By this time Phillips was sure the man was an escapee, so he offered him a ride.

In downtown Huntsville, they came up behind a military church parade. Phillips slowed down and informed the sergeant at the end of the line that the man in the car was an escaped German prisoner. The marcher didn't even break stride. Instead, he told the reporter to tell one of the officers.

During this exchange, the POW jumped from the car and ran.

Phillips angrily sped to the head of the column, stopped a lieutenant and asked for help. The officer's response was even more incredible than the sergeant's: "You follow him," the reporter was told. "We'll catch up to you after the parade."

By this time, Phillips didn't know whether to laugh or cry. He had captured an escapee and no one seemed to care. Finally he drove to a police station and told his story. Less than half an hour later, Chief William Carson of the Huntsville police department took the German, whose name was Ron Kempe, into custody. Phillips continued his story for the *Star*'s readers:

Kempe was still amiable when he was returned to the Huntsville police station. He readily admitted his identity. Chief Carson took from his pockets a few half-eaten carrots, a tin of fifty cigarettes, two road maps, a steel mirror, a pocket knife and a German-English dictionary.

"You are an army officer," Kempe told me. When I denied this, he demanded: "Why do you lie to me? It is all over now. You can tell me the truth."

Chief Carson tried to convince him I was a newspaperman. Picking up a copy of the *Star*, the chief told Kempe that I wrote for the paper. Headlines describing Royal Air Force successes caught his eye.

"Lies," he declared. "Why do you write such lies? We are the strongest in the air." The incident seemed to help him regain the arrogant sullenness which marks the German prisoners.

He refused the offer of food from the chief. After giving his name and age, he refused to tell his rank, service or where he had been captured.

"The guards have all those things," he said. "Why should I tell them to you."

When a crowd began to gather outside the cells, he was again surly.

"Why don't you charge them money to see me," he told the chief.

Later he told me that he had found food by the side of the road and that in the time he had been at large he had not been hungry. He would not say where he had been or how he came to get the road maps in his possession.

"I escaped alone underneath a garbage truck," was all that he would say.

Senior officers at the camp later demonstrated how Kempe secreted himself underneath the truck. He had taken a piece of board about two and a half feet by six inches and jammed it under the floor of the truck.

The space into which he cramped himself was not more than six or eight inches deep and a foot and a half to two feet wide.

Local reaction to the capture of Kempe and other escapees was more or less typical of the reaction of most Canadians to the fact that there were Germans, albeit under guard, on Canadian soil. People came out to stare at Kempe because he was an object of curiosity. He was the enemy and they wanted to see him.

Elsewhere, reactions were much the same. Maritimers stood at dockside and watched the POWs leave the ships that brought them here. Children playing road hockey in Gravenhurst interrupted their games as the prisoners marched past. Farmers on the prairies clustered at grain elevators and watched the prison trains arrive. Few bothered to protest. The world was at war and these prisoners had been part of it. But now they were under lock and key.

Even Canadian Jews were remarkably silent about the presence of German soldiers in this country. "We might have wished they were somewhere else," a Jewish businessman told me, "but we didn't have much say in the operation." "It was done too quickly for any real protest," added another.

And it *was* done quickly.

In most cases, the time between the selection of a camp site and the arrival of the men who would live in it was very short: several days or perhaps a couple of weeks, in locations where facilities already existed. Under such circumstances, there was almost no time to mount any organized opposition. People who lived close to a particular camp might complain, but for the most part, their complaints were ignored. The camps opened, the POWs arrived, and the war went on — as did the life behind the wire.

FOUR

Behind Barbed Wire

Whether the location was Fredericton or Monteith, Île Ste-Hélène or Medicine Hat, life within all POW camps was in many ways the same. As soon as the front gate was closed, the prisoner entered an artificial world — a world where women, children and the old did not exist; a world where the horizon began at the barbed wire and ended with whatever the inmate imagined was on the other side. It was a world where reality was something one remembered, something an ocean, a different culture and another language away. It was a world where the roll call, the censored letter and the guard tower were all that mattered. And most of all, it was a world where freedom was as chimerical as a dream.

It was a world where the day-to-day routine was the same; where the events of one day blended with the events of all the other days; where the activities of one year were the activities of a year earlier.

In the fall of 1942, a prisoner in Camp 30 at Bowmanville described the life in a letter to his mother:

My daily routine is really very simple: We get up at seven a.m., have roll call at seven-thirty and breakfast at eight. I take an English and a Spanish lesson for an hour each, then read until dinner at eleven-thirty; from one to one-thirty I often swim, and until our second roll call at three, we read or walk. Occasionally we have a coffee party in the dining room, and after we have talked ourselves out there, we go back to our rooms to work for an hour. By that time it is nearly a quarter to six and time for supper. In the evenings we read or write letters. Sometimes we play *Doppelkopf* in the old German fashion with a great deal of talking, or sometimes we drink a glass or more of beer. The daily routine includes sports, concerts and lectures. Since we manage the whole camp ourselves, we have similar food to what we had at home. We still get a good bowl of porridge in the morning.

The day-to-day routine for the guards at any camp was often just as predictable as it was for those they watched. They spent a fixed period of time, often four hours, on duty and then had two to four hours or so off. Some veteran guards watched from the towers. Others, called scouts, patrolled the fences and went inside the camps to keep a sharp eye out for clandestine radios, escape paraphernalia and the like. The scouts were generally the first to discover tunnelling activities.

From time to time, in the event of an escape, camp routine was disrupted, and off-duty guards were called out to search for escapees. And even though it was their job to contain the POWs inside the wire, escapes were not always unwelcome. They were a break in routine.

For the most part, relationships between prisoners and guards were good. Despite rules against them, some friendships developed between the Canadians and their charges, particularly in the bush camps. At an Ontario camp, a guard by the name of Davis was supervising several prisoners who were involved in a road-building project. One day Davis and a couple of prisoners were standing on a rocky ledge, trying to decide where to pile some tree limbs in order to burn them. After a decision was made, the three began climbing down to the roadbed, but partway there Davis fell and shattered his right ankle. His loaded rifle ended up several feet away from him, but it did not go off.

The prisoners immediately ran to their guard's side. One who had been a medic in the German army examined Davis's leg and, using some wood and strips torn from his own shirt, fashioned a temporary splint. Then four POWs gingerly picked up the guard and placed him in a wheelbarrow. Two of them wheeled him back to camp — one pushing the wheelbarrow and the other carrying the guard's rifle. Just outside the gates of the compound the fellow with the rifle decided he should not be carrying it, so he placed the weapon across Davis's knees. As soon as the POWs had taken their patient to the infirmary they went back to work — for fifty cents a day.

A somewhat similar incident happened to Veterans Guard officer Ron Schamerhorn. He and another soldier were sent to meet a train at Thunder Bay. Arriving on that train was a POW from a bush camp near Nipigon, Ontario, who was in need of medical attention for what turned out to be a hernia. Two guards from Nipigon accompanied the prisoner.

The train arrived on schedule and several passengers got off. For a long time, however, there was no sign of either the POW or the men who were with him. Finally, just when Schamerhorn and the man with him were starting to wonder if they had met the wrong train, the German prisoner came down the steps to the platform — carrying a rifle in either hand.

Without a word, he handed the weapons to Schamerhorn, then turned back to help his keepers down from the coach. Both of them were so drunk they could hardly stand.

Inside the camps, guards sometimes marvelled at the way some of the POWs treated each other. A fellow the guards called Boston Johnny was notorious. The man was a prisoner who had been a merchant marine captain when the war broke out. His ship had been taken over and he was suddenly stripped of command. The man was an officious braggart who swaggered around the camp, ordered others around, and in general earned and merited the hatred of almost everyone who encountered him.

He had been given his nickname by the guards because he loved to brag about how he had taken a damaged ship into Boston harbour without the loss of anyone on board. No one knew whether the story was true or not. Former guard Ed House recalls: "He'd be marching some of his own men around when some of them would kind of balk. Old Johnny would yell, in English, for us to hear: 'Come alive, goddammit, look alive! They do things different in this part of the world. Here you could be prime minister if you tried. Get a move on! This isn't Germany.' " House recalls, "I used to listen to him, and Christ, I often wondered if he'd get back to Germany before his own men killed him. They sure hated that guy."

Early in the war, when the Germans were still certain of victory back home, two prisoners were threatened with punishment because they had saluted a guard with the outlawed straight-arm Nazi salute. That evening during roll call, the two repeated the offence. When the guard protested, several others saluted the same way. Finally, in utter exasperation, the guard stomped away. Two hundred laughing, saluting POWs watched him go.

A short time later however, the two ringleaders were put in detention and the matter ended.

But not all exchanges between guards and prisoners were as easily resolved. On at least one occasion, officer prisoners in a camp lodged a protest that seems almost unthinkable to us today. Unfortunately, the protest was not only tolerated at the highest levels, but was immediately acted upon by Canadians.

The incident in question occurred in June 1941, at a time when German officer prisoners were billeted in Fort Henry (Camp F or 31) in Kingston. These men, some of whom had been in the fort for weeks, were disgruntled with their lot and were extremely unhappy with the spartan existence the fort offered. They hated the place, the ringing cement parade square, the dungeon-like casements and the ugly walls of naked stone on every side. Most felt that confinement in such a building was inhumane, and therefore tried in every way they could to seek redress. Most chose to pretend they had never heard of places such as Colditz in Germany and Stalag VIIIB in Poland, camps where Allied prisoners were held — but under far more dreadful conditions. In some of those camps, Canadian soldiers were beaten, tortured, starved and shot. In his book *The Great Escape*, Paul Brickhill tells of Allied prisoners being murdered simply because the German High Command was angered by an escape. But regardless of conditions in Europe, Germans in Canada had little hesitation about lamenting their lot.

On Sunday, June 15, the guard contingent changed at Camp F. Company 3A of the Veterans Guard of Canada was transferred from the fort and Company 4A moved in. Included in the latter unit were three blacks, men from the British West Indies who were regular members of the Guard. These three were soon noticed by the prisoners. Two days after the guards changed, Generalmajor Georg Friemel, the senior German officer at Kingston, met with his advisers. At the close of their meeting, on the morning of June 17, they sent the following two-sentence letter to the Canadian commanding officer, Major C. J. Carruthers:

I protest earnestly against the guarding of German officers and other ranks by negro soldiers as it is done here in Camp F since two days. I ask you to send on this protest to the Authorities of the Internment Operations to stop further watching of POWs in Canada by coloured people.

(Sgd.) Friemel, Generalmajor[1]

Three days later Captain W. R. Shanks, adjutant to Carruthers, contacted Internment Operations headquarters in Ottawa for a ruling on the complaint. Carruthers and Shanks, both of whom had reputations for honesty and fairness, were embarrassed by the protest and were at a loss as to exactly what to do about it.

On June 24, Internment Operations director Colonel Hubert Stethem replied. His letter to Major Carruthers said, in part:

> Will you please inform Generalmajor Friemel that this office received word on June 20th that three West Indian soldiers were members of the Company which took over guard duties at Camp F, and the Director communicated immediately with the Adjutant-General requesting that they be transferred to another station. . . .
>
> While they are members of the Canadian forces, it is not felt desirable that they should be placed on guard duty in connection with the German officers, and, until a transfer is effected, it would be appreciated if they could be employed where they would not come in contact with or under the observation of the officer prisoners.[2]

Ironically, the fact that Canadian soldiers were sent to Europe to fight Hitler's racism never seems to have occurred to anyone in connection with this incident.

Occasionally, members of the press were allowed into POW camps. A Montreal *Gazette* reporter told his readers what he saw and heard inside the wire in a story published on October 10, 1940. The camp was Fort Henry.

> Following guides, we trooped inside the prison yard and strolled around. Some of the men grinned at us, others turned aside and mumbled remarks that caused their neighbours to regard us with grins. With a guide I looked through one of the cells. The place was clean, the beds neatly covered with grey blankets.
>
> My guide answered questions as we went. He was asked about trouble with the prisoners. "A little at first," he said. "They're pretty cocky when they arrive and usually tell us it's a waste of time to lock them up because within a few days the war will be over, they will have won and we'll be going into the prison."

The reporter mentioned that a camp spokesman was the only prisoner allowed to speak to the visitors. Among other things, the German told the press people that Hitler would, of course, win the war.

"Two plus two adds up to four, doesn't it? He's sure to win, and soon. We all expect to be out of here by Christmas. The Canadians treat us all right, but we naturally don't like prison. The food is good but they only give us one newspaper a day. This paper usually has some stories censored — cut out. . . ."

Shortly after the first POWs came to Canada, the Red Cross became the official channel through which incarcerated Germans communicated with their homeland. The Red Cross also monitored the extent to which Canada adhered to the terms of the Geneva Convention on the treatment of prisoners of war. Any violation of the terms of the Convention was immediately noticed by the POWs, who voiced their grievances to the Red Cross. That organization, in turn, investigated the complaints and reported their findings not only to Canadian officials, but to Berlin as well. Needless to say, Convention regulations were seldom broken. Canada had no desire to leave the way open for reprisals against any of the 1,864 of our troops who had been taken prisoner in northwest Europe.[3]

The Canadian delegate to the International Red Cross was Ernest Maag, a native of Switzerland who came to Canada in December 1926. An engineer and former officer of the Swiss army, Maag, thirty-five years old at the time of his appointment, was both liked and respected by those who knew him for his fairness and decisiveness. Part of Maag's job was to visit and inspect POW camps in Canada to check on their adherence to international regulations, and to mediate prisoner complaints. Occasionally the prisoners may have questioned his objectivity, but on the whole they accepted his judgments.

A key to Maag's success seems to have been his impartiality. He sided with the inmates as often as he sided with the guards. This may be seen over and over again in his inspection reports. If a camp was good, he said so. If not, or if prisoner gripes seemed warranted, the senior Canadian officer soon knew it. As far as this country was concerned, however, Maag's criticism was never harsh. In a note in the spring of 1941 to Norman Robertson, then under-secretary of state for external affairs, Maag discussed the approach he took to his job and expressed his views about Canadian camps and conditions in those camps. His letter said, in part:

Although it may be questioned in certain quarters, or even called biassed, I really try to shake all sentiments when I enter through the gates of internment camps, and I sincerely assume the role of a neutral. . . . I can truthfully say that I have never yet seen a condition in an internment camp in Canada, which I, as a former officer of the Swiss Army, would not have found perfectly acceptable for the mode of living in any army.[4]

Apart from minor inconveniences and personal grievances that they can recall, most former POWs tend to be in agreement with Maag. They also played jokes on him occasionally.

In one instance at the camp at Lethbridge, Alberta, the inmates had complained about crowded living conditions. Maag went to investigate, and informed the prisoners that they had no real grievance. To aid him in his report to his superior, he took several photographs, which showed that camp standards were quite acceptable. Because the prisoners realized that Maag was not going to side with them, they let him take all of his pictures — and then stole his camera and film.

Like the Red Cross, another organization sent representatives into POW camps. The World Committee of the Young Men's Christian Association spent many thousands of dollars ministering to the needs of the prisoners of war in more than thirty countries, Canada among them. Unlike the Red Cross, however, which dealt mainly with accommodation, food supplies and official prisoner complaints, the YMCA concerned itself with everything from the intellectual to the recreational and religious needs of the POWs.

The YMCA was responsible in large measure for establishing educational courses of various kinds in the camps. It sought and obtained donations of books, located sports and musical equipment, and ordered handicraft supplies for POWs. Movies, guest speakers, religious services and Christmas packages were all provided by this organization. Jerome Davies, who worked for the YMCA during the war, described his job for the publication *The Christian Century.*

Perhaps the easiest way to understand our work is to think of an American college or university campus. The YMCA provides, behind the barbed wire, all activities that usually belong to college life — educational, musical, athletic, recreational and religious. Take the matter of libraries, for instance. Books have been donated from individuals, college and city libraries, religious and other organizations all over the United States and Canada. Classes have been organized under the leadership of able teachers who are prisoners. In many of these camps the men who graduate are given certificates which will be recognized in their home country. . . .

In the field of music, the Church of the Brethren donated a piano for each camp. We also provide gramophones, records and musical instruments for an orchestra. In recreation we furnish a few indoor games, including ping-pong, the men often making their own tables. In most of the camps we provide boxing gloves and skates, but usually only twenty-four pairs to a camp of a thousand. The men sign up for these as one would for a tennis court. . . . For those who can occupy themselves with arts and crafts, we find materials for all sorts of activities. . . . The articles the prisoners make are often sold and the money given to the men.

In the religious field, we have tried to meet the needs of all groups, including Protestant, Roman Catholic and Jewish. We have sent in Bibles, hymn books, altar cloths and Communion sets.

Various odd situations occur. Recently I had to notify one prisoner that the death of a relative had brought him a bequest of six thousand dollars, and another that he had been married by proxy in Germany. Last December we made arrangements for sending in over eleven thousand dollars' worth of gifts from relatives and friends in Germany.

For Christmas we were instrumental in distributing packages to all the prisoners. Each contained a few nuts and raisins, a toothbrush, toothpaste, a box of chocolate, a few cigarettes and a handkerchief. I spent Christmas in one of the camps attending the Christmas party where these were distributed. There were tears in the eyes of many of the prisoners as they received their packages. As they stood around the Christmas tree and sang "Silent Night, Holy Night," one could not but realize that the distance between men of every nation is perhaps less than we think.[5]

From time to time, YMCA and Red Cross personnel were asked why they bothered to assist the incarcerated enemy. The answer was always the same. German prisoners were helped so that Berlin would be more humane toward the Allied troops who were being held in Germany. And to a certain degree, the reciprocal agreement worked — particularly insofar as the Red Cross was concerned. Canadian POWs in Germany were allowed to receive Red Cross parcels, and in many cases owed their lives to the gifts.

The YMCA film programs were always well received by the prisoners. Certain POWs worked out the camp schedule for the showings, set up the screen and chairs, and ran the projector. The films themselves were often first-run American and British movies such as *How Green Was My Valley* and *Yankee Doodle Dandy.* Quite often these features were seen in the camps before they were shown in moviehouses in Canada's largest cities. All films shown were in English. One evening, a minor problem occurred at Fort Henry when the movie to be shown opened with a spirited version of "God Save the King." After the prisoners protested, the objectionable lead was removed and the film ran without incident in several other camps.

In some cases, however, particular problems were not always solved in precisely the way the prisoners wished. One such dispute centred on the type of clothing POWs were permitted to wear. In the early fall of 1940, German POWs in Canada were confident that the Allies not only would lose the war, but would be defeated before winter came. As a result, many officer prisoners in particular continued to wear their summer uniforms in camp. They believed that they would be free before winter and would not need warmer clothing. But with the actual arrival of cold weather, they started to complain. By this time, of course, regulation prison garb had been distributed to them. Those who had their German uniforms were allowed to wear them, including the particular rank badges and other insignia. They could also wear any parts of the uniform that arrived by mail.

But they were not allowed to wear civilian clothing. Those whose uniforms had worn out, or who were not wearing a uniform when captured, were issued with a standard internment uniform; both the summer and the winter issues were dark blue and had a wide red stripe on the right leg. The blue undercoat and the blue overcoat had large red circles on the back, which the prisoners often referred to as the target. Some of them used to say jokingly that they would never be shot in the chest because the guard could not see the target.

The shirts worn by POWs were dark grey or blue and also had circles of contrasting colour on the back. The circle was rather large, seventeen to thirty-five centimetres in diameter. The size was chosen deliberately in order that no circle could be removed without almost wrecking the garment.

In some of the rural areas of Canada, POW shirts and jackets were a commonplace sight after the war. Farmers, loggers and construction workers often wore them, as much for their serviceability as for the fact that they sold for as little as twenty-five cents at war surplus outlets.

courtesy Siegfried Bruse

Captured U-boat crew seen as they were about to be taken ashore at a Scottish port. The original caption to this wartime magazine photo read: "Most of the forty-three prisoners expressed distaste at their task of sinking defenceless ships and seemed glad that their share in this type of warfare is finished."

Siegfried Bruse, today a successful realtor in North Bay, Ontario, is fourth from the right.

courtesy Ed House

German officer prisoners march on arrival through the streets of Gravenhurst, Ontario. Camp 20 at Gravenhurst housed 400 men in a converted sanatorium.

Public Archives of Canada

Escapes from POW camps were far fewer in the winter, when harsh weather, especially in isolated northern locations, discouraged even the hardiest prisoners. Pictured here is the camp at Neys, Ontario, on the north shore of Lake Superior.

courtesy Ed House

A Canadian soldier examines a tunnel dug by prisoners at the Espanola, Ontario, camp.

The camp at Seebe, Alberta, housed 650 POWs chiefly in tents.

courtesy Horst Braun

Thousands of prisoners spent their captivity in smaller transient bush camps, where they worked at outdoor tasks like logging and road-building. Pictured here is the mess at a northern Ontario camp.

Luftwaffe ace Franz von Werra escaped from a prison train bound for the camp at Neys, and successfully crossed the half-frozen St. Lawrence River to reach the still-neutral United States. Although von Werra glamorized his story for reporters, there is no doubt that his was one of the most daring escapes undertaken by a POW in Canada.

POWs stacking wood.

Farmers in many communities were grateful for POW labour while young Canadian men were in short supply. Prisoner Walter Woehr is second from the left in this farm family photo.

courtesy Bill Lesniak

Prisoners joked about the large red circle on the back of their shirts, referring to it as a readymade target for authorities intent on stopping escapes.

courtesy Ed Billet

Theatrical performances with POWs playing all roles were a staple of camp entertainment programs. Arrayed in medieval garb are the German officers at Gravenhurst.

Cut off from their families and from their country's war effort, the Germans' only contact with home was the mail, which, although heavily censored, was eagerly read and reread.

The YMCA was chiefly responsible for prisoner recreation and educational programs. Classes in a wide variety of subjects were available to help pass the long hours of incarceration and divert the POWs from planning escapes. Note the Nazi emblem over the door in this photo.

At the Bowmanville, Ontario, camp, 750 prisoners were housed in a boys' reformatory. This building was the principal scene of the Battle of Bowmanville: German officers barricaded themselves inside for three days to protest the shackling of prisoners, which was ordered subsequent to the failed landing at Dieppe.

Kingston's Old Fort Henry during its time as a POW camp. The men were housed mainly in the upper tier, with stores and privies on the ground floor.

In discussing the apparel today, most former prisoners remember with some amusement what they once wore. "We were not going anywhere anyway, so there was no need to dress up," one Gravenhurst veteran recalls. "Who cared if we looked like clowns? I know I never cared," he added.

One aspect of the clothing regulations that Stethem missed turns up in a later memo from the adjutant-general's office. Mercifully, no one recalls now who it was that asked for a ruling on the matter. We do know that Major-General B. W. Browne busied himself on May 27, 1941, writing the following:

It is not considered any special marking need be placed on the summer underwear or shorts worn by Prisoners of War as, should they escape in their underwear or shorts, they would be reasonably conspicuous.[6]

The document was originally classified as "Secret." Canada's war effort was obviously in good hands!

Even though many years have passed since the Germans were here as prisoners of war, they still recall diverse incidents of the time. Things that occurred in the small work camps are sometimes the most vivid of all.

A doctor in a bush camp north of Lake Superior happened to be Jewish. In his job, it occasionally seemed as if he was trying to make up for some of the wrong done to his people by the Nazis. If an injured prisoner was particularly cocky, the medic's bedside manner generally left something to be desired. He would then examine a bad bruise or a sprained ankle by pressing on it or perhaps twisting it, at the same time asking: "Does it hurt when I do that?" or "Do you have any feeling there?" When the injured party cried out in pain, the doctor would say, "Oh, I'm sorry."

One day a POW whose leg had been cut by an axe was brought in for stitches. The fellow didn't particularly want to be looked after by a Jewish doctor, but he had no choice in the matter. The doctor was aware of the way the man felt, so he cleaned the wound and sewed it up without any anaesthetic. Some time later when the leg was healed, the POW pretended to be sick. As soon as he found himself alone with the doctor in the examining room, he reminded the physician of the stitching incident and then slugged him. A guard rushed in, grabbed the assailant, and dragged him away. The POW later served six months in jail for what he had done. On the day of his release, he was heard to say how great it was to be back in a prisoner-of-war camp.

Former POW Ed Billet remembers his brief escape from a work camp. He also recalls the French-Canadian girl he met in the interval when he was free. He told his story in the Toronto *Globe and Mail* of March 11, 1976.

I came to Canada in 1942 as a German prisoner of war and was sent to a POW camp in Northern Ontario. Facilities were excellent in view of our situation, and although we were well treated, and I and others should have felt happy to have escaped what would eventually have probably ended in death or mutilation, the well-guarded fences of our camp soon began to close in on us. Only those who were at one time or another forcibly confined to a restricted area will be able to understand such a feeling. I often woke up at night to the nostalgic whistle of a train passing through the town nearby, and I visualized what it would be like to travel through that vast, sheer unending country out there, free to go or free to stay. Then, in the summer of 1943, I was one of the first volunteers to leave for a lumber camp in northwestern Ontario. My dream of roaming the vast, open spaces of God's country had come true.

We were sent to a minimum-security lumber camp where our daily tasks gave us ample time for our interests, and where we were allowed to move about at our own discretion, since the camp was many miles away from the next village. This was the most exciting and fascinating period I spent in Canada. It was the time when I began to live again after years of mental oppression and when my mind opened up to an unknown sense of freedom and adventure. Sometimes I felt like a child that sees for the first time the world around it. Self-made skis and canoes enabled us to travel the countryside and the lakes, and during our extended trips we discovered two more lumber camps, one occupied by other POWs and the other by Canadians. Time went by and the end of 1944 signalled the end of the war. Sooner or later we would be sent home. But I had different plans — fantastic but unrealistic — motivated by these facts. I wanted to go into hiding until grass had covered my tracks and I would be able to return and live as a civilian. This crack-brained scheme was further emphasized by the fact that I had met a French-Canadian girl in one of the neighbouring camps with whom I had a secret intimate relationship. I escaped, was picked up by the RCMP a few weeks later, and was sent back to my base camp. Thus ended one of the most exciting and adventurous periods of my life.

Horst Braun, the former wireless operator on U-434, spent two years in bush camps near Nipigon, Ontario. While he has generally pleasant memories of those years, he now looks back on a POW "strike" as one of the highlights of the time:

> The woodcutting should only have been a winter operation — because of the bugs. We had to work summer and winter and in the summer they gave us black dope to smear on ourselves to ward off the bugs. We also tried nets and gloves and so forth, but we found it almost impossible to work that way.
>
> In July 1944 we went on strike. The CO from Port Arthur came in, lined us up, and told us if we did not go to work we would be locked up in the cooler. He gave us time to think it over. Then, those of us who still refused were put on a truck and shipped to Port Arthur. Then we were put into the barracks under guard. The guard was active military — not the Veterans Guard. We walked into the barracks and saw the bunk beds and so forth and thought everything was beautiful. We got twenty-eight days, the standard detention. Then we were all called out on roll call. When they let us back in, the barracks were empty — no beds, nothing! We were given a couple of blankets and told to sleep on the floor. We slept three together so we could use three blankets for the mattress and three over us — the nights were that cool.
>
> Every few days the CO came in and asked the same question: "All right, are you ready to go back to work?" When we would answer, "No sir!" his response was always the same. "Three days of diet number one." Diet number one was bread and water. And you didn't get all the bread you wanted. You just got all the water you wanted. We went through this procedure four times. They had to give us three days of full meals and then we were asked again. Then it was back to diet number one. This was still better than the heat and the blackflies and the mosquitoes. We knew that. After twenty-eight days we said we would go back to the bush because we knew in August the blackflies were pretty well gone. After that, things were good.

Things were also good in other ways for Horst Braun. During his second winter in the bush, he was transferred from Nipigon to a camp near Longlac, 240 kilometres northeast of the earlier location. While here, the enterprising young corporal actually set himself up in a thriving, albeit illegal, private lumber business.

At the time, each POW was expected to cut and pile one cord of wood per day. However, ambitious individuals who wished to earn more money for their accounts often cut two and sometimes three cords, using the receipts to buy mail-order watches, rings, pen sets and the like. Braun did some extra cutting himself, but realized that while there were plenty of dead trees lying around, the company was only interested in green wood. That was when he started to look around for ways to sell dead trees.

One day during a conversation with a truck driver from outside, Braun mentioned the dead wood and asked if it could be sold somewhere. The driver's eyes lit up at the idea and he said he would see what could be arranged. A week later, the man returned with a plan.

Since trucks were coming and going from the camp on a regular basis anyway, the driver doubted anyone would object to one extra trip in the evening. Several cold, moonlit nights that winter, the truck came to the camp and drove to where Braun had cut and piled four or five cords of dead wood. Because prisoners were left pretty much on their own in the bush, the German would help load the wood, and then go with the driver to the town of Geraldton for the unloading. The trucker had a number of contacts there, so selling the wood was not difficult.

Braun and his partner were paid eight dollars a cord for their efforts, and they simply split the proceeds. After each load was sold, the two men often drove to a local hotel for a quiet beer. Then the driver would take Braun back to camp.

At about the same time as Horst Braun was logging in the North, a man by the name of Francis Olde operated a farm near the southwestern Ontario POW camp at Fingal. Like many of his neighbours, he employed prisoner labour during the busy summer months, mainly because there were few Canadian farmhands around. Most of them were in the army. While several Germans worked for Olde at various times, one of them made more of an impression on him than the others.

Hans Modrow was a highly skilled ear, nose and throat specialist who found himself in March 1941 working as a ship's doctor on a merchant vessel near the Lofoten Islands in northern Norway. On Tuesday, March 4, just as he was performing an emergency appendectomy on a sailor, Modrow's ship was attacked by a British destroyer. Because of his decision not to interrupt surgery, Modrow was captured, as was his patient, who subsequently recovered in a prison camp.

Many months and several POW compounds later, Modrow had a chance to exhibit the same surgical skill on Francis Olde's farm. Operating conditions were still far from satisfactory, but again the patient recovered. Olde recalls what happened: "I had a cow that got infection in one of her teats. Even though she was a good cow, the veterinarian told me to get rid of her, as the problem, according to him, was cancer. Modrow disagreed and asked me if I would let him try to save her. He operated using a straight razor and sewed up the wound with a black thread. The cow recovered, had several more calves, but we never told the vet. We needed him after the war. Modrow had amputated the infected teat."

In the many areas of the country where prisoners helped on farms, the relationship between the farmer and the POW quickly moved from a formal tolerance of each other to an acceptance and then to a warm friendship. Several farm operators have told me they were truly sorry to see the prisoners leave when the war was over.

David Carter referred to these friendships in his book, *Behind Canadian Barbed Wire*.

In some instances, relationships between the farmer and the POW became so positive that the POW would be left for days on end with the farm, livestock and children in his care. Some POWs were sponsored back into Canada after the war by their farmer friends. Some married the farmer's daughter.[7]

After he had spent several weeks in the Medicine Hat camp, Walter Woehr, the former army Unteroffizier captured in North Africa in 1943, was one of those allowed to go to work on farms throughout the district. Initially the POWs were picked up at the camp by local farmers, and taken to the place of work for the day. Gradually this practice changed. "Eventually we simply lived with the family, almost like sons," recalls Woehr. "We were treated so well."

Woehr remembers many other kindnesses shown by his hosts. "Another guy and I were given the run of one place. The woman of the house fed us so much. Her husband told us as soon as we got there: 'There is the beer. There is the whisky. We don't have too much, but what is mine is yours.' We slept under the stars and we worked as hard as we could for him. He grew sugar beets.

"Most of the farmers were the same. Sometimes they took us

into town with them. One night a number of prisoners who were working on area farms even went to a dance. One farmer had a very beautiful daughter of eighteen or so. She knew the dance was on and she went to all the farms in the area and invited us," Woehr recalls. "We found everything so strange for the first while. Then we started dancing and had a wonderful time. Germany seemed so far away. That's where the Canadian boys were. After the dance, a girl I met took me to her home and I met her family. Some relatives dropped in and I met them, too."

In the artificial society of the POW internment centres and bush camps, the absence of women and children was felt. But even though a certain percentage in any group can be expected to have homosexual tendencies, neither former guards nor prisoners recall many incidences of overt homosexual activity.

One who does is Max Schoellnhammer:

"I remember one case at Monteith," he says. "A navy man from a destroyer made a play for another fellow in a washroom one night. I guess the wrong man was approached, however. The next morning the sailor had his face smashed and both his eyes blackened. This was the only one I can remember."

At Gravenhurst two men were known to have engaged in homosexual acts. In this case several prisoners knew what was going on but they simply turned a blind eye. When the guards became aware of the matter, however, the men in question were each given twenty-eight days' detention.

By contrast, Eric Koch, in his book *Deemed Suspect*, claims homosexual love was an everyday occurrence in the alien camps where he spent sixteen months.

> By far the greatest number of love affairs were between men who before and after internment were perfectly straight. If you had played a policeman in a play, as one of my friends had done, and you celebrated your triumph at a party in hut 4 after opening night, you probably could not take your hands off the boy who had played and looked exactly like Mitzi, the luscious chambermaid.
>
> As to the urgency of our libido, to keep it within bounds we were convinced that bromide was added to our soup, or possibly our coffee. It was perhaps this widespread assumption of the use of chemicals that served as an explanation why many of us found our libido surprisingly docile and relatively easy to sublimate.[8]

In almost all camps, there were stories connected with the use of radios. At one point during the war, Internment Operations decided they should move the bulk of the Gravenhurst prisoners to Fort Henry. So many officers in Muskoka had attempted to escape that it was felt the Kingston camp would be more secure. The move was not a welcome one for the prisoners, but they had no choice. They were simply informed of the move and told to get ready.

To some, the change of camps presented no great difficulty. To others, however, the transfer presented problems. In Gravenhurst, as in virtually all of the camps, the POWs had constructed a receiving set from bits and pieces of radio parts. One man had the responsibility for keeping the device hidden — and that man was one of the people involved in the transfer. Because the officers had no desire either to leave the radio behind or to allow it to be discovered, they decided that, if possible, the set should be smuggled out of the camp during the upcoming move. Unfortunately, getting the device past at least two sets of searches — one in Gravenhurst when leaving, and another in Kingston on arrival there — would be difficult.

The radio committee met several times to assess the problem. They listened to and dismissed one idea after another for getting the machine to Kingston. The most popular idea was to take the thing apart, hide sections among the personal belongings of several men, and hope that much of the set went undiscovered. While this suggestion seemed far from foolproof, no one seemed able to come up with anything better.

Then, just two hours before the first men were to leave, someone hit on a novel idea. In one of the common rooms in the camp, there were several large decorative plants the prisoners had cared for. The POWs took one of these and gently removed it and the supporting clay from the container. Then, using waxed paper from the kitchens, they carefully wrapped the radio and hid it at the bottom of the flower pot. The plant itself was then returned to the holder and the clay repacked. Extra dirt was flushed down a toilet.

When it came time to move out, the officers lined up and were counted, searched and marched to the waiting trucks. As the search moved closer to the man with the radio, those who knew what was happening talked to and joked with each other and the Canadians.

"We'll miss you," yelled a prisoner to a guard some distance away.

"Yeah, no more tunnels to find," the man called back.

"Now you won't have anyone to watch," laughed a Luftwaffe tunnel expert.

"You'll never get out of the Fort," came the rejoinder.

Soon the banter was contagious. Neither the guards nor the Germans seemed to take the searching seriously. Prisoners danced around, joked with the guards, and one or two broke into paroxysms of laughter during the body searches. Eventually the man with the plant came to the head of the line.

"Where's your stuff?" asked a guard.

The POW indicated that the man behind was carrying an extra bag.

"Why aren't you carrying it?"

"Because of this," he answered, referring to the plant.

"Is that all you've got?"

"No. I have a secret radio hidden in here and it's heavy. It's all I can carry." He peered down through the leaves.

The guard hesitated, not really knowing what to say. Then he laughed and waved the prisoner through. The story was so preposterous it was actually funny.

Later that day the radio arrived intact in Fort Henry.

Other incidents ended differently.

On the morning of August 19, 1942, a five-thousand-man Allied expeditionary force composed mainly of Canadian troops attacked the town of Dieppe, on the coast of France. The attack was repulsed, and by the end of the day there were 3,367 Canadian casualties. In addition, 1,946 officers and men were taken prisoner. Even the detailed military plan for the debacle fell into enemy hands. Unfortunately, it was this plan that sometime later gave rise to a series of reprisals on either side.

Included in the scheme was the proviso that prisoners might be tied up so they could not destroy their documents. The British War Office later cancelled the order, but by then the damage had been done. On October 8, nearly two months after Dieppe, the German High Command had a number of Canadian and British prisoners bound. Hours later, and without consulting Canadian officials in advance, Winston Churchill ordered similar reprisals on German prisoners. On October 10, this directive went into effect in a number of camps in Canada. Unfortunately, Canadians suppressed whatever doubts they might have had about the idea, so that publicly, at least, they could maintain a semblance of solidarity with Britain over the matter. Privately, the situation was much different. Canada opposed the move and the British knew it.

Men were shackled in four camps: Gravenhurst, Monteith, Espanola and Bowmanville. In Monteith and Espanola, the move caused no real problems. The POWs protested but did what they were told. In Bowmanville and Gravenhurst, however, reaction was totally different. It was also the reaction that the British should have anticipated.

The prisoners at Gravenhurst removed the handcuffs almost as quickly as they were put on. Some of the locks were picked while others were simply broken. There were also a few opened with keys that sympathetic guards "happened" to drop. The situation became so bad that within a couple of days the number of broken and missing sets made it necessary to order new ones.

In Bowmanville, the reaction not only lasted longer, it was much more violent as well. At noon on Saturday, October 10, Lieutenant-Colonel J. M. Taylor, the commanding officer at Camp 30, advised the German camp leader, Generalmajor Georg Friemel, that a number of prisoners were to be shackled. The general listened politely to what Taylor had to say, but then replied that no German in the camp would voluntarily submit to handcuffing.

"Then we will do the job by force," Taylor is said to have retorted.

With that, Friemel returned to his quarters and met with his senior advisers to decide how best to oppose the decree. Taylor also held a hurried conference on the matter. The Canadians decided to try to reason with the Germans, but if that proved to be ineffective, to use stronger measures.

Half an hour later, an unarmed German-speaking Veterans Guard officer entered the compound and began explaining the shackling order directly to the POWs themselves. As the Canadian spoke, the Germans began to crowd around him. Then, on a prearranged signal, they sprang forward and grabbed the man.

"The fellow we took was a captain, I believe," recalls Siegfried Bruse. "He was fairly young, too. Within two minutes he was knocked cold. We bound him and put him in a corner, and he became our prisoner of war."

This act in itself probably did more to boost the morale of the prisoners than any other event during the momentous weekend that followed. The Germans now felt they had luck on their side and the advantage in the dispute was theirs. They had not only told the Canadians what the response to the shackling would be; they had backed the protest with action. The next move was up to Taylor.

While the Canadian CO was a good officer and a decisive leader, he was unprepared for this sudden turn of events. And even though the shackling order was certainly not his idea, he had to live with it and somehow enforce it.

At three o'clock the same day, the Germans were ordered out for roll call. They refused to appear. Instead, they barricaded themselves inside their quarters and propped steel lockers, heavy cupboards and even bedsprings against the windows and doors. By this time they had also armed themselves with sticks, baseball bats and any rock they could throw.

Taylor felt defeated. He and his veteran guards were more than able to police the camp if everything was going all right. Now, however, he realized that forcibly ejecting hundreds of much younger, athletic, and well-organized prisoners from the compound buildings was beyond the capability of his men alone. At one point in the afternoon, the veteran guards made an attempt to clear the mess hall. The foray came to nothing as they were pelted with a hail of stones, a baseball or two and even some kitchen crockery. The Canadians retreated, nursed their wounds, and called for help.

As early as midday, Taylor had been in telephone contact with officials at Military District 3 in Kingston, and as a result, a number of troops at nearby Barriefield had been put on standby in case matters worsened at Bowmanville. When the news came that the situation had in fact deteriorated, 212 officers and men were immediately dispatched to Camp 30. In the meantime, the veteran guards watched and waited, all night and through a muggy Sunday morning. At nine, when Taylor ordered a roll call, the POWs didn't budge. The large two-storey red-brick and stucco buildings were still tightly sealed. Pathways through the compound were deserted, as was the well-worn cinder track next to the warning wire around the perimeter of the camp. Except for the fleeting appearance of a face in a window now and then, the buildings looked empty — empty and ominously silent.

Inside, the Germans waited to learn what the Canadians would do, knowing all the while that sooner or later, attempts would be made to evacuate the buildings. In the meantime, the tension, suppressed excitement and heat were affecting everyone. Men talked in nervous, staccato whispers and chain-smoked; some pretended to read. They ate little, and during the previous night had barely slept.

Among the prisoners, officers such as Tony Kleimaker, Siegfried Bruse and many others recall this time as one of the more memorable periods of their captivity. This was because prison life with its inherent sameness had, for one weekend at least, become exciting, mildly dangerous and almost fun. The shackling itself had become secondary; it was the resistance to it that was now important. The whole thing had become a game, a diversion that both sides — prisoner and guard — would long remember. And though it was a game, the rules favoured the guards, who, whether alone or with help, would ensure that the POWs would eventually lose. In reality, the only factor not apparent from the outset was the length of the contest.

When the first group of reinforcements arrived from Kingston, an assault was made on building 5, the structure that Taylor and his men felt was the centre of most of the resistance. The Canadians got a door open, but as soon as they did, they were assaulted by prisoners with clubs, baseball bats and hockey sticks. The Canadians carried the same type of weapons but after several intense, heated skirmishes, made no more headway than they had in their previous assaults. A lot of the fighting was done just inside the doorway to the building, and because of the confined space, neither side gained much. At one point, however, the situation threatened to escalate into something far more serious.

"I was in one of the guard towers directly in front of where the fighting was taking place," recalls Bill Kennedy, a Veterans Guard scout. "A chap by the name of Bill Portice was with me. As we watched, the pushing and shoving seemed to get worse and there was a lot more cursing and swearing.

"Then somebody inside the door yelled something in German, and the prisoners started to march out with one of our men in front of them. It was the guy they'd grabbed the day before. Bill hollered at the column to halt. Instead of stopping, they slammed our man up against the building and cut his face.

"When that happened, Portice swung his rifle around and fired one shot. He hit one of the leaders in the leg and he fell. Then they let our man go and raced back inside and stayed there. The whole thing was over in a few seconds.

"Because he did the shooting, Portice had to be tried. He

naturally said that he had to shoot to protect our man. And that was true. It didn't do any good, though. He was convicted of the shooting of a prisoner and given fourteen days' detention. Actually, all they did with him was send him home on fourteen days' leave. They had to get him away from Bowmanville right away. He came back later."

The prisoners had grabbed their fallen comrade and dragged him inside the building. There, one of the two German doctors in the camp stopped the bleeding and dressed the man's wounds and the various cuts and abrasions suffered by others in the melee. At the same time, every POW able to do so began securing the doors and reinforcing the already barricaded windows on the ground floor.

When it became apparent that no further assault would be made on their stronghold before nightfall, the men within the compound posted lookouts and attempted to sleep.

Outside the enclosure, very few Canadians were sleeping. Instead, their pride hurt because of their failure to break the deadlock in the camp, they again conferred with Kingston. Additional help was requested and this time 150 more troops climbed on trucks and in the dead of night set out on the two-hundred-kilometre journey to Bowmanville. They drove to within a kilometre or two of the camp, where they left the trucks and formed up behind a copse in a farmer's field. When the time came, they would move in on the enclosure from the rear, thereby concealing their presence as long as possible.

At noon on Monday, October 12, the combined operation was launched. The seventy-five Veterans Guard personnel posed largely as screens, while the two regular force units provided the main thrust of the attack. About half of the latter carried rifles with fixed bayonets. Many of the remainder had clubs.

For the second day in a row, the initial operation was directed at building 5. When the attackers failed to get the door open, however, they moved quickly to other buildings. One by one the remaining quarters were cleared and the prisoners marched to the parade square. Finally, when the rest of the barracks were completely empty, the Canadians returned to number 5.

Because the structure had withstood the brunt of two major assaults, it began to look more and more like a fortress. The windows were still sealed and untouched, but the solid oak door at the front was now badly scratched and gouged, particularly where an attempt had been made to pry off one of the hinges. The concrete steps were littered with pieces of rock, a splintered baseball bat and several broken bottles. Yet the building itself looked as impregnable as ever.

At this point, Taylor and the two other senior officers in the operation, Major D. F. Adams and Captain T. J. Wallace, met to confer concerning their next move. The discussion was brief. Taylor phoned the Bowmanville fire department and borrowed their equipment. Ten minutes later, the front door of building 5 was broken open with an axe. At the same time, men from one of the Kingston units threw ladders against a rear wall and climbed onto the flat roof of the structure. As far as the POWs inside were concerned, the game was over.

In no time, a hole was chopped down into the attic and several of Wallace's men clambered through. The nozzle of a high-pressure fire hose was handed to them. Then, as the water was turned on up on the roof, tear gas was lobbed through a broken downstairs window. Almost immediately the two prisoners who had been closest to the gas stumbled from the front door, tears streaming down their faces and handkerchiefs over their noses.

The sounds of shouting, cursing, coughing and breaking glass inside rivalled the whine of the pressure pump on the lawn. Then, singly and in groups of three and four, the POWs gave up the fight and agreed to go outside. One navy man tried to prolong the affair but gave in when a bayonet sliced into his ribs. A few others threw a punch or two, but real resistance was now short-lived.

"We had no choice because we were unarmed," recalls U-boat officer Siegfried Bruse. "Then the Canadians made sort of a barrier away from the front door. There were two lines of guards there and we had to walk down through the centre. As we did so, they hit us on the head with clubs. It wasn't fair, but they were mad because it had taken three days to end the whole thing."

Generalmajor Friemel was also incensed at the way the fracas had ended. In a later communiqué to the Swiss Consul General's office, the German camp leader said, in part:

Injuries were suffered on both sides. Forty-six prisoners of war suffered casualties up until the time the resistance was stopped. I do not fail to recognize that the authorities have tried to avoid bloodshed. However, I must confirm that only after resistance ended

not less than 107 Prisoners of War (Officers and men), while a great
part put up their hands, were beaten with sticks and rifles or were
injured with bayonets. Among these defenceless were found a doctor
distinguishable by a Red Cross armband and a lieutenant wounded
before and lying on a stretcher. One officer suffered a head wound
with concussion of the brain and probably a fractured shoulder
blade. Another an injury of the lungs through a stab with a bayonet.
It must be pointed out that some Canadian officers and soldiers,
especially those of the present camp staff tried to protect the
defenceless prisoners of war against mistreatment. . . . I petition you
to make complaints to the Canadian Government with regard to the
treatment of German soldiers after the cessation of the fight.[9]

The protest went through the various official channels, and on
October 20 was replied to by Lieutenant-Colonel Taylor. His side of
the story is somewhat less than candid. For one thing, he never
really got around to addressing the major complaint — that of
POWs being beaten after the fight was over. In his words:

There was considerable confusion and excitement. Most of the
fighting was at close quarters, and because of the nature of the
buildings the space, available for action in most cases, was rather
limited, and it was during the melee that went on in each of the
buildings in turn, and before the prisoners surrendered and agreed
to come out voluntarily, that most of the casualties on both sides
took place. It should be realized, that while in some instances the
prisoners in one or two rooms would surrender, fighting continued
in other parts of the same buildings, adding to the confusion, in so
far as the troops were concerned.[10]

Although there is some confusion over what happened at Bowmanville that day, Bill Kennedy tends to agree with the German
general. "We had to try to herd the prisoners out of each building," says Kennedy. "As we did this, we were told not to touch or
hurt any of them in any way. But by this time, some of the fellows
from Kingston were pretty worked up. One of them, who had been
punched in the eye by a prisoner, was clubbing the inmates over
the head as they came out the door. Then an officer ordered him
not to hit anyone whose hands were up. 'Okay, sir,' this chap
answered. But when the next German came out with his hands
up, the same man yelled: 'Put your goddamned hands down!'

The POW did so and was slugged on the back of the head with a tent peg. There was a lot of that sort of thing."

Finally, all the quarters were cleared. The three-day "Battle of Bowmanville" was over, but nothing had really changed. The veteran guards were again in control; the POWs were still inside the compound; and the handcuffs would now go on. Most of the prisoners knew that sooner or later the shackling would be done, yet they also knew that now even the great Winston Churchill would learn what Bowmanville POWs thought of his order. In fact, Churchill already knew.

Shortly after the last prisoner reported to the parade square for roll call, the various buildings in the camp were thoroughly searched for weapons and other forms of contraband — notably escape paraphernalia and radio apparatuses. While several home-made clubs and caches of rocks were found, no one today remembers much of anything else. On the other hand, the Canadian soldiers who did search the premises helped themselves to dozens of personal items that they had no right to touch. Included in the haul were watches, rings, fountain pens, uniform insignia and several battle decorations, including an Iron Cross with Oak Leaves belonging to the U-boat ace commander Otto Kretschmer. Later on, when they were allowed to return to their quarters, the Germans reported the pilfering to Taylor, who in turn passed the word to his men. Eventually a few articles were returned, with the explanation that these had been found on barrack floors and picked up "by mistake." The bulk of the material was never returned.

As soon as the camp settled down to a semblance of normality, several of the ringleaders in the protest were transferred out of Bowmanville. After their departure, no difficulties were encountered with the handcuffing, and on December 12, the shackling order itself was cancelled.

While the whole affair seems a tempest in a teacup to us now, it was far from that in 1942. A number of "Secret" and "Most Secret" cables flew between Ottawa and London, and, because of a two-hundred-word item in *Time* magazine,[11] between Ottawa and Washington as well. Because of the newsmagazine article and the Canadian government's protest about it to the U.S. State Department, stories on the entire subject of prisoners of war in Canada had to be submitted to Canadian censors before publication. The *Time* description of the "battle" had not been — primar-

ily because the editors in the United States felt that POW stories
did not have to be censored.

In the main, the short piece had been reasonably accurate,
if a bit overplayed. "When the Canadians came with the mana-
cles, the big blond boys at Camp Bowmanville put up an awful
fight," gushed the story. And later:

> After the prisoners had gone two days without food, the energetic
> future commandoes [from Kingston], hooting like Indians, carried
> out a planned campaign. They battered through the camp door
> with a telephone pole, chopped a hole in the roof, bayoneted the
> windows, turned a fire hose on. After thirty-five minutes of high-
> pressure water and tear gas, the Nazis marched out smartly in
> military formation.

Reporters who had been assigned to describe the event for Canadian newspapers were unsuccessful in their attempts to publish
what they wrote. The Toronto *Star* assigned seven people to the
story and rented rooms at a downtown Toronto hotel so that the
team could collate the information as it came in.

Years later, *Star* reporter Gwyn Thomas recalled the incident.
"I remember crawling through an apple orchard near the prison
camp and being warned by a guard with a fixed bayonet to get
out, or else. We filed stories to the *Star* for four days, but
the censor . . . had his orders from Ottawa and nothing was
published. It was frustrating as hell."[12]

For its part, the Canadian government was forced to admit
publicly that there had in fact been some trouble at Camp 30.
After that, the incident was forgotten. The press and politicians
turned to other problems, and the extra troops went back to
Kingston. At Bowmanville, the POWs coped with the shackles and
the guards with the POWs.

In addition to problems with the press, Internment Operations
had to cope with problems connected with POW mail, both to and
from the camps.

As the war moved into its second and third years, the list of
restricted persons and organizations from which mail could be
accepted grew. Many names were aliases and several address
changes were evident. In some cases, mail from a particular
address was refused, no matter who the sender claimed to be.
The bulk of such restricted addresses were in the United States,
although Canadian, Mexican, Paraguayan, Brazilian and Argen-

tinian locations were included. While some of the organizations were openly pro-German — the American Committee for German Relief in New York, Philadelphia's Kyffhauser Bund — others like the Chicago Knitting Club or the Meyer Seed Company of Baltimore were less obvious.

Occasionally, materials emanating from Germany gave cause for suspicion. Two weeks after Christmas 1940, a packet containing fifty-three Christmas cards sent by a German *Gauleiter* (Nazi Party district leader) arrived in Ottawa. The cards, all addressed to known Party members in several camps, looked suspicious. Internment Operations turned the lot over to the RCMP, who ran the standard lab tests for hidden messages. The tests themselves proved negative, but some of the cards were permanently stained by the chemical used in the testing procedure. However, all the greetings had been distributed by the end of February. No record exists of how welcome they were.

Now and then photographs accompanied letters. When that happened, the prisoner was doubly pleased. Occasionally, though, a photograph caused more pain than joy. A friend of Tony Kleimaker once sent him a picture of herself. At first the pilot thought the photo had escaped the censor. Two weeks after the picture arrived, however, a huge X made by the censor with some type of chemical appeared and completely obliterated the girl's face. "I almost wished she had never sent it," said Kleimaker of the incident. "There was nothing I could do or say."

Often, self-styled Good Samaritans wrote to the camps. Such letters were legion, and their content must have caused some amusement when received. The following note from a girl in Rochester, New York, was answered by Internment officials but was never shown to any POW.

Dear Sir:
Would you please send me the names and camp addresses of two or more German aviators who are prisoners of war. I would like to correspond with them. These men must naturally be able to read and write fairly well in English. There may be some aviators who know how to read and write some English but would like to improve. This would be a good opportunity. Believe me when I say I have no ulterior motives in writing these men, it just seems fun and rather interesting. These letters might help entertain idle hours which might otherwise be spent in planning "excursions." I know prisoners are allowed to send only a limited number of letters a

month. That is quite all right since I'm rather slow replying myself. I understand these fellows are rather difficult to get on with. But if any proved friendly enough to write me, I might send cigarettes and magazines later. If no aviators will come down to earth and write to me, you might try some sailors, although aviators are preferable.

Thank you.[13]

Some of the most curious letters received by Internment officials concerned a man who was never a prisoner in Canada, although for a time both POWs and their guards thought he might be brought here.

On the night of May 10, 1941, Rudolf Hess, the deputy leader of the Nazi Party under Adolf Hitler, flew alone to Scotland on what he said was a peace mission. His Messerschmitt 110 crashed near Glasgow, but Hess bailed out before the aircraft went down. The German was interned in Britain for the duration of the war and since then he has been held in Berlin's Spandau prison, where today he is the only inmate.

But not long after the flight of Hess and his subsequent imprisonment in the Tower of London, a rumour began to circulate in Canada that the deputy Fuehrer was not in England, but in Fort Henry in Kingston. Not only the newspaper people but others outside the media heard the story and believed what they heard. Dozens of letters came into Internment headquarters about the Hess imprisonment, but few received replies. In one case, RCMP intelligence officers visited a correspondent in Toronto who had said in a letter that he would be contacting Hess about an important message. The "message" was rambling nonsense, and the man who concocted it turned out to be a wino who lived in a downtown flophouse. When he found that the police laughed at his story, the wino did not seem to mind. Instead, he told them he would just have to contact Hess in another world.

An American organization that wanted to correspond with POWs showed how resourceful and ingenious people can be. The Chicago Knitting Club sent dozens of letters and parcels to several of the camps. In most cases, a covering letter to the authorities was included, and inside the various packages were hand-knitted woollen socks, generally two pair to a package. Such generosity was appreciated and the socks were popular among the prisoners.

It was only after several such parcels had been distributed that government mail censors learned why the socks were so welcome. Hidden far down in the toes of some of the socks were tiny balls of paper. On these papers, in minute letters, were printed the names and addresses of contact persons who lived in the United States and who would help POWs during an escape attempt. After this discovery, the Chicago Knitting Club was placed on the restricted list as far as correspondence to and from the camps was concerned. During the research for this book, I found several socks stored among POW materials in the Public Archives in Ottawa. The fact that the socks went undelivered indicates that mail censorship did have some effect.

"Whether we had a great deal of effect will probably never be known," says one former censor. "If we look upon censorship as security, then the business of the censor is to remove from correspondence anything that would be detrimental to the war effort.

"The incidental effect was to gain intelligence. This worked in various ways. There were two things that we gleaned from prisoner-of-war mail, and in my opinion we did so reasonably skilfully. Certain prisoners were assigned to certain censors. The censor therefore got to know 'his' prisoners quite well. He became familiar with the personal codes these POWs used, and so on.

"For instance, I recall one censor who worked with me who started noticing occasional references to the uncle of a POW, who every so often went on a journey to a farm. The censor started keeping track of the 'farm visits' until through various stratagems he learned that the uncle was a U-boat commander, and every 'farm visit' referred to the man and his ship going to sea. This type of information was helpful to the Navy.

"The other thing that was learned from mail sent to POWs was the state of mind of the German civil population. We monitored their morale, their optimism and so forth. Occasionally letters from the camps hinted at possible disturbances the guards could expect."

The censor recalls an unexpected outgrowth of the censorship that was very useful. "If a censor noticed that particular prisoners were happy, or reasonably happy with their lot, they were often approached by our people in military intelligence. Individual POWs were then asked if they were interested in taping messages to be broadcast to their relatives in Germany. Initially the reaction was rather guarded, but before long, men in several camps recorded greetings for their families and the messages were broadcast by the BBC in London.

"Because the German population was not supposed to listen to the BBC, the whole scheme was somewhat chancy at first. From the letters of POWs who had made broadcasts, however, we knew that relatives in Germany were told about the broadcast greetings. Presumably the German censors deleted most such references, but we know some got through. A lonely mother or wife would write to her man in camp and tell him she had heard him on the radio.

"Our purpose, of course, in all this was to get as many of the German people listening to these broadcasts as possible, in order to show them that the propaganda they had been fed for so many years was a lot of bunk. If we could get them to not hate us, our reception once we moved into Germany would be a bit easier.

"From time to time, rather amusing things cropped up concerning the censorship. A friend of mine had been assigned a particular assortment of letters written by men at a camp in Quebec. One of the men who wrote regularly complained in his letters that the censor who read his mail was too severe, and that too much of every letter was cut out. At that point, every censor had a number, and the number was written on every letter read. So the censor wrote a different number on this prisoner's next letter, in order to see what would happen. The POW's next note to his wife mentioned that he now had a new censor and 'everything was much better.' "

Though the war has been over for several decades, the letters and snippets of information garnered from the mails to and from POW camps have not disappeared into a void. I was given access to much of this material in the National Archives — and while it may seem somewhat exciting to read someone else's mail, the novelty lasts for only a short time. The bulk of the letters that went undelivered because of the war contain no more information than the name of a city, a mention of a new CO in the camp or an expected transfer to another location. Taken out of the context of the time, such facts seem rather innocuous. The remainder of the letters contain such things as family news: Uncle Peter's health, Mother's cooking at Christmas, young Helga's latest love, and so on. A few minutes spent reading these and similar mundane trivialities give us a certain admiration for the censors who devoted literally years to their work.

While not all mail entering or leaving the camps was censored, a certain portion of it always was. However, there were not enough censors to read everything; the volume of mail was overwhelming. But censored or not, that mail was very important to the prisoners.

Several former prisoners told me how excited they were when they got mail from home. "One day just before Christmas, two letters came for me," recalls a man who was in Camp 23 at Monteith, Ontario. "I took the first letter and read about ten words. Then I actually stuffed the thing away and read a few more words the next day and so on. It probably took me two weeks before I had read it all, but that way, I had mail every day. Then, on Christmas Day, I read *all* of the second letter. What a treat that was! Especially since I was so lonesome."

Another prisoner wrote to tell his parents about mail call. In a letter from Camp 30 on September 20, 1942, he said:

> So that you have an idea what happens when we receive mail, I'll tell you what happened to your last letters. I was sitting in my room rolling cigarettes; there was a knock at the door and a comrade came in with four letters in his hand. Naturally I stopped rolling cigarettes. First I examined the letters carefully, looking at the postmarks and the addressee's name. I was glad to see that you know the address of this camp at last. Now you think I would open the letters. No! First I rolled ten more cigarettes to prolong the excitement. Then I read the first letter. Between each letter I rolled ten cigarettes — spinning out the excitement of receiving mail as long as possible.[14]

While prisoner arrivals, camp openings and the Bowmanville shackling debacle were the stuff of news reports when they happened, there were also a thousand lesser tales in every POW camp. Few such stories ever made the papers, but they circulated among the guards and prisoners like gossip at a bridge game. Very often the incident that underlay a particular anecdote was rather insignificant in itself, but over a period of time became so embellished that the story took its place in the lasting folklore of internment life. For example, during my research for this book a number of former guards told me what happened to one prisoner who insisted on using the Nazi salute whenever he wished. The man was told the salute was unacceptable, and was warned that he would be reprimanded if the practice continued. Apparently the practice must have continued, because the German was seen a day or so later with his right arm broken below the elbow. But the guards who told the story insisted that the incident happened at Neys, Kingston, Gravenhurst and Monteith. Either the same man had his arm broken several times, or the tale was the result of someone's wishful thinking.

The prisoners at Gravenhurst built a small zoo and collected squirrels, chipmunks, a seagull and a couple of snakes for display. One night somebody noticed a porcupine in a pine tree outside the compound fence and thought the animal should become part of the camp collection as well.

The following morning just after roll call, a volunteer took an old burlap sack and, with both prisoners and guards watching him, made his way up the tree toward the animal. When he reached the porcupine there was a wild skirmish and the man dropped the bag. A minute or so later, the would-be captor came down, but by this time *he* looked like a porcupine. He had quills in his hands, wrists, shoulder and neck. It had been impossible to get the animal's head into the sack.

In all camps, roll call, which was generally taken in the early morning, at noon and in the evening, was an accepted and necessary routine that no one, prisoner or guard, particularly liked. Counting men was like counting cattle, you ended up either with a number or as a number. Unlike cattle, however, the prisoners were capable of ingenious stratagems to frustrate the procedure. Such ploys generally grew out of a sense of boredom, of frustration with the monotonous, mindnumbing dullness of camp life. Often they were enjoyed as much by the guards as they were by the prisoners — though not necessarily at the same time or for the same reasons.

In almost every camp there were instances of prisoners answering to the wrong names or claiming numbers other than their own. This procedure was often an integral part of an escape attempt. By the same token, however, prisoners often played games when no escape was in the offing, in order to confuse the guards. Sometimes the POWs shifted ranks, fainted or pretended to faint in the hot sun, paraded too quickly or too slowly, or pretended not to hear an order. In one camp, a group being counted all started to laugh at an overly officious guard. The more they laughed, the more he blustered. Finally, when the Canadian started to withdraw privileges, his charges grew silent. The whole act was played out on three successive days before the guard came around.

At some time or other, every camp seems to have had at least one still. Using high-quality copper pipe removed from toilets and showers, fresh water and such things as sugar and raisins stolen from the kitchens, the prisoners had no trouble producing alcohol. Each camp had several men who had made liquor in the past, or who knew enough basic chemistry to turn out a potable product. There were also enough prisoners with plumbing experience that relocating water pipes was a simple matter.

When copper tubing was commandeered for a still, the POWs sometimes covered up the operation by bypassing one toilet completely or hooking up two water tanks to one main line. Now and then a toilet would stop working. When this happened, Canadian maintenance personnel would simply install new piping and leave the facility to be vandalized all over again. In most camps, guards who got a share of the booze turned a blind eye when copper piping went missing. And in at least one case, in Bowmanville, a guard provided all the copper the prisoners needed.

The guard in question was befriended by a couple of POWs who had learned that the man liked to drink. When the prisoners first offered the Canadian a sample of camp brew, the gift was declined. Eventually, however, the guard's resistance lessened and he accepted the bait. A month or so later, he was hooked. Then the Germans cut off the supply. The guard was told that more copper pipe was needed by the distillers — and would he happen to know where such pipe might be obtained. When he seemed uncertain, he was reminded that his senior officers would not react too favourably to the news that he had been drinking with the prisoners. The man found the copper pipe — several times.

At Bowmanville, there was so much illegal liquor around that the camp atmosphere became more and more like that of an exclusive country club. Beer was legal in camp anyway, but any prisoner who preferred liquor had little trouble obtaining it. As quickly as the guards located and destroyed one still, another was started. Often, of course, the searches were rather haphazard. The guards overlooked as much liquor as they found.

Luftwaffe officer Tony Kleimaker still recalls with amusement the amount of drinking at Bowmanville and the types of parties that were held there: "In our room we had a man who today is a very famous lawyer in Germany. His job was to order all supplies, and he often ordered sugar, raisins and the like. We made liquor out of everything. At times the still was in our clothes closet, and at times it blew up. Then there was this terrible stench over everything. Of course, the guards knew we had liquor, but they hardly ever interfered. We often traded things with them, our cigarettes and so forth, for liquor. Very often we had parties where we drank this stuff, which must have been ninety percent alcohol, and after half an hour everybody was drunk. One night after one of these binges, the guy in the bunk above me woke up screaming, 'I'm blind. I'm blind.' He couldn't see anything because he was still stoned drunk, but it was pitch dark and nobody could see anything.

"In Bowmanville at one time we had so much liquor around that our commanding officer said it was a disgrace and was afraid we all would become alcoholics. He ordered all the booze disposed of, but he didn't say how this was to be done. So we drank it all. That evening, half of us couldn't even get out for roll call. Some staggered out; some were dragged out. Even the Canadian guards helped us. I know of one Canadian guard who actually held a prisoner's head while the guy threw up in a washroom."

Siegfried Bruse was running the canteen at Bowmanville when the authorities decided that the POWs should have beer in camp. "They came to me one day," said Bruse, "and asked me what brand we wanted. I didn't know anything about Canadian beer so I asked the guards to let us have a sample of whatever was available. A day or so later they showed up with ten or twelve cases, all different. We tried them all but Kingsbeer was the favorite. We were allowed some breakage, but most of it was consumed in somebody's room after the canteen closed. We had fun."

Twelve weeks after his capture in the hospital bed at Narvik, Max Schoellnhammer and nine hundred other-ranks POWs were herded into a converted factory at Espanola, Ontario. This was in July 1940. The camp had just opened, and at first, conditions were primitive. "For some time," says Schoellnhammer, "we didn't have enough things like toothbrushes and cigarettes. I didn't smoke so it didn't matter to me. However, the fellows who did smoke were getting desperate. They dried leaves and so forth but that was no good. Finally, someone decided to scrape some mahogany shavings off an old piano that was there. Imagine — a piano but no toothbrushes! Anyway, they used a vegetable grater and scraped down more and more of the piano. The shavings were old and dried and burnt well. For paper they used toilet paper. One day a guard noticed that the piano was gone. Don't forget, there must have been about five hundred smoking it, bit by bit. When he was told that the prisoners had smoked the piano, the guard thought the Germans were really crazy people. He didn't know whether to believe it or not. After a couple of months, each prisoner got real cigarettes."

The camp in Gravenhurst was on Lake Muskoka, in the heart of one of Ontario's most beautiful tourist centres. Every summer hundreds of vacationers from the United States and Toronto swarmed into the area for their holidays. To these outsiders, the POW camp was an object of curiosity, and the men who worked there were looked upon as having the key to the mysteries behind the wire. Guards were constantly asked about the prisoners, the escape tunnels, the Nazi beliefs, the camp routine and so on. Often such talk led to requests for photos of the camp, and ultimately for souvenirs. A man was a big shot in Toronto or Cleveland if he had a ship in a bottle on his mantel. Not just any ship, of course, but one made by "an ace U-boat commander," or "one of Rommel's top officers captured at Alamein." In the face of this great demand for artifacts from the camp, guards invented several stratagems to satisfy the curious.

Clandestine photos taken from guard towers were coveted and popular. So were the ships in bottles, and, perhaps most cherished of all, battle medals. As these were rare, however, it wasn't easy for the guards to get them. Understandably, few prisoners who won honours wanted to part with them. But, because one or two Germans actually did trade minor decorations for radio parts, interested guards soon guessed what the street value of an Iron Cross might be.

A handful of other ranks at Gravenhurst then showed themselves every bit as resourceful as their jailers. "We borrowed a real Iron Cross," says Ed Billet, "and we made a pattern from it. We then made a clay mould, melted lead, and filled the mould. The replica was painted black and looked just like the real thing. Then we exchanged these with the guards for anything we wanted. It took quite a while before someone found out we were just making fake Iron Crosses. A guard eventually realized what was happening and he put us out of business. Too bad. I still have a tie that a tourist smuggled in to me for something or other."

Another incident involving German prisoners occurred near Farnham, Quebec, after the war was over, but before the POWs could be sent back to Germany. In September 1946, a farmer who had purchased a small wartime airstrip from the government advertised an air show and talked three German paratroopers who worked on nearby farms into making a jump to entertain the crowd. The soldiers agreed — provided their identities were not divulged. They did not want to be punished later for their actions. The farmer accepted the condition and paid the trio ten dollars each in advance.

On the day of the exhibition, however, certain complications developed that affected the agreement. The jumpers gave their money to a couple of locals, in exchange for liquor. By the time the jumps were to take place, the Germans were drunk. The farmer saw what had happened, became annoyed, and decided that his promise was no longer binding.

The POWs managed to get their parachutes on and then were helped into the jump plane. None of them was in any condition to leave the ground, but the effects of the alcohol erased all sense of danger. The aircraft taxied to the runway.

As soon as the plane was airborne, the crowds in attendance were told over the public address system that "three famous German ex-paratroopers" would be jumping from a plane for the entertainment of the spectators. The names of the three were then announced.

Fortunately, the jumps were all successful, and the POWs were apparently never reprimanded. But it is doubtful that they would have been let off so easily had Internment officials known the three were blind drunk before they ever left the ground.

With the possible exception of the United States, Canada was, in the minds of most German POWs, the country where it was best to be a prisoner. The food was excellent, the accommodation generally adequate or better, and the educational, recreational and cultural opportunities as good as or better than those found in any prisoner-of-war camps anywhere. The only reason a few former prisoners gave for wishing they had been locked up in the United States was that they felt escape possibilities were better there, because of the proximity of some of the southern compounds to Mexico and South America. Food, living quarters and other amenities were no better in the United States than they were here.

Some former POWs who spent time in Canada told me they were glad they were sent here because they were left alone; the guards rarely interfered with the day-to-day routine inside the compound. Prisoners could organize their own sports activities, cook their own Germanic dishes and participate in such things as

German musical and dramatic presentations if they wished.

While the time behind the wire may not have been idyllic, it was not unpleasant. This can readily be seen in some of the letters the prisoners wrote home.

To his parents — Camp 30, October 18, 1942
On account of the quiet and regular life one gains weight at first but later on gets back to one's former weight through sport, sunbathing and swimming. I got accustomed very quickly to the much better bread we get here as well as in England.

To a girlfriend — Camp 30, October 15, 1942
Autumn here is just as wonderful as at home — the trees, the foliage and the warm sun. Don't worry about me. We've had a Bach and a Beethoven concert — both were excellent.

To his parents — Camp 30, October 3, 1942
In the course of a year we have built up four orchestras — a symphony orchestra of fifty performers, a light orchestra of twenty-five performers, a dance orchestra of sixteen players and an orchestra for march music, which I am conducting. In the first two I play the clarinet and in the dance orchestra the saxophone.

To a wife — Camp 30, September 27, 1942
Engineers and artists have, in recent weeks, with much care and work, fixed up a room in the dining hall where we are entertained with a miniature stage program which changes each month. Our camp newspaper *The Bridge* (Die Brucke) informs us every week concerning political, economic, technical and cultural events in the whole world.

The stock in our zoo is now three raccoon, two monkeys, one alligator (sixteen years old), several tortoises, four linnets, two canaries, one brown bear.

To a wife — Camp 133, October 15, 1942
Today we had a party and I felt great. For two hours I almost forgot I was a prisoner of war. I have a wish and wish you could satisfy same and send me an Italian grammar for beginners — also some table-tennis balls.

To a brother — Camp 23, September 18, 1942
We have arranged our camp very nicely in the course of the summer. Beside the sports field was built a bear cage (for two

representatives of the Western Rockies), a handsome duck pond
(populated by a dozen examples of this proud feathered tribe) and a
rabbit hutch (which already had to be enlarged). Our quarters are
surrounded by fresh green lawns and flower beds.[15]

But no matter how green the lawns and beautiful the flower
beds, there were some prisoners in every camp who were never
satisfied with their lot. They complained to each other, to their
guards, to the Red Cross and to the commanding officer. And no
matter what was done to address their grievances, they were
never satisfied.

While no Internment official in this country ever maintained
that Canadian camps were particularly utopian, most agreed
with most POWs that life in the compounds here was as good as,
and for the most part far better than, internment camp in Germany ever was. Almost without exception, former POWs interviewed for this book were of the opinion that if they had had to
become prisoners of war anywhere, then Canada was the place to
be. But even though this country might have been the place to
live, living in POW camps did not suit everyone — least of all those
who tried to escape from them. Several prisoners broke out of
POW compounds, and others got away before they even arrived
in camp. One of these was a German baron named Franz von
Werra.

FIVE

Von Werra's Escape

On September 5, 1940, Luftwaffe Oberleutnant Franz von Werra was shot down into a flat stubble field in Kent. The Messerschmitt 109 was barely damaged; its cocky pilot not at all. There was no fire, no panic and no chance to escape. Von Werra calmly unbuckled his seatbelt, pried the cockpit open, and climbed out. Then he took off his helmet and walked around the plane, marvelling at how lucky he had been.

As he stood there, trying to decide what to do next, he noticed a number of people running toward him. Almost immediately, several men from a nearby anti-aircraft battery surrounded the aircraft and von Werra was captured. The German offered no resistance as he was led away as a prisoner of war. Instead, he joked with his captors and complained that it was just a freak shot that had brought him down.

Even though they were not sure how to react to him, the British soldiers who took von Werra regarded their quarry with both interest and pride. Interest, because to them the gregarious stranger was the first enemy flyer they had ever seen; pride, because they had prevented the man from getting away. They also had the fairly intact plane in their possession. They had done their duty and a day or so later got their names in the paper. Von Werra was interrogated in London and then shipped north by train to Grizedale Hall.

For all its beauty, the countryside near that prison camp was wild and, to the outsider, terribly lonely. The windswept, often barren hills stretching away in every direction seemed to offer little protection for any would-be escaper. Scrub brush, thorn thickets and piles of stone dotted the hillsides. Unrelenting dampness, mist and endless days of bone-chilling rain made staying indoors very appealing. But not to von Werra. He wanted to be outside — outside the compound, the area and England itself. He had to escape somehow — and soon.

Some days after his arrival, when he and twenty-three other officers were on an escorted exercise march near the compound, von Werra dived over a low stone wall that bordered the narrow road. Two other prisoners had created a diversion by starting an argument and in doing so managed to momentarily distract the attention of the guards. The ruse worked. On one side of the wall, the remaining prisoners eventually regrouped and rather nonchalantly prepared to walk back to their camp. On the other side, the prisoner crouched, his heart pounding, hardly daring to breathe. Then the others trudged on without him. He listened to their boots on the gravel as they got farther away.

Then as soon as the detail disappeared around the first bend, von Werra raced along behind the wall, darted across the road, and clambered into a nearby grove of trees. After that, he stayed out of sight as much as possible, travelling by night and sleeping in the underbrush during the day. His destination was the west coast of England, where he hoped to be able to talk his way on board a ship bound for Ireland. Von Werra's charm and good fortune would, he believed, be his greatest assets.

But even before the remaining POWs completed the march back to Grizedale Hall, von Werra's absence was noted. One of the guards ran to a nearby house and phoned the camp, and within minutes, dozens of searchers, some with vicious tracking dogs, began combing the area. Their progress was slow and then a teeming rain made the job harder. The search was widened and extra men were brought in, but von Werra had apparently disappeared. His name, age and physical description were circulated to the various police and military authorities throughout the country, and all persons living on the moors and in the lonely villages near Grizedale Hall were warned to be on the lookout for him. Finally, six days later and several kilometres from where he got away, von Werra was spotted by a local farmer. The police closed in and the exhausted and bedraggled-looking German surrendered. That ended his first escape. As punishment, he was given twenty-eight days' solitary detention, the maximum allowable under the terms of the Geneva Convention. He used the time to take stock of his situation and to build up his physical strength by doing push-ups, sit-ups and knee-bends.

Shortly before the twenty-eight days were up, von Werra was moved to another camp, Swanwick, twenty kilometres northeast of Nottingham. On the very night he arrived, he discussed the possibility of escape with some of the senior officers there. Six weeks later, he did get out. He and four others crawled through a shallow tunnel while their comrades behind the wire executed one of the loudest and best choral offerings ever heard in the camp. The boisterous singing distracted the guards long enough for the escapers to clear their tunnel and disappear into the gloom. The tunnel had taken the Germans weeks to construct, but unfortunately for them, none got completely away. Yet von Werra came close.

He struck out across the country in the direction of an airfield some thirteen kilometres away. Posing as a Dutch pilot who had just crash-landed, and calling himself Captain van Lott, he relied on luck, lies and his great natural charm to get himself onto the RAF base at Hucknall. There, no one knew quite what to make of the man. He was closely questioned about his "crash," as no crash had been reported in the area in the previous twenty-four hours. Von Werra recounted detail after detail of his story. He claimed he had become lost and while he had been trying to orient himself, his plane ran out of gas. Because he could not see where to land, he bailed out and from the air watched the ship blow up on a hillside. His story *sounded* plausible, particularly as he told it with such attention to detail — and in such a sincere, straightforward fashion.

He described his terrible fear of death as the reading on the gas gauge became lower. He told of his momentary panic as it seemed his chute would not open. He also recounted for his listeners his attempts to make his way to help. Finally, as a still skeptical Hucknall official started making telephone inquiries regarding him, the German ducked outside, sprinted across the tarmac, and climbed into the cockpit of a parked Hurricane, which he planned to steal and fly to France. He was grabbed as he sat there, frantically trying to start the plane's engine. As he was led away, he thanked the men who had captured him and wished them luck when Germany overran their country. Then he was put in a van for the trip back to prison.

Less than a month later, early in January 1941, von Werra was
sent to Canada.

Like most of the ships bringing POWs across the Atlantic, the
Duchess of York was alive with rumours of an impending takeover. Nothing came of the stories, though, so von Werra, his
friend Peter Krug and a thousand other young Germans on the
ship arrived in Halifax in late January 1941 without incident.
Long before they reached Canadian waters, however, most of
the would-be escapees were making plans to break free in the
Dominion. Von Werra was among them.

Because he spoke reasonably good English and could talk his
way out of almost any predicament, von Werra was able to
ingratiate himself into the company of a couple of unsuspecting
guards and one of the ship's cooks. These liaisons were most
helpful. He practised his English, garnered a small amount of
money in return for the sale of rank badges and the like, and
picked up bits and pieces of information about Canadian folklore,
customs and geography. In addition, he and another officer obtained a rudimentary map of eastern North America. The map in
particular would soon prove to be invaluable. Later von Werra
looked back on the voyage as a successful lark.

As was customary at all prisoner landings, the Germans were
given a somewhat superficial search in port, counted, and
loaded onto rather drab-looking railway coaches drawn up at
dockside. Disembarkation took several hours, but just at nightfall
all the prisoners were finally ready for the long journey west.
Guards signalled the all-clear and the train pulled out of Halifax
at 4:30 on Wednesday, January 22, 1941. Outside it was snowing.

Von Werra and the others tried to get accustomed to their new
surroundings as the outskirts of Halifax fell behind them. The
train coach was overheated, and most of the prisoners stripped
down to shirtsleeves. Outside, the cold caused the windows of the
train to frost over, and only by scraping frost off the inside could
the Germans see much of the countryside they were passing
through. From time to time they asked guards questions about
Canada, but depending on the mood of the guard, an answer
might or might not be forthcoming. In all, the trip was to last
sixty-four hours and would bring the POWs to Camp W at Neys,
Ontario, on the north shore of Lake Superior. The first leg of the
trek took them across Nova Scotia to Truro, then to Moncton,

north and west of the state of Maine to Quebec City and Montreal. It was west of Montreal that von Werra made his break.

The prison train followed the Canadian Pacific line, which ran almost arrow-straight between Montreal and the town of Smiths Falls, Ontario, sixty-five kilometres southwest of Ottawa. The distance from Smiths Falls to the St. Lawrence River is slightly more than forty kilometres, and across the river lay the United States, still not at war for several months. Von Werra would head for the border.

It was dusk when the train steamed out of Montreal. The next stop was Smiths Falls. For von Werra and another flyer named Otto Hollman, it would be the last stop. Both jumped from the windows as the train moved slowly through the local railyards. Neither was hurt, but only von Werra actually got away. A railway employee witnessed Hollman's escape and alerted two police officers who were nearby. They raced after the fleeing German and one brought him down with a flying tackle. He got to his feet, brushed the snow from his grey overcoat, and surrendered. Then he was locked in the town jail, where a Canadian Press reporter met him an hour or so later.

The twenty-five-year-old prisoner said he had been shot down off the coast of Scotland three months earlier and, after spending more than two days floating around in a collapsible boat, had finally reached shore. He said he had been well treated in British POW camps, and that it had been easy to escape from the Canadian train.

Hollman said that before the war he had spent several years in England, where he had trained as an actor. With the outbreak of war, however, he returned to Germany and the Luftwaffe. As he talked, he munched on a chocolate bar and even offered to pay — in English currency — for the coffee the reporter brought him. His only complaint was that he was behind bars.

"This is my first time in jail," he said. "I have committed no crime. I am an officer, and it is the duty of a German officer to escape if he can."[1]

There is no record of Hollman's ever getting away again.

As soon as von Werra's escape was noticed, search parties began combing the town and the outlying districts for him. The police warned farmers and those living in the country that bitter cold might drive the German to seek shelter wherever he could. During the night, buses, trucks and scores of cars were stopped on area highways and country roads, and identification demanded of their occupants. The escapee was not among them. Von Werra eluded the dragnet.

In fact, he was almost nabbed several times. Even though he had been ahead of Hollman in the blind dash away from the train, he later stumbled around a corner just as his friend was being led away. Fortunately for von Werra, the policemen were going in the opposite direction and did not see him.

Later, a farmer's dog surprised the fugitive as he attempted to hide in a barn. Fearing that at any minute the dog's wailing would alert its owner, von Werra ducked into a nearby grove of trees and ploughed frantically through knee-deep snow, away from the danger. He fell several times.

Two hours after his escape, he was exhausted, hungry and colder than he had ever been in his life. His face was raw from the wind, and the pellets of blowing snow that drifted across the open fields stung his cheeks and half blinded him. His left hand was numb, because the first time he fell he had lost a glove. By the time he found it, his hand was stinging. After that, it never really did warm up.

Because it had been so warm in the train, he had forgotten to bring anything to wear on his head. His ears stung, and the bitter wind on his neck and forehead made his head throb with cold. Once when he stopped to urinate, his hands were so numb he could barely unbutton his pants.

Somewhere he heard a siren, at first far away and then closer and closer. He emerged from a small gully, which had afforded some shelter, and saw a police car, its headlights like beacons in the gloom, racing along a road in the direction from which he had come. In the distance, the lights of Smiths Falls shone opaquely through the storm. The sight convinced him that while he might not be a prisoner, he was far from being free. Obviously the police car might not be where it was because of him, but he could not take chances. His only consolation was that the auto had been going the opposite way.

And the car had been moving fast.

This observation made him realize that the snow that was so deep in the fields must have been cleared from the road. Obviously, walking would be better on the road, and if a car approached from either direction, he knew he would see its headlights and have plenty of time to hide in a ditch or by one of the fences that paralleled the highway.

Von Werra floundered through the drifts to the nearest fence, clambered over it and slid down a snowbank to the roadway. Here the right-of-way seemed to have been freshly cleared, so he turned into the wind and walked on, for what seemed like hours. Every so often he would run for a few moments, in an attempt to get warm. Once when he was running, the sound of his footsteps and laboured breathing almost drowned out the sound of a car that approached from his rear. He saw the lights of the vehicle in time, however, and dashed into some roadside bushes. As he crouched out of sight of the road, he noticed a barn a couple of hundred metres back from the road. A darkened house was farther away.

By this time, the earlier encounter with the dog had been half forgotten, so von Werra decided to seek shelter in the barn. He knew he needed rest, food and above all, protection from the biting wind and blowing snow. He knew he would be warmer in the barn, and surely if whoever owned the building kept cattle in it, the place would be warm enough to risk allowing himself to rest. He had some dried apricots in his pockets and a small hunk of chocolate, and though neither was a feast, they would have to do. He headed for the barn. A large doorway faced the roadway, but as he got closer, von Werra noticed that the snow was piled up heavily against the door itself. He moved around the barn to the side closest to the farmhouse. A smaller entrance had been shovelled clear and the door looked well used. Von Werra stood stock-still, listening for sounds from the barn, particularly straining to learn whether a dog might be loose inside. He knew a dog would have detected his approach by now, but would likely have made some sound, growling or whimpering.

The door opened easily and a warm cloud of pungent steam wafted toward him from inside. The steam carried with it a mixture of animal smells, manure and hay — and the effect was momentarily overpowering to von Werra. He caught his breath and, judging that no dog was in the barn, gingerly stepped inside, closing the door behind him.

At first he could see nothing whatsoever. Gradually vague outlines of shapes appeared before him. Muffled movements on either side told him there were cattle in the barn, but as the sounds came no closer, he judged that the animals must be in pens. He seemed to be in a passageway that ran down through the barn. He groped forward, guiding himself by holding on to what he presumed was a manger. About four metres from the door his feet brushed up against something on the floor. The

German reached down and grunted with delight when he touched what he knew had to be a pile of hay. He eased himself down and burrowed deep into the pile. In less than a minute he was sound asleep.

Several hours later, the sound of a car horn jolted him awake. Von Werra jumped to his feet, scaring two cows that were in the pen closest to him. He looked at his watch and was shocked to learn that it was almost eight. Because he had slept so soundly, he would have to leave the barn in daylight, thereby greatly increasing his chances of being discovered. But his luck held once more.

A car horn tooted again, but by this time von Werra had scraped enough frost from a stable window to see a car moving down a driveway toward the road. A woman stood at the doorway to the farmhouse, waving to someone in the car. Then she turned and went back inside. An instant later, von Werra shot out of the barn, raced around behind the building, got his bearings and headed for the road.

Perhaps we shall never know how von Werra actually evaded detection. He would later recount some of the adventures of his journey away from Smiths Falls, but at times his story seems a bit incredible. We know he hitched rides from passing motorists; he even claimed one such ride was with a policeman who took him to Ottawa.

Strangely enough, newspaper reporters who later met von Werra never seriously questioned this and his other rather fanciful descriptions of his break for freedom. One thing is reasonably certain: a stranger walking alone on a country road and speaking English with a German accent would surely have made any police officer near Smiths Falls pause. After all, a manhunt was on at the time. What is more, the flyer would have no reason to go north to the capital when, in fact, he was intent on getting to the United States.

While von Werra's actual route to the border is unknown, the most logical way for him to have gone would have been east from Smiths Falls along Highway 43 to the town of Kemptville, then south on Highway 16 through the hamlet of Spencerville to the frozen shoreline of the St. Lawrence River at Johnstown, five kilometres downriver from the town of Prescott. The nearest community on the American side is the city of Ogdensburg, New York.

Though no one knows what time von Werra actually arrived in Johnstown, one thing is certain: he waited until it was dark before he attempted to cross the river on the ice. According to his biographers, he thought that the ferries between Prescott and Ogdensburg would not be running because of the St. Lawrence ice. In fact, the ferries were running, as they did every winter until they were replaced by an international bridge in the early 1960s. What is more curious today is the question of how von Werra passed his time until it was dark. After all, the journey from Smiths Falls to Johnstown was not a long one. Even if his luck in hitching rides had not been too good, he could have made the journey in two or three hours with ease. Since he would have been seen loitering along any roadside, he presumably sought shelter. The question is, where? In researching this book, I stumbled onto one possible answer, which is presented here as an intriguing theory only.

As early as two days after von Werra's disappearance from the train, rumours about the escape began circulating in the town of Prescott. These rumours began when the police questioned a German-Canadian who resided in the town and who worked as a gardener and handyman for a prominent local businessman. The businessman in question owned a summer cottage on the shore of the St. Lawrence at Johnstown. A woman who once worked as a maid for the family told me that the cottage owner rarely went near the place in the wintertime, but that the hired help had access to it all year long. It is known that the German gardener spent long periods of time at the cottage, and could have been there when von Werra arrived. It is entirely possible that even if the two had no prearranged contact with each other, the flyer could have been seen by the gardener and sheltered in the cottage during the daylight hours. It is also said that the gardener's views on the war did not exactly coincide with those of most people in Prescott. If that was the case, perhaps he would have welcomed the chance to assist a former countryman to gain freedom.

Unfortunately, though the cottage itself is still there, it has changed ownership and the businessman has gone. The German gardener left the area years ago also, and today no one seems to know where he went. And for his part, whether he was helped or not, von Werra didn't say. Obviously, the limelight was brighter when he didn't have to share it. Then too, anything he said would only have implicated the gardener.

Alone or not, von Werra soon found that crossing the St. Lawrence River in winter was not easy. Anyone who is familiar with the Johnstown area and the location where the German found himself can easily visualize what he was up against. The St. Lawrence is about one and a half kilometres wide at this spot, and because of strong currents, it is rarely frozen all the way across. It is, however, often frozen for well over a hundred metres out from the Canadian shoreline. Von Werra waited until dark and then started walking across the ice.

At first the going was easy. The ice near the shore was frozen evenly and there were few ridges or snowdrifts to contend with. On the American side of the river, even the neon signs at Ogdensburg were visible, as were the headlights of cars entering that city. Von Werra rejoiced because by crossing on the ice, he would not have to contend with the Canadian officials who would undoubtedly be present had he crossed either at a bridge somewhere or on the ferry upstream at Prescott. He paused for a moment to look back at the country where he had been a prisoner. He wondered where his friends were now; how far the train he had been riding had gone. And though he missed the fellowship of his colleagues, he did not miss the fetters that bound them. He then turned, shielded his face against an unexpected snow squall, and almost fell headlong into open water.

The river was not frozen in the centre!

To von Werra, the shock was like a kick in the groin. He staggered back, momentarily stunned, unable to comprehend the sudden turn of fortune. He then picked up a clump of snow and tossed it ahead of him. The snow plopped into the water like a sponge. The German stood still, listened to the wind and tried to estimate the width of the channel. He guessed it was at least a hundred metres or more. What a few seconds earlier had been a simple matter of walking on ice suddenly became an impossible nightmare. He knew he could never hope to swim the rest of the way. A few seconds in this frigid water would kill anyone. Bitterly disappointed, he turned on his heel and walked back to Canada. Somehow, the cold seemed more severe now.

In 1941, there were a number of summer cottages along the shore of the St. Lawrence at Johnstown. Von Werra went from one to the other in hope of locating some type of boat so that he could complete his escape. Finally, as he was at the point of giving up his quest, he located an overturned rowboat, half covered with snow. After managing to free the craft with a wooden picket from a nearby fence, he somehow succeeded in dragging it out onto the river ice. He intended to use the picket as a paddle.

The struggle to get the boat to open water was a difficult one.

He alternately pulled the thing along by the bow and, when he tired of doing this, went to the stern and pushed. The farther he went, the harder and slower his journey became. Once or twice he slipped and fell headlong across the ice. With each fall, he felt that his plight was worse than it had been a few minutes before. Here he was, midway between two great nations, one as foreign to him as the other, one of which would toss him in prison if he returned to it; the other that might or might not accept him if he ever reached it. The chasm he had to cross was one of the greatest rivers on earth, and now, to this puny, desperate and terribly cold alien, was as unforgiving as the sea it eventually joined.

Somehow, after he knew not how long, von Werra got the rowboat to the water. He half stepped, half fell into the craft and was on his way.

Then he lost his paddle.

It had been in his hand as he was getting into the boat, but during his struggle to maintain his balance and keep the rowboat from capsizing at the same time, the paddle had slipped out of his hand. A second later, it had disappeared.

Now he was *really* at the mercy of the elements.

The boat drifted with the current, past chunks of floating ice, then out into the frigid black water, farther and farther from any place to land. The combination of fast current, the relentless biting wind and the lashing of icy spray spun the little craft in an apparent aimless series of circles. The German held on grimly, his hopes fading as surely as the lights of Ogdensburg receded in the distance.

But then he realized that those lights were *not* farther away. In fact, the little boat was veering closer to the American shore and to the ice that stretched out from it. Suddenly, and with almost no warning, the boat bumped up against solid ice, the impact so unexpected that von Werra was momentarily too stunned to realize its significance.

The German clambered out of the rowboat, stumbled toward shore, and gratefully stepped onto the soil of the United States of America. He was almost directly across from Johnstown, on the grounds of a large New York state mental hospital. Today any one of the thousands of tourists who cross the river on the huge international bridge can look down and trace von Werra's route. On a quiet evening, the swish and swirl of fast water can also be heard far below. Perhaps it is this, the terrifying sound of this great river, that drives home to the casual onlooker the sheer gutsiness of von Werra's actions. Although one might doubt his credibility, he has to be given full marks for bravery.

As soon as he got his bearings on the American shore, von Werra noticed a car parked nearby. He walked over to the vehicle and asked the driver, Al Crites, a Canadian working in the United States, for a ride into Ogdensburg. Crites dropped his passenger on a downtown street and immediately called the police. Von Werra had been bragging about his escape and Crites was not sure what to do with him. Unfortunately, no one will ever know much about this brief car ride, or what von Werra told the driver, as Crites died in 1973. Von Werra, who dictated his memoirs to a writer friend, skimmed over his conversation with Crites.

When Ogdensburg police officers Delduchetto and Richer approached von Werra, on the downtown corner of Ford and Patterson streets, the German offered no resistance. On the contrary; he told them that he was glad to see them, that he was happy to be in the United States, and that he assumed they would do all in their power to be fair to him. He also said he wanted to get back to Germany at the earliest possible opportunity. The policemen were not impressed. They arrested the flyer on a charge of vagrancy and asked him to come along. The time was 10:15 p.m., January 24, 1941.

The arrest card made out for von Werra is still on file at the police station in Ogdensburg. On it, the German's age is shown as twenty-six, his address as Cöln-C-Vorgebirgstr, and his marital status as single. His occupation is given as "German Aviation Pilot — unemployed." The vagrancy charge is listed, and below it the words "No visible means of support."

The Ogdensburg police station where von Werra was taken that night is essentially unchanged today. It is found in a small, cramped part of town behind the city hall. The usual entrance, and certainly the one through which von Werra would have been taken, is approached on foot through a somewhat obscured walkway between the city hall and an adjoining store. It is doubtful, however, that the flyer took much note of these surroundings. He was too intent on making a good impression and on pleasing reporters, who started coming to the station within minutes of his arrival there. As soon as he found he had an audience, his garrulous, indiscreet, publicity-seeking nature took over. Reporters jollied him along, fed him leading questions, flattered him and, in a way, tricked him. Von Werra played right into their hands. In the words of his biographers, von Werra "committed one indiscretion after another. He boasted, bragged, exaggerated outrageously and spoke of the British war effort with contempt. If this performance had been limited to the night of his arrival, it would be easy to overlook it, but it was continued throughout the next day."[2]

The Toronto *Star* reported on January 25, 1941, that von Werra said he had gone to Ottawa after his escape, and that he had lunch there in a restaurant on Bank Street. Whether von Werra thought the Canadian reporter might check the facts of such a story is not known. For whatever reason, American and British papers repeated more or less what von Werra told them. On January 25, 1941, the *New York Times* said that von Werra "jumped off the train at Mount Laurier [*sic*], 98 miles north of Quebec [and] . . . hitch-hiked from Mount Laurier to the banks of the St. Lawrence." In reality, Mont Laurier is two hundred miles — more than three hundred kilometres — from Quebec City.

In London, *The Times* of January 27, 1941, quoted von Werra as saying he had escaped when he did in order to "take part in a knockout blow against England." He also said that any United States help would be too late to save Britain, and that a complete German victory was a certainty.

Von Werra was kept at the police station only long enough for the authorities to try him on the vagrancy charge. The trial before Judge John H. Wells, in the case of *The People of the State of New York* vs. *Baron Franz von Werra of Germany* lasted only a few minutes. The defendant pleaded guilty and received a suspended sentence. A somewhat relieved police department immediately turned him over to the immigration authorities at the Ferry Building in Ogdensburg.

From this time onward, von Werra's future became the subject of international debate. Naturally enough, the Canadian and British governments wanted to get him back. German consular officials, acting on orders from Berlin, were determined that, because he had indeed escaped into a neutral country, he should not have to go back to Canada. The United States was caught in the middle.

German Consul Hans Borchers appealed for and succeeded in obtaining the flyer's release on the charge of entering the United States without reporting to an immigration officer. Borchers posted a $5,000 bond in the matter and took von Werra to New York City — presumably to get him away from the Canadian border as quickly as possible. By this time, the Ontario Provincial Police at Prescott had become involved. OPP Constable Alex MacLeod filed a warrant in Ogdensburg, charging von Werra with the theft of a rowboat valued at thirty-five dollars, in a vain effort to have von Werra extradited to Canada.

Meanwhile, von Werra was already closeted with German officials in New York and Washington, for the purpose of compiling as much information as possible on British and Canadian internment techniques and practices. Later on, von Werra's recollections were used to advantage by the German Luftwaffe in briefing sessions for pilots. His experience in captivity had been more or less typical of what German POWs could expect. Because of von Werra, those who came after him had a better idea of what to say and what not to say during interrogation. From then on, much less information was gleaned by the Allies from captured German airmen. A number of former Luftwaffe POWs told me they remember being given a stepped-up briefing program shortly after von Werra's exploits became known.

In Canada, the escape had received extensive coverage in the press. The daring break from the prison train, the dash to the border and the heroic night crossing of the St. Lawrence all sparked the imagination of readers. "TITLED FLYER SEIZED AFTER HE PADDLES ACROSS RIVER," said one paper. "ESCAPED NAZI PILOT FINDS HAVEN IN U.S.," trumpeted another. Almost every story mentioned von Werra's claim that he had "flown over England so many times" he was "unable to count the number." To anyone who would listen, he mentioned that the damage done to London, England, by the Luftwaffe had been "terrific," and that the Allies would surely lose this war. He kept asserting that it was "only a matter of time" before England was invaded. Experiments being done in Germany with bombers towing gliders loaded with troops would provide "a knockout blow" to England when the gliders landed and armed men emerged from the machines.

In Ogdensburg, the local *Journal* mentioned that the German had bragged that England would be invaded. He claimed that he wanted to get back to his squadron as quickly as possible "to take part in the all-out invasion." Ogdensburg Police Chief Herbert S. Myers taunted the German and told him to "put it in writing." Von Werra wrote "May 12, 1941" and said, "Remember what I am telling you, on May 12 — that will be the big day and I will be back flying over England with my squadron."

"Von Werra was idolized as a hero and trailed by crowds of sympathetic admirers after he was apprehended," added the *Journal*. Initially, the fact that von Werra was a member of the armed forces of a hostile power seems to have mattered little. Gradually, though, this point of view started to shift. Editorial opinion became more sombre, more realistic. However, when it appeared that von Werra would not be returned to Canada, the press started to protest. An editorial in the Kingston *Whig-Standard* on January 27, 1941, assessed the situation, and then added an almost prophetic warning about difficulties Internment officials might face if von Werra were not returned.

It took just two hours for the German consulate to swing into action with $5,000 bond for the liberty of Baron von Werra, who escaped from the train conveying Nazi prisoners to the internment camp and crossed the St. Lawrence River at Ogdensburg. This incident raises a most important test case. If von Werra is retained in the United States for the duration, there will undoubtedly be a veritable epidemic of Nazi attempts at escape, especially during the summer months. If for no other reason than to break the monotony of internment camp life, there is ample inducement for planned escapes on the part of young men as enterprising as pilot officers and submarine commanders have to be to qualify for their jobs. But if to prospective relief from monotony is added the chance of escape to a neutral country containing all the wonders publicized in film and literature about the United States, the lure of seeing the great world will be as dynamite in the minds of the young Hitlerites. In addition, freedom from enemy confinement is looked upon as an achievement in itself.

The necessity of closely guarding these prisoners has been brought home to the authorities before, and there will likely be no intensifying of their problem if the United States authorities return von Werra promptly to the Canadian side of the line. If they do not, it spells future trouble for Canadians on guard duty.

The appeal was wasted. Von Werra remained in New York for several weeks while his case was considered. Finally, two months to the day after his arrest, he took off again — this time with funds provided by the consulate in New York. German officials there were apparently afraid their guest might be ordered back to Canada, so they decided to help him disappear.

They put him on a train for El Paso, Texas, from where he

crossed into Mexico a couple of days later, dressed as a migrant farm labourer. From then on, von Werra was really free. He made his way southward from Panama to Peru, then to Bolivia and eventually, by mid-April, to Rio de Janeiro. He flew home from Rio. Six months later, Canada's most celebrated POW escapee of all died in a plane crash while on a routine Luftwaffe patrol off the coast of Holland. He was only twenty-seven.

SIX

Breakout at Fort Henry

Winter in a Canadian prisoner-of-war camp was generally a quiet time. Prisoners spent most of their days indoors and only went outside to walk the exercise path, shovel snow or play hockey. It was just too cold to escape. Depending on the camp location, a winter escape could be just another form of suicide — slow, bitter and utterly pointless. Why leave a warm, clean, reasonably comfortable living compound for the shrieking white-out of a prairie blizzard, or the rocky wastes and mind-numbing cold of northern Ontario? Most prisoners had no intention of doing so, and the guards knew it. In the north and west, and to a lesser extent in eastern Canada, a winter escape was insane.

In southern Ontario, however, the same obstacles were not always there. For one thing, the cold was less severe. But there were also more roads, more railways and far more people. A man could get out of Bowmanville or Gravenhurst and very quickly get lost among the thousands of strangers who poured into Toronto every day. The road and rail systems connecting the city with the rest of Canada were the busiest in the country, and boarding a train or bus or hitch-hiking was comparatively easy — certainly far easier than breaking out of any northern camp would be.

It was for these reasons that many escapers or would-be escapers from Gravenhurst and Bowmanville picked Toronto as their first destination. They may not have intended to stay in the city for long, but at least by going there they could attain a reasonable degree of anonymity not possible in a small town. In this way, many of them hoped to remain undetected long enough to plan their next move, whether it was a dash to the United States through the border towns of Niagara Falls or Windsor, Ontario, or a journey by train to Halifax or Vancouver in order to board a ship and quit the country that way. Whatever the plan, its chances of fruition for many were so unrealistic as to be nonexistent. This, however, was not the case for two prisoners who fled Fort Henry late in March 1941.

Friday, March 21, was a mild, overcast day in Kingston, Ontario. For the first time that month, the snow and cold of a bitter winter seemed past. But although Lake Ontario was open as always, the St. Lawrence River immediately in front of the fort was still frozen, and snow drifted from shore to shore.

In the prisoner-of-war camp that afternoon, a spirited game of snow soccer ended with most of the participants soaked to the skin by the slippery slush on the playing field. When the match ended shortly after five, the players trooped indoors to change before the evening roll call began at six. Inside, other prisoners read, played cards, studied or retold the same stories of a war that now seemed as remote as the moon. So far, the day had been normal, routine and dull — for everyone except Bernhardt Gohlke and Heinz Rottmann.

Gohlke and Rottmann were small-statured, lean, athletic naval officers who shared not only a warm comradeship, but also an intense desire to resume someday their role in Hitler's war. For weeks now they had talked of only one thing: escape. They had examined every bit of the nineteenth-century fort. On their exercise periods they walked all over the camp, watched the guards, and made note of every visitor and vehicle that came near. They kept track of the weather, the river ice conditions and each day's times of sunset and sunrise. Finally they found a way to escape.

There are only three ways of getting out of any prisoner-of-war camp: over the wall, under the wall or through the wall. Gohlke and Rottmann decided to go through.

From the time of its founding in 1812, and during the various reconstruction programs in the years that followed, small embrasures had been built into the outer walls of the fortress. Because these openings were an integral part of the defensive system for the structure, they were still there in 1941, as they are today. Each such vertical opening is about ten centimetres wide and three or four times as high. They are a metre or so apart.

In 1941, as today, the moat that surrounds the fort was empty, but the nine-metre stone wall on its outer side presented a second barrier for the Germans to conquer before they were really free of the place. This wall, though, was not the primary obstacle that faced Gohlke and Rottmann. The main problem was the narrowness of the opening they had to squeeze through.

During the days that led up to their escape, the two sloshed boiling water, then ice water, then more boiling water against the wall around the opening. Gradually, small fragments of stone began to crack, and, with the most painstaking of chisel work, the ten-centimetre aperture was widened. By the middle of March, the two men believed they could squeeze through the opening. While the moat wall was still a problem, scaling it would not be difficult.

The prisoners commandeered a sturdy metal support from one of the mess tables. They fashioned the support into a kind of grappling hook, sharpened one end and tied the other to a plaited rope of cotton and canvas odds and ends. The rope itself took days to make. Finally, on the morning of the escape, the pair fashioned their own white bed sheets into outer coverings for themselves so that they would be less visible against the snow.

It was while the snow soccer game was in progress that they made their break.

Getting through the embrasure was the worst. Both men scraped their shoulders and hips against the stone, and for a time it looked as if Gohlke would never get out. He got his head through and then became hopelessly jammed. The more he struggled, the worse his predicament became. All the while, the thought of being found wedged in the wall, in the midst of an escape attempt, was terrifying. Under the circumstances, both men found it difficult to ignore the surge of panic they felt. Finally Gohlke inched forward, partly on his own and partly because a couple of other prisoners grabbed his legs and pushed. At last, he lurched through the hole.

But once through, the escapees were still far from free. They crouched in the dry moat, caught their breath, and turned to face the outer wall. Rottmann coiled the homemade rope in his hand, held one end and tossed the loop toward the top of the wall. When he tugged on the rope, the hook pulled loose from the top. Seconds wasted. He threw again. No luck. On the third try the hook held.

The men then clambered up the wall, pulled the rope after themselves, and quickly hid it under the snow. Then they took off down the bank toward the pine trees at the river's edge.

The escape went unnoticed by the guards for more than an hour. When roll call came at six, the POWs deliberately took their time turning out for the count because any time gained now would enable Gohlke and Rottmann to get farther away. Six men stayed in their bunks and pretended to be asleep when they should have been forming up outside. A couple of others suddenly claimed to be sick and raced to the latrine. At least one told the guards that all his clothes were wet from the soccer match and he was waiting for them to dry. And after all of these were finally accounted for, the prisoners began shuffling ranks and answering to the wrong names. Eventually, the alarm was sounded before the authorities knew exactly who or how many were missing. The actual method of escape was still unknown.

Once it became known that at least two prisoners had disappeared, the hunt for them began, both inside the fort and outside it. Several guards, singly and in twos and threes, started to search every corner of the fortress. Another party tramped through the deep snow around the walls while twenty others under Captain Graham Thompson prepared to patrol the area down to and along the St. Lawrence River and the United States border.

Thompson loaded his men on an army truck, drove down through lower Kingston to a point where they could have access to the river, then headed out across the ice to Wolfe Island, the large Canadian-owned tract of land in the middle of the St. Lawrence. The truck lumbered across the island, then over more ice to Cape Vincent, a small American village in New York State, some twenty-four kilometres south-southeast of Fort Henry.

By this time reports were reaching the camp that two men had been seen walking on the river ice. Timothy O'Shea, a resident of Wolfe Island, told the Kingston *Whig-Standard* the next day that he had seen two men who "were walking quite briskly and gave every appearance that they were in a hurry." When he saw them they were "about half a mile from the island shore," he added. O'Shea's wife managed to get a better look at the men on the ice and she was "sure they were not wearing overcoats and they appeared to have a sort of windbreaker." After he had talked to the fort, O'Shea phoned several of his neighbours and told them to be on the lookout for the escapees. This was about seven-thirty in the evening.

In the meantime, Graham Thompson and his veteran guards had driven onshore at Cape Vincent. In his words: "We arrived there at night. A terrible trip. Cold as bloody be damned. We were met by a United States border patrolman — a nice fellow — and I told him what my problem was. I asked him if we could remain there and wait in case any of the prisoners landed on United States soil. That was before the Americans were in the war and here we are, all armed, and walking around in a foreign country. Anyway, the patrolman gave us permission, so I stationed my men all along the shore, from west of Cape Vincent, right down to the village of Clayton, New York, about thirty kilometres downstream. I got off there myself and the guy from the Border Patrol came with me.

"It had not been too cold in the cab of the truck, but outside it, the wind went right through you. As soon as we had oriented ourselves, we walked out on the ice but saw nothing and heard nothing, so we decided to stand beside a lighthouse where we would be out of the wind. As we stood there, we chatted about the escape and how silly we probably were. Two grown men, both armed, half frozen, crouched out of the wind on the ice of the river. And by this time it was eleven o'clock at night. The whole thing was a joke.

"Then suddenly there was a crunch in the snow, some distance in front of us. I remember saying, 'There they are now,' as if the whole thing had been prearranged. I told the patrolman that I would have to take the men because I had to get them back to the fort. He told me okay, so we decided to see what had made the noise.

"I took my flashlight and swept it over the snow a few feet in front of me. Then, after we walked about fifty metres upriver, we saw two white mounds on the ice. It was the bloody Germans! Those guys were only half dressed really, but they were lying down with white bed sheets wrapped around themselves. They were damned near frozen. We could hardly believe what we were seeing," Thompson recalls.

"Then things got complicated. The patrolman changed his tune and told me he'd have to take charge. He said he never really thought we would make the capture, and now that we had, he would have to be responsible. He pointed out that we *were* in the United States.

"I had no choice in the affair, so we ordered the escapees to get up and we took them in to Clayton, to the local police station. When we got there I phoned Kingston, reported the capture, and told the CO that the border patrol people had taken over. Then I climbed in the truck, picked up my men, and came back to the

Fort. It was almost morning when we got there."

Immediately after Thompson's phone call to Fort Henry, Colonel C. G. Carruthers, the camp commander, contacted the director of Internment Operations in Ottawa, Colonel Stethem. For his part, Stethem got in touch right away with the Department of External Affairs, who conferred with Washington on the situation.

For the next few hours, negotiations for the return of Gohlke and Rottmann continued at a frantic pace. There were more calls between Ottawa and the American capital, hurried conferences, counter-proposals and, for the escapees, bad news at the end of the night.

At four in the morning, the Americans told Stethem that Canada could have the two Germans back, provided he came to the border by six and got them himself. If they were not picked up by then, they would be held in the U.S. on a charge of illegal entry. Five minutes after he was given this news, the director and an RCMP officer were on their way out of Ottawa.

Four police officers on motorcycles accompanied Stethem on that wild ride down Highway 16 to Prescott, then west along Highway 2 to the Ivy Lea Bridge, near Gananoque. At one point, the race almost came to a tragic halt. Stethem's car skidded on a turn, grazed a bridge abutment, and ended up half buried in a snowbank on the roadside. The escort stopped and got the car back on the road, and away they went. The entire incident was over in a couple of minutes. No one was hurt.

At the border, Rottmann and Gohlke were handcuffed and waiting. When he saw the shackles, Stethem ordered them removed immediately. He also refused to allow American news photographers to take any pictures of the prisoner transfer. The escapees were then packed into Stethem's car for the trip back to Kingston. For their part, the POWs were obviously disappointed that they were not allowed to stay in the United States, as Franz von Werra had been. However, the American attitude toward Germany had become increasingly hard-line in those months before Pearl Harbor. Rottmann and Gohlke were simply not welcome in the United States of America.

The journey into Kingston passed quickly and without any rancour. The Germans chatted amiably with their captors. Stethem offered his passengers cigarettes and avoided discussing the escape — and in particular, the return of the two from what was still a neutral nation. Instead, the conversation dealt for the most part with fishing and other sports in Canada. At Fort Henry, the prisoners were received without hostility. However, the episode was not quite over.

Because he was ultimately responsible for the proper security and management of his camp, the camp commander of each prisoner-of-war internment centre was answerable for any breach of discipline or other infraction by those under his command. Each CO knew and lived with this fact. Nevertheless, those under his control were not able to accept the situation so easily. Graham Thompson remembers being quite annoyed when, just after the escape, Colonel Carruthers was told he was facing a court-martial because of the escape. "Carruthers ran a tight ship, and there was of course no possible way he could have known of the scheme, or prevented the two Germans from getting out. The escape was well planned and terribly well executed," says Thompson now.

The subsequent court of inquiry was held at the fort and the hearings went on for several days. From the outset, none of the guards was sure how the escape actually came about. They found the embrasure, of course, but couldn't believe any grown man could get through it. Fortunately for Carruthers, no other way out was found.

For its part, the court did look at the gun slit, but the examination became something of a farce. According to Thompson: "When the court was there, we proved a man couldn't get out through the opening. We had one of our guys try it and he could hardly get his feet through. Therefore, if the two did not escape, Carruthers could not have been responsible. Finally he was let off simply because no one could show for certain how the Germans got out. No one could prove they escaped."

There were other breakouts from Fort Henry that were just as ingenious as the one perpetrated by Rottmann and Gohlke. One of these took place the day after a concert at the fort. Again two POWs were involved, although this time only one of them actually gained a measure of freedom — and that was short-lived.

Some time before the concert, a POW spokesman approached the guards and asked if two pianos might be rented for a few days. The instruments would be required for one night only, but the two pianists involved wanted to be able to practise before-hand. Both were accomplished musicians, said the spokesman, but without a piano at the fort, they were afraid that their talents had become rather rusty.

The guards felt the request was a legitimate one, and they passed it along. A day or so later the C. W. Lindsay Piano Company in Kingston trucked two instruments up to the camp. The prisoners seemed overjoyed.

During the few days before the scheduled recital, both pianos were in constant use. Several POWs were excellent players and they made use of the opportunity to exhibit their talents. Had the guards taken closer notice, however, they might have seen two other young men who often looked carefully at the instruments but rarely played them. Lieutenants Hans Strehl and Siegfried Schmidt, twenty-three and twenty-five respectively, had more on their minds than a tune.

The night of the concert came and both pianos figured quite prominently in the recital. Several veteran guards in the audience applauded as loudly as anyone when it was over. These Germans were good! They certainly knew and loved music.

Shortly before noon the next day, the Lindsay company sent their truck for the pianos. When they realized only two company men were along, several prisoners crowded around the vehicle and helped with the loading. Less than five minutes after its arrival, the truck departed with the first instrument. The driver said he would be back after lunch for the second.

The trip downtown was quick. So was the unloading. The truck was backed up to a ramp and the piano simply wheeled out. No lifting was needed. Then with the first part of their job done, the men swung the ramp door closed, picked up their lunch pails, and went to eat.

About twenty minutes later, the Lindsay bookkeeper, a Mr. Mallory, had to go to the company stockroom to check an invoice number. There he heard a muffled cough, which seemed to come out of the piano the men had just delivered. The bookkeeper came to an abrupt stop. Then, like the lid of a coffin opening in a horror movie, the top of the piano was slowly raised and the astonished Mallory found himself staring at the face of a German airman by the name of Hans Strehl. At first neither was able to speak. Then Strehl burst into laughter and surrendered to Mallory. The fort was alerted and Schmidt removed from the other piano.

The greatest escape of all from Fort Henry did not take place until a couple of years later. That breakout is vividly recalled at the fort; the red-tunicked student guides there still mention the event when they give their spiel to the tourists who go through the place each summer. The guides talk excitedly about the method of escape, the numbers who got away and the circumstances surrounding the occurrence, as if it had happened just last week and not nearly forty years ago.

On Friday, August 27, 1943, the two-inch banner headline on the front page of the Kingston *Whig-Standard* read: "WAR PRISONERS ESCAPE FORT HENRY." The story that followed went on to describe how nineteen prisoners at the fort had tunnelled their way to freedom the previous night. At first the news was greeted with absolute incredulity by the townspeople. They were reasonably familiar with the fort and could not understand how anyone, let alone a group of nineteen men, would be able to get through those two-foot-thick walls, particularly in view of the supposedly strict security of the compound. What happened, in fact, was that the escapers did not go through the walls; they went under them. And they did very little tunnelling: that had been done for them long before.

Like most historic buildings of its kind, Fort Henry was built in stages. The structure of 1943 was the result of extensive restoration efforts begun seven years earlier when the ancient structure had shown signs of falling down completely. With the outbreak of hostilities in 1939, and the urgent need to use the fort as an internment centre, restoration ceased and the first internees were moved in. At the time, no one really paid much attention to what the building might have looked like in an earlier age, or how it had been constructed in the first place. Above all, the authorities did not have the time to examine the building as closely as the prisoners of war caged there would examine it. The prisoners stumbled upon an old plan of the fort amid junk left behind by the restorers. Ironically, the plan was passed around among the prisoners for some time before anyone realized its value. One day, however, someone noticed a series of light dotted lines leading from inside the walls, apparently through the walls and down to the water's edge on the Kingston side. At first no one realized the significance of the lines. Then a prisoner wondered aloud if they might indicate the location of either old foundations or some kind of an underground drainage system.

The second explanation was too good to be true! But if it was!

Several prisoners pored feverishly over the map, checked distances, locations and the apparent width of the wall or ditch or whatever it was. If the marks indicated a buried wall, there was no cause for excitement. But if indeed there was a tunnel down there . . .

That night the search began. Eventually it was determined that the lines led to a lower room near an exterior wall. Fortunately for the prisoners, the room was not frequented by the guards, so a thorough search could be made of the floor area. At first nothing was obvious. The floor looked like all the others in the compound, greyish in colour, slightly damp and seemingly as permanent as the building itself. But then someone started chipping away a layer of concrete and found bricks under it. No foundation wall this!

In the days that followed, a makeshift cover was built for the excavation, so that when a guard came anywhere near, the hole could be covered, dirt swept over it, and the escape route concealed.

At this time, George Fehn of the German merchant navy had been in the fort for several weeks. "I was one of those who took part in the digging," he says today. "We worked like hell, but it was very slow going. We put the dirt in the garbage, a little at a time, because there was no other way to get rid of it in that place. When we finally broke through into the old drainage tunnel, we all felt like cheering. But then we found that the thing was so small, only little guys like me could fit into it."

Preparations for the escape were made over a period of several days, but Fehn recalls, "None of us really expected to get too far away anyway, so there was no real hurry. We were just bored looking at the same grey walls of the place and we needed some excitement of some kind. One thing I know for sure; none of us were dangerous."

The breakout began a short while after evening roll call on Thursday, August 26, just after there was darkness enough to provide cover. The first man left the tunnel at nine-thirty and the last, less than five minutes later. Most were very excited and momentarily stunned by the darkness and the realization that they were actually outside the wall. They scrambled away from the tunnel mouth and into the gloom downriver. As yet, no alarm had sounded.

At about the same time as the breakout, a Kingston fireman named Harold Pitman was visiting a Boy Scout camp on Cedar Island, a speck of land just off Kingston. At nine-thirty he noticed how dark it was getting, so he said goodnight to the youngsters there, climbed into his rowboat, and headed for home. The evening was rather cool, and the low clouds reflected the lights of the city. There was little wind.

Pitman rowed quietly, admiring the view and mulling over in his mind the events of the day. Then, as he approached the tip of land where Fort Henry stood, he heard voices from the shore — by now less than fifty metres away. He stopped paddling and listened, trying to figure out why anyone would be walking around on that rocky headland at that time of night. The voices became clearer, yet Pitman couldn't understand what was being said. The language wasn't English.

Suddenly he knew exactly what was happening. The language he was hearing was German, and at that very minute an escape was in progress.

The fireman dug in his oars and the little boat jerked forward. The oars bit again and again as he strained to increase his speed. Where in hell was the nearest phone?

The hundred metres around the front of Fort Henry seemed to last forever. Up ahead, half a kilometre or so away, Pitman saw a woman walking along the shore. He sped over to her, blurted out what had happened, and asked her to phone the police. He could do nothing more.

The woman's call was the first indication the police and the Fort Henry authorities had of any escape. Most of the POWs still in the fort knew about the break, of course, but they weren't talking. On the other hand, most of them were decidedly pessimistic about their colleagues' chances of really getting away.

Within minutes Kingston and the area immediately surrounding it became a restricted travel zone. Cars, departing buses and trains and all trucks passing through it were stopped and searched. In all, the Ontario Provincial Police, the RCMP, city police and more than five hundred officers and men from the various military establishments at Kingston were called out. They closed all roads leading to and from the general area of the fort, scrutinized and questioned every traveller, and turned back hordes of curiosity-seekers who wanted to see where the escape originated. Three teenagers in a canoe were told to steer clear when they paddled too close on the river side of the camp.

The search efforts soon paid off.

Minutes after Harold Pitman's warning had reached them, three police officers raced to the St. Lawrence and started combing the thick underbrush that obscured the shoreline downriver from the fort. There were a few cottages in the area and the trio checked these as they went along.

At first they neither saw nor heard anything suspicious. However, just as they finished circling the third cottage in a row, a flashlight picked out the form of a man crouching under the foundation of the fourth. He was ordered out, searched for weapons and questioned. When he heard the commotion and realized what had happened to his partner, a second man inside appeared on the doorstep with his hands up. Both admitted they were POWs, but neither wanted to talk about their method of escape. There were too many others involved to give the plot away this soon.

All through the night, during the next day and for four days afterward, the hunt went on. Singly and in twos and threes, the escapees were rounded up and returned to camp. Some were disappointed at being caught. Others were relieved that the hunt was over, while a few were surprised the end had come so soon. None offered any resistance.

George Fehn remembers hiding out all night, not far from the fort. When morning came, he dodged a couple of patrols and made his way into downtown Kingston. Without food or money to buy any, he just wandered up and down Princess Street, the city's main thoroughfare; he looked into store windows and once overheard two local merchants talking about the "big escape at the Fort."

"I never really expected to get anywhere," recalls Fehn today. "I acted more like a tourist, I suppose. I had a good look at the city, which was a lot more exciting than the grey walls back at the camp. Still, by midmorning I found myself thinking more of food than of escape. Perhaps that was why I found myself walking slowly back in the general direction of Fort Henry.

"At the lower end of Princess Street, the main highway curves to the left, just above the point where the Holiday Inn is today. I walked along there, as far as the causeway bridge on Highway 2. Up ahead I could see a roadblock.

"While I was trying to think of what to do next, I stood on the bridge and admired the view out over the harbour. Then, out of nowhere, a jeep with a couple of MPs [military police] raced down the road; they glanced over at me and went on. Something must have sunk in, however, because the next thing I heard, the brakes went on and the jeep was skidding to a halt. It roared backward and stopped. One guy jumped out, grabbed me, and ordered me to get in. He didn't even have to ask if I was a prisoner of war. I still wore the jacket with that crazy circle on the back. They gave me breakfast and I started my twenty-eight days in the cooler."

Fehn's experience was quite similar to that of the other escapees. Some of them managed to elude roadblocks and get some distance away. Others were picked up near the fort or, at most, a couple of kilometres away from it. Two were walking along a road east of the city just as a transport truck was going by. When the driver saw them, the pair jumped into a ditch and crouched down behind some bushes. The trucker simply hailed a passing police car, and the escapees were arrested on the spot. Two others were sighted and taken into custody at Seeley's Bay, thirty-five kilometres north of Kingston. They had hitch-hiked that far.

Throughout the area, news of the breakout dominated conversation and provided the local media with a major story. A mere glance at newspaper coverage of the escape indicates that they certainly rose to the occasion. Man-on-the-street interviews, detailed descriptions of the missing POWs and extensive coverage of every sighting and capture were spread across the pages of the *Whig-Standard*. Radio station CKWS was just as thorough.

The newspaper also used the escape as the basis for its lead editorial on August 28, two days after the break.

After drawing attention to the "uneasiness" and the "exceedingly disconcerting sense of insecurity" suffered by local residents because of the escape, the paper went on to criticize the management of Fort Henry and the apparent inefficient vigilance found there.

"When nineteen prisoners of any institution are able to escape in a body," the paper thundered, "then something is radically wrong . . . something is extremely inefficient." The editorial continued:

> It may be the prison itself, it may be the staff; it may be the
> administrative framework, or those who man it. We make no
> accusation on any of these points; that is not our province. We do
> feel, however, that this newspaper, speaking both for itself and on
> behalf of the people of Kingston and district, has every right to
> demand an intensive and exhaustive investigation of this prison
> break — and immediate and drastic elimination of the inefficiency
> which permitted it, regardless of whether that ineptness is shown to
> be manual or mechanical, animate or inanimate.

The newspaper got what it wanted. Even before the last missing POW had been located, a three-man board of inquiry had been appointed by Ottawa to investigate the escape. As was the case following other prison breaks, the sitting of the board was as much a device to ease public anxiety as it was a method of ascertaining why the prisoners got away in the first place. The board merely learned how the nineteen men got out and how ingenious the escape was. Culpability for the affair was harder to pinpoint. In the end, each escapee was given twenty-eight days' detention, a few minor security measures were suggested, and the whole thing was forgotten. A few days later, the last of the missing men were rounded up in an apple orchard in Clayton, New York. They surrendered without incident.

SEVEN

Angler: The Greatest Escape

Sheets of cold rain swept in from the lake, lashed the huts, and passed into the bleakness beyond. Except for the perimeter lights, the buildings were in darkness. On three sides, the oldest hills in the world continued their mute and lonely surveillance. Trees, rock, swamp and brush stretched to the horizon. It was spring on the north shore of Lake Superior, but the screaming wind promised snow.

Inside the camp, the 559 German prisoners finished their evening meal, trudged back to their quarters, and pretended to retire. Outside the muddy enclosure, the Canadian guards cursed the weather, smoked and prepared for a boring night. Thus ended Friday, April 18, at prisoner-of-war Camp X at Angler, Ontario. The year was 1941.

It was almost one in the morning when a tower guard heard a noise in the bush behind him. He peered into the blackness to see what was there but, because the snow had already started, could discern nothing. He listened for a few seconds, then decided to climb down and investigate.

The terrain on that side of the camp sloped gently down from the barbed wire to a small gully a few metres away. Beyond the gully were trees. At first the guard walked slowly along the fence; when everything seemed normal there, he moved into the gully. In the gloom near the bottom he kicked something half hidden by the snow. When he reached down to see what was there, he found himself staring into the mouth of a tunnel from which twenty-eight prisoners had just crawled to freedom. The guard raced back to his tower, took the steps two at a time, and phoned the guard room.

This twenty-eight-man escape from Angler was the largest ever from a Canadian camp. It had been planned for weeks, executed in minutes, yet almost cancelled a few hours before it was to begin. And in the end, only a fraction of the more than one hundred potential escapees made it. Of those, two got almost two thousand kilometres away. Two others, however, would never see the camp again. They were shot a short distance from Angler and their corpses brought back by dogsled three days after the breakout.

In any discussion of the Angler escape, one finds three separate yet interconnected stories: the planning and construction of the Camp X tunnel, the successful (for a time) escape of the two POWs who managed to get farthest away, and the still controversial sequence of events that culminated in the deaths of two Germans and the wounding of three others.

Angler was one of the loneliest and most remote POW compounds in Canada. The area surrounding it was desolate and virtually inaccessible except by rail or crude logging road. All building materials, supplies and personnel came in by train.

In the spring and summer, blackflies and mosquitoes hung over the bush in swarms. By September the nights were already cool, and before the end of October the first snows swept the low hills along the lakeshore. From mid-November until April, the land and all who lived in it were locked in a never-ending struggle against the bitter cold. Temperatures of forty below zero were commonplace. In a word, it was the ideal place to put a prison — 400 kilometres northwest of the city of Sault Ste. Marie, 300 east of Thunder Bay and at least 150 by water from the United States. The settlements closer to the camp were either Indian villages or small railside communities where no escaped German prisoner could ever hope to hide.

The first POWs arrived at Angler on January 10, 1941, not long after the Nazi Blitzkrieg had swept across Western Europe. Hitler's war machine at the time was still well oiled, well equipped and victorious, and it was no wonder the men who had fallen from it were resentful: locked up, thousands of kilometres from home and an ocean away from the action. All prisoners of war want out; perhaps none more than these men at Angler. They discussed, discarded and dreamed up escape schemes from the moment they arrived in camp, but of all the realistic and not-so-realistic plans for escaping Camp X, the 1941 "tunnel job" was certainly the most daring. It was also the most successful.

Planning for the break began four months before it took place. Initially, a handful of men who had known each other for some time met to draw up plans for a tunnel. They surveyed their domain, measured distances, watched the routine of the guards, and memorized the soft spots in camp security. The apparent density of the outlying bush, the surrounding terrain and the composition of the soil beneath the compound were all noted. So was the location of the Canadian Pacific line and the approximate distance to each community the railway served.

By the end of February, the general outline of the scheme had been decided upon. Lists of necessary materials — compasses, maps, civilian clothing and so forth — were agreed upon and their construction started. The manufacture of each and every item posed some kind of a problem. Either the raw material was unavailable, the design rudimentary, or the security difficult. For example, maps of northern Ontario did not exist anywhere inside the wire. A map had to be stolen from the guards, hastily copied and put back. A trusted POW employed to sweep Canadian officers' quarters was the thief. Compasses made from magnetized strips of razor blades stuck on the ends of needles were far from reliable. Dozens of suits of civilian clothes, which would be needed once escapers were away from the camp, were almost as hard to conceal as they were to manufacture.

But the most serious problems involved the tunnel.

At first, each member of the escape committee had his own ideas of where the tunnel should be built. Then the size it would be, the kind of opening or trap door it would have, and the method by which excavated dirt would be hidden became contentious items. Endless meetings were held to resolve each difficulty. Eventually, however, even with the restraints of time — the men wanted to give Hitler a surprise and escape on April 20, his birthday — and the differences among prisoners from the three services, procedures were agreed upon and digging got under way.

The buildings in Camp X were constructed in such a way that no barrack block was an entity unto itself. Instead the buildings — H huts, as they were called — were built in pairs, with interconnecting washroom areas joining one barrack with the next. They stretched in rows leading away from the main gate.

For that reason, the structure farthest from the front entrance was the building under which the prisoners decided to construct the tunnel. That area of the camp was also closest to the bush, where the necessary cover would be available once the men were out.

One factor in the design of the compound made Angler an excellent camp for tunnelling. As any man who was ever a POW knows only too well, disposing of excavated soil under clandestine conditions can be difficult; in some camps, virtually impossible. There are only so many places to hide the stuff. At Camp X, however, disposal was never much of a problem.

Every one of the prisoner barracks had been built about a metre above ground. In the summertime, anyone attempting to hide, much less dig a tunnel, under a building would stand out like a neon sign. But during the winter there was no such danger. Boards were placed around the foundation of each hut for warmth. Then snow piled against these boards acted as an additional insulator. With such cover, tunnelling operations could not be seen, and the piles of rubble that were excavated were completely hidden as well.

Before starting the tunnel leading out of the camp, it was decided that short passageways should be dug between each pair of unconnected huts so that every barrack block in the compound would be linked together. Roll calls that winter were done within the huts, and almost without fail, these counts began with the first building inside the main gate and proceeded to the one farthest from it. The guards who did the counting didn't check faces too closely; they were more interested in obtaining a proper head count. This gave the prisoners the notion to dig cross-tunnels, so that they could duck from one hut to the next, giving the impression that each barrack was full when the guards doing the count arrived. Several times that winter this manoeuvre was practised, until a dozen or more men could dash underground between any two barracks in a few seconds. The cross-tunnels were helpful as well for hiding food caches and other items needed for the breakout.

The entire camp at Angler was built on sand, so there was no problem in cutting into the sand and burrowing through it. But ensuring that the sides and particularly the top of the tunnel did not come crashing down was not so simple. Virtually every inch of the structure had to be reinforced with floor joists stolen from the barrack blocks. When the floors had been laid originally, they had been so well supported that a missing joist or two now caused no great problem. But by the time shoring timber had been cabbaged for the tunnel, some huts had floors that actually sagged in spots.

While prying the joists away from the floor boards was reasonably easy, cutting them into lengths suitable for use in the tunnel was difficult and rather slow. At first, most of the cutting was done with knives stolen from the kitchen and sharpened enough to penetrate wood. Later on, thin metal springs that had been removed from camp gramophones and tempered were stretched between two handles and used as saws. One team of men would remove a joist, and a second would cut it up. Then the teams would switch roles and do the next one, and so on. At times, the actual digging proceeded at whatever pace the woodcutters could maintain.

The opening under hut 5B was begun the day after the last cross-tunnel was completed. At first, a two-metre-square underground room was dug under one corner of the building. This room served several purposes. The men doing the tunnelling used it as a place to rest when they were not actually digging. In addition, sand from the tunnel face was dragged back here for disposal up above. As well, any shoring timber that had been cut but not yet installed was stockpiled in this room.

For the most part, the digging proceeded with little interference from the Canadians. A Veterans Guard officer who was at Angler that winter remembers that a few periodic spot checks were made of the prisoner huts, but at no time were any illegal activities discovered. As far as the guards were concerned, the POWs seemed content, so it was decided to leave them alone. Anyway, it was felt that only a fool would try to go anywhere in midwinter.

Fools or not, two men, Horst Liebeck and Karl-Heinz Grund, *were* particularly eager to get away from Angler. They felt they had been there too long. Both hated being caged and they fought against the alluring temptation to relax and live out the war in the safety and comfort of this or any other POW camp. For these reasons, Liebeck, Grund and many like them wanted to get away, and the sooner the better. Any day now, one of the spot checks might alert the guards as to what was really going on in the camp.

During one such check, several prisoners were almost discovered in the tunnel. The floor trap was lowered and a card table and chairs were barely thrown over it by the time a Canadian captain touched the door handle. Most of the time, however, a series of signals agreed upon before digging began eliminated chance discovery. A lookout posted near the front gate took note of unexpected visitors in the compound, then relayed the news to a second man posted closer to 5B. The same set of signals were used for a day or two at most.

For the first few days the digging went well and the tunnel moved ahead several feet. Gradually, however, progress became slower and slower. The farther the digging face was from the underground room, the harder it was to bring the sand out and get the shoring timbers in place. Often large chunks of the tunnel roof would come crashing down, half burying the diggers and making it necessary to remove more sand than expected. Each time this occurred, the diggers feared that the ground in the compound would drop as well and expose the excavations. They all knew that if that happened, there would be no break in the spring.

In order to get the sand out of the shaft, a wooden cart was constructed, with a rope tied to each end of it. When the cart was full it was simply pulled out of the tunnel, emptied and hauled back in again. Without the cart, sand removal would have been almost impossible. From time to time, even the cart caused difficulties. Unless it was pulled slowly, carefully and in a straight line, the corners tended to catch on the sides of the tunnel. Once when it caught, the man who was doing the pulling jerked the cart harder than he should have and tore two side timbers out of the walls. Because they were also roof supports, the roof at that spot collapsed, and several hundred kilograms of sand suddenly blocked the tunnel, cutting off the man at the digging face and literally burying him alive. Several frantic minutes went by before the digger was rescued and the damage repaired. The experience left several men badly shaken, but no one left the tunnel team because of the incident.

Lighting below ground was never really a problem. Makeshift candles for the tunnel were produced from tin cans, kitchen fat and underwear drawstrings. Liquid fat was simply poured into a tin around the drawstring wick. As soon as the substance congealed, the candle was ready to go. Dozens of these were used during the course of excavations — three or four at one time in the workroom, and others in the tunnel itself. While not the best illumination, they were portable, easy to construct and readily obtainable inside the compound.

During the excavation of the workroom and the first section of the tunnel, the quality of air underground was reasonably good. As the digging moved farther and farther away from 5B, however, problems arose. Men working at the face complained of headaches and, in one or two cases, actually passed out from lack of oxygen. To remedy the situation, milk tins from the mess hall were linked together to form an air duct running the length of the tunnel. Toilet paper soaked in a mixture of flour and water was wrapped around the pipe to make it tight, and a hand-operated fan in the workroom blew fresh air down to the digging crew. The method was crude, but it worked.

As the tunnel grew longer over the weary winter weeks, the tension in the camp escalated. Tempers flared over occurrences that normally would have been laughed off or ignored. Card games were more serious, individual habits more irritating, and altercations on the ice rink more commonplace. What once might have been a momentary shoving match between two hockey players had now become a full-fledged brawl. Slurping coffee at meals, loud snoring at night or unconscious humming while someone was trying to read were quirks that often resulted in heated arguments.

Suddenly spring came — too quickly.

Because the break was scheduled to take place on the Fuehrer's fifty-second birthday, all the plans and preparations of the winter were aimed at the April 20 target date. Normally, the ground on the north shore of Lake Superior would still be frozen at this time, and travel in the area would not be hampered by either severe cold or insects. What the POWs did not count on was the rain.

About the middle of April, a low-pressure weather system swept across the upper lakes, bringing with it milder temperatures, fog and rain. In the internment camp at Angler, the massive snow banks started to shrink, rivulets of water collected in muddy puddles on the footpaths, and the insulating board skirts around the prisoner barracks were suddenly laid bare. But worst of all, from the prisoners' point of view, drops of water started to seep into the precious tunnel. At first the trickle was hardly noticeable. Then it became more and more alarming. Finally, by the morning of Friday, April 18, when the rains stopped, one section of the tunnel was awash in fifteen centimetres of water, with more pouring in all the time. If this continued, escape would quickly become impossible and all the hard work of the winter would be in vain. Yet April 20 was only two days away.

An emergency meeting to consider the situation was held in 5B. Several prisoners argued that the escape should proceed as planned and no earlier. Any change now, or so they felt, would not be wise — or safe. Last-minute arrangements were still not finalized, they argued, and to go out half prepared would only increase the chances of being caught.

The argument shifted back and forth for some time, but in the end the rising water was the determining factor in the decision to go. By noon, the flooded section of the tunnel bottom was submerged to a depth of thirty centimetres, and the boards overhead were soaked for a metre or more in either direction. A long section of the roof appeared ready to fall.

All through the day, the tunnel engineers kept checking the low spot. By midafternoon, some hours after the rain had ceased, leakage below ground had also ended. The wind shifted into the north and the temperature dropped. Snow clouds hung over the lake; a few hours later they would move inland.

Once the decision to go was made, feverish last-minute plans were set in motion. Tools and equipment that would be needed to open the tunnel were moved down the shaft to the face. Food caches, civilian clothes, compasses and maps were sorted and made ready. The order of departure was reviewed, and the movement from hut to hut via the cross-tunnels practised. POWs who would be left behind rehearsed the cover system worked out weeks before.

By mess time that evening, those who were going to go out were showing their excitement in various ways. Some were unusually talkative; others became virtually mute. Several found it impossible to eat, and a couple threw up what they did eat. All were scared.

Horst Liebeck remembers that he was apprehensive because of the tunnel flooding, but felt that because the men had worked so hard preparing for this night, some of them *had* to get out. "I found it hard to concentrate on the everyday things we had to do," he recalls. "At first the day of the escape seemed as if it would never end. But by evening there was so much excitement in camp that the time really flew. I don't remember ever seeing so many guys go to the toilets so often. Some were really worked up. It was exciting being part of the whole experience, though."

Outside, the rain had begun again, but now it was icy, wind-driven and torrential. In the escape shaft, the water was slightly higher, meaning that every man who got out would probably be soaked before he ever left the tunnel. Yet it was this terrible night — or not at all.

As soon as roll call was over, the first groups began moving into the tunnel. These were the people who would have to excavate the final metre of dirt at the tunnel's end. Following them, and going into the tunnel for the first time, were those who had made candles, distributed sand, and made the maps. Most of them were terrified. The fifty-metre-long, metre-square underground passage seemed so small, so very long and so much like a grave. Still, they did their best, fighting down panic, claustrophobia and the urge to retreat. And once in the tunnel, they waited — and waited.

Up at the face, digging was slow. It had to be done in absolute darkness because even a pinpoint of light coming from the ground outside the wire would be seen immediately. The longer the digging took, of course, the greater the anxiety level in the tunnel. Waves of fear affected everyone — particularly those who were well back from the face and had no way of knowing what the delay was. Someone was sure the break had already been discovered. A young navy man was certain he had heard a shot. Could it be that the escapers were being killed as they emerged? Then, finally, word came back that the diggers had broken through. Outside it was snowing.

Twenty-eight men got away from Angler that night. Twenty-eight individuals — each with his own hopes, fears, inner resources and personal plans for remaining free. Some of these plans had been well thought out. Some, such as the one of rowing across Lake Superior, were foolhardy. Others, even though they seemed workable when first presented, were good for just a few days. One almost succeeded. Those who didn't get out before the tunnel was discovered simply stayed behind.

When they had first discussed their scheme a few weeks earlier, most of the prisoners who listened to Liebeck and Grund thought the two were mad. After all, who in his right mind would leave Angler and head for *Japan*? Even if that country was friendly to Germany, it *was* on the other side of the world! Why not try for the United States, still neutral and a mere 150 kilometres away? Sure, it was 150 kilometres of rock, bush, snow and water — but it wasn't a continent and an ocean away! However, the two clung to their plan, worked it out, modified it — and then almost made it work.

Years later, Liebeck, now a successful Toronto businessman,

described how he and Grund decided on their unique idea.

"Even though the U.S. was not technically at war, we knew it was useless going there. After von Werra's escape, none of us thought we would have much chance of getting away there. The States was just too big, and besides, they were already starting to turn escapees back. Grund and I decided to go to Vancouver and talk our way on board a Japanese ship, or a ship going to Japan. Neither of us knew any Japanese in British Columbia who might have helped us. We just thought if we could somehow get to Vancouver, we would head for the harbour and simply try our luck.

"Others planned to go north, some east and a lot south. We thought it would be best to get on the first train we could and get the hell out of the area. Any other way would have been difficult — with the wilderness, the weather and so on. We had concentrated food with us, prepared by the food committee. We also knew the timetable of the Canadian Pacific, which passed fairly near the camp. We could tell from the sound the trains made that there must have been a bend and then a hill somewhere close by. All the trains slowed down. We also timed the trains. Of course, we had nothing else to do."

Liebeck also remembers what it was like to go through the tunnel, and what he saw when he emerged from it: "In the tunnel we were all very tense. We also hoped and prayed that nobody made a mistake and that everything would go well. We were convinced that if we were seen leaving the tunnel, we would be shot. In fact, we were sure of it. There was a tower close by. We believed we were gambing with our lives. We were fully aware of the danger, but at the same time, the tunnel was probably the safest and most conventional way of escaping.

"After I got through the tunnel, I was soaking wet. I recall lying there in the brush in the blizzard and looking up at the silhouette of a guard in a tower. But he was behind me and I was *free*! It was a great feeling. I was on the other side of the fence and I felt like cheering.

"The weather was terrible. Wet snow and wind. I remember looking into the blackness in front of me and feeling scared and damned cold."

The two men crawled on their stomachs deep into the bushes. Finally, when the underbrush was thick enough, they stood up and tramped on toward the railway. As yet there was no sound behind them, but far ahead they heard the faint whistle of a steam train.

"We made it to the railroad on time. Somehow, we also got to the right place, a sharp bend in the tracks. We ducked down in a ditch as the engine passed, then we climbed up the embankment beside the train. I remember that it was quite long and moving fairly slowly. I don't recall whether there was a caboose or not. We were too busy to look, I guess."

The two stood transfixed for a few seconds as car after car swept past. Then, when they had caught their breath, they jumped toward two boxcars and grabbed the steel ladders on the sides. Painfully, hand over hand, each slowly pulled himself upward. "My hands were on the second rung, but my feet were actually bumping on the railbed." Liebeck grimaces as he tells of the incident. "If we had not been young and in fairly good shape, we would have been thrown off. As it was, my ankles were cut and bruised from being dragged on the cinders."

Finally both men managed to get themselves up the side and onto the roof, where they could rest and decide what to do next. They had brought makeshift tools with them: a tiny saw, hammer, pliers and screwdriver in order to force their way inside a boxcar. Originally, the plan had been to cut through the wooden floor of a car, but this idea was quickly dismissed as impossible. As it turned out, all attempts to pry a door open were just as hopeless. They moved along the train and tried door after door after door, but were unable to budge any of them. Eventually, in utter exasperation, they climbed back up to the roof to see if there was any hope of getting in from the top.

Few cars had doors on the roof, so the possibilities of locating one that might open seemed slim. Nevertheless they succeeded on both counts. A third of the way down the train from the engine, they found a round hatch that seemed less secure than anything they had tried so far. They crouched by it, one in front and the other behind. Then, using the tools they had brought along, they started to remove the steel locking device.

Their working conditions were terrible. Because the train had picked up considerable speed, the cars were swaying so sharply that Liebeck and Grund had to work with one hand each, holding on with the other. The momentum also increased the discomfort from the driving snow. Biting, stinging ice crystals cut into their faces and coated their clothes. Flying cinders half blinded them. Every so often the smoke from the engine would stream back along the roof and engulf them in an acrid, sooty, choking cloud.

But they didn't give up. Their hands numb with cold, they pried and hammered and cursed the hatch lock until it finally gave. Slowly, with one man pulling and the other pushing, they eased the heavy steel plate open. Liebeck, who had been sitting with his back to the engine, held the cover up while Grund fumbled to make sure the broken lock would not close itself and make it impossible to open from the inside. With all they had gone through so far, they had no desire to get trapped inside a railway car.

Suddenly Grund looked up and screamed, "Get down!" The words were hardly out of his mouth when the train roared into a tunnel.

"Another second or so and it would have been all over for me," recalls Liebeck now. "The hatch was fairly large and I was half kneeling, holding it. I'm not sure just how much space there was between the train and the roof of that tunnel, and I never want to know. When Karl yelled, I didn't realize what was wrong, but I knew from the tone of his voice I shouldn't ask. We just flattened ourselves and held on. Inside the tunnel we could hardly breathe because of the smoke. After that, we watched where we were going."

By the time they were sure the hatch would not close on its own, the train was approaching another of the short tunnels that dot the CP tracks along the Lake Superior shore. The men were ready this time.

As soon as the second tunnel was behind them, Grund reached into the car to see what it carried. Because his hands were numb, he was unsure at first of what he touched. Then Liebeck checked. Whatever was inside seemed to be smooth, hard and cold.

"All we found in there," recalls Liebeck, "was ice! There may have been something down underneath, but we never saw it. All we found were hundreds of blocks of ice. We were so damned cold, that's all we needed!"

Feverishly the two started pitching the blocks out of the train in order to make enough room to get inside. When they had a sizable cave dug for themselves, they climbed down into the car and closed the hatch behind them.

"We knew that as soon as the escape was discovered, every train that passed the camp would be checked," recalls Liebeck, "so we decided to burrow back into the ice so that if the hatch were lifted, we would be out of sight. We had one of the fat lamps with us, and by using it we could see what we were doing. It took a long time, but finally we figured we'd done the best we could. We were a couple of metres away from the opening, and there was a solid ice wall below the hatch."

The train sped on. Past Jack Fish, Schreiber, Rossport to Nipigon. Liebeck and Grund ate some of the rations they had brought with them, sucked some of the ice for water, then, huddled for warmth, drifted into a half-conscious somnolent state brought on by the exertion and excitement of the night. Every so often they lit the candle, in order to check the level of oxygen in the car. They knew that if the candle would not burn, the hatch would have to be opened slightly, danger or no danger.

Then the train started to slow down. The rocking from side to side lessened, and the squeal of brakes could be heard. Both men were instantly wide awake. They felt a lurch and the train was still.

"Almost immediately, we heard shouts that sounded like military commands," says Liebeck. "Then there was a lot of movement outside and the sound of doors being opened. We knew the boxcar in front of ours was opened because we could hear the door being pulled back."

Liebeck and Grund lay there, hardly daring to breathe, terrified that any minute someone would climb up on the train and check the hatch covers. But no one ever did. Once or twice they heard threads of muffled conversation, and on one occasion, a soldier shouted an order an arm's length from the hiding place.

After what seemed two hours, but was in reality little more than a quarter of that, a whistle blew and the train started to move. They had been missed in the first check.

"Because of the search, it was obvious the escape had been discovered," Liebeck says. "We were fairly sure it had been, but now we were certain. We knew that from now on, the police would be watching for us. Still, it was great to be free. Twice more the train was stopped and searched. We were lucky, I suppose. They never found us."

At Kenora the escapers decided to get out of their refrigerator. The train had been stopped for some time, and no voices could be heard near it.

"We had lain there on the ice for so long that we were afraid we'd freeze to death if we didn't get out," Liebeck remembers. "But we found that we could barely move. Karl must have taken five minutes just to get the candle lit. He dropped the first three matches because he couldn't hold them between his fingers. Our legs were stiff, and there seemed to be no feeling in our feet at all. We eventually had to punch each other to get the circulation back."

Slowly, very slowly, the men cleared the ice from under the

hatch. Grund raised the cover a tiny bit, and a sliver of daylight penetrated the car. It took him a minute or two to get accustomed to the brightness outside, but once he had done so, he was able to get some idea of where they were. The car was on a siding, still coupled to the rest of the train, but the engine was no longer in front. Some distance to the rear, two men were piling boxes of something or other onto a truck. As Grund watched, they completed their task, climbed into the cab and drove away. No one else was around. The freight sheds were two hundred metres away on one side. On the other, across a tangle of tracks that seemed to curve every which way, was a pile of oiled railway ties. Beyond the ties was the bush.

The men climbed out through the hatch, closed it behind them, and dropped quickly to the ground. Satisfied that they had not been seen, they darted across the tracks, paused momentarily behind the pile of ties, then dove into the trees.

"We walked deep into the bush," says Liebeck. "Then when we were sure we were absolutely alone, and far enough away that no one would likely come along, we got a few sticks together and lit a fire. Eventually we got ourselves thawed out. Then we found some water and began to clean up. We even shaved."

Both men were carrying extra clothes with them in waterproof bags. They changed and buried what they had been wearing under some leaves and brush at the base of a tree trunk. Then, after some hot food and rest, they decided it was time to move on.

Getting onto a train was easy this time. While Grund acted as a lookout behind the pile of railway ties, Horst Liebeck casually crossed one set of tracks, ducked under a stationary tanker, and vaulted through the open door of an empty boxcar on an adjoining siding. As far as Grund could tell, the movement went unobserved by anyone else. A minute or so later, he followed.

Only after they were inside the car did it occur to them that they did not know the direction the train might be going. At that point, no engine was attached.

Just as they had decided they would drop off the freight if it started moving eastward instead of west, the train on the next track lurched forward. The two men looked at each other for an instant, then, barely glancing to see if anyone was around, jumped from their hiding place, raced alongside the second train, and dove into the first open door they found. The freight shunted its way onto the main line, gathered speed and headed west. The Germans cheered — for a couple of seconds.

Over in one corner of the car, a middle-aged man sat watching them.

The man in the corner said nothing at first, although it was obvious to Liebeck and Grund that he was mildly curious about them. They in turn wondered about *him*, thinking that he was some kind of police officer. Finally Liebeck, who knew English and had taught the language to others in Angler, moved over and spoke to the stranger. To the German's immense relief, the man was not a policeman but an unemployed vagrant riding the rails. He didn't question the story Liebeck gave him about their being geology students who were heading west to do some prospecting in the mountains. Today Liebeck wonders if the man would have reacted any differently had he known he was sharing his train carriage with two escaped prisoners from the German air force.

The hobo's presence was annoying at first, because the escapees had to be careful of what they said to him. On the other hand, they learned a certain amount of geography from the man — particularly about the route the train would follow through western Canada. The fellow mentioned that he had many friends in towns and villages across the country. Liebeck and Grund were pretty sure the "friends" were other tramps running from work, conscription or both. At one point he startled the two by mentioning that there were "fewer men riding on the trains now. It's because of the goddamned Krauts." The POWs smiled, looked at each other but said nothing. They were relieved when he got off at Dryden.

When they arrived in Winnipeg, Liebeck wanted to look up some distant relatives to see if they would provide a hiding place and shelter for a few days, until the manhunt died down. The pilots left the train and located the address in the city, but found that the house was occupied by someone else. Liebeck learned years later that his relatives had been interned at the time.

After their dreary months of captivity, the Germans found Winnipeg an exciting place. It was busy, colourful and friendly. The two did some sightseeing there, shopped, drank in a local hotel, and bought a newspaper at a street-corner kiosk. From it they learned that a total of twenty-eight men had gotten out of Angler, and that several of them were still at large. The paper also mentioned that the authorities were sure all escapees were still in the vicinity of the camp.

"We were happy to read that story," says Liebeck, "but it probably did more harm to us than if they had said they had no idea where we were. Because the paper said the search was near Angler, we were less cautious. I remember walking past a cop in Winnipeg and whistling 'Deep in the Heart of Texas.' The same day Karl tried to buy some cigarettes with *English* money. In a way, we were just asking to be caught."

Because the search for Liebeck's relatives had been futile, the POWs decided they might as well leave Winnipeg. Gradually they made their way across Manitoba and Saskatchewan, into southern Alberta. Then, at Medicine Hat, their luck ran out.

"We were sitting in a boxcar on a siding there," recalls Liebeck. "We were talking, trying to figure out whether to leave our hiding place in daylight or wait for darkness. A railway cop came along and asked who we were and what we were doing. Karl gave him a story and the guy seemed convinced. He told us to move along."

The Germans were not sure whether they were really in the clear, so they left the rail yards and headed into town. No one followed them, but neither felt particularly at ease.

"We stopped at a house for some water," Liebeck says. "Then we found a road leading out of the town toward Lethbridge. We were walking along there when a cruiser pulled up beside us."

The man in the car was an RCMP officer who had been alerted by the suspicious railway policeman. Five days after their escape, the two "vagrants" were taken into custody and lodged in the Medicine Hat jail. Then their true identities came out.

For the next few hours the Germans were treated like celebrities. A local newspaper reporter arrived at the jail and interviewed them. He asked about their escape, their journey and their capture. "We told him we had pretended to be Dutch miners heading for Calgary," Liebeck recalls. "Why we picked Calgary or why we decided to be Dutch, I really cannot remember. The whole thing was somewhat of a lark. We were treated like celebrities and we both enjoyed the experience. If I was in the same circumstances again, I would do the same things."

So would Karl Grund. In an interview at his home in Bremen, West Germany, in 1964, Grund described the escape and its aftermath for reporter Peter Desbarats.[1] He looked upon his and Liebeck's capture as being unique.

"It was the craziest part of the escape," he said. "We felt more like Hollywood celebrities than recaptured prisoners."

At someone's suggestion, a clergyman was brought in to offer guidance to these two errant souls. The minister probably meant well, but to the Germans who had never pretended to be particularly religious, and who had little or no contact with religion in the Angler camp, the approach of the cleric was particularly incongruous. The minister shook hands with the two escapees, sat down on a bunk beside them and stared at Grund. Finally he asked, "Do you believe in God?" The Germans were at a loss for words.

Later, some soldiers came to talk. A couple of collectors wanted souvenirs. A handful of townspeople asked for autographs. Dozens more just gawked.

Then the word came from Angler. Liebeck and Grund were to be taken under guard back to Camp X. That night, a large crowd yelling "Good luck!" and "See you after the war!" was on hand as the train carrying the two prisoners pulled away from the Medicine Hat station. This time, the train was eastbound.

EIGHT

Cover-up at Angler?

Horst Liebeck and Karl Grund had been little more than a hundred metres from the tunnel mouth at Angler when the breakout was discovered by the guards. After them, only five others got away.

As soon as the Canadians knew what was happening, the entire camp came alive. All available Veterans Guard personnel were immediately alerted. Singly and in twos and threes they raced to the guard room, got their orders, and fanned out across the grounds. The tunnel exit was sealed almost as soon as the alarm sounded. Additional guards were mounted in the towers, and foot patrols tramped around the wire, both inside and out, double-checking that no second avenue of escape existed.

Five minutes after he was informed of the break, Major Charles Lindsey, the crusty commanding officer at Angler, was in his office issuing directives to his men and initiating the early search procedures. All police and military authorities in the area were contacted right away, and a couple of hours later Internment Operations headquarters in Ottawa received the news. Lindsey's first telegram indicated that thirty prisoners were out. This delay in reporting and the error as to the numbers involved were both direct results of the difficulties experienced in trying to conduct an accurate roll call.

While the POWs would normally have tried to frustrate the count in every way possible after any escape, the fact that the mass break they had planned was not altogether successful made them even less inclined to line up and be counted now. Because the escape had been discovered so soon, many of them were angry, bitter and terribly disappointed. For every man who got away, three more who had planned to get out were left behind. These prisoners had no intention of cooperating with their jailers.

Active Company 2A of the Veterans Guard, the unit that policed the camp at the time, tried at first to count the prisoners inside the barracks. The correct number of prisoners was found in the first hut. But in the second, two were missing. In the third, the guards found five *extra* men. There were also one too many prisoners in the fourth hut. The second time around, one man was missing from the first barracks, but three extras turned up in the second. The cross-tunnels were a success!

Finally, in utter exasperation, the Canadians ordered the POWs outside. This in itself took some doing. The prisoners took their time getting dressed, joked with one another, and tried to play games with the guards. A few lagged behind in the latrines, and a couple feigned illness and asked to remain in bed. No one stayed in the tunnels. They were afraid they would be shot if they did.

Once everyone was outside, the roll call was slow because the Germans shifted ranks, responded to the wrong names, and danced around in the snow. It was four in the morning before a completely accurate count was completed. Then the laborious task of ascertaining just *who* was missing began. This aspect of the job was not finished until almost daybreak. But by this time, Liebeck and Grund were far away.

Once he was certain the camp was secure, Lindsey ordered patrols established on the CPR line. All trains, passenger and freight, eastbound and westbound, were stopped and searched, and their crews were warned to be on the lookout for any escapees. After one train in either direction had been halted, others entering the area expected to stop and did so. In all the searches, railway employees obliged in every way possible.

Incoming trains also brought assistance. Veterans Guard reinforcements, Ontario Provincial Police and RCMP officers converged on Angler. At midmorning, two officers and fifty men of the Algonquin Regiment, a unit of the regular army, arrived from Thunder Bay.

Then the brass showed up.

Colonel Hubert Stethem, director of Internment Operations, was in Toronto when word of the escape reached him. He flew to North Bay on a military aircraft but was forced to leave the plane there when it was grounded by fog. He continued his journey by rail and reached the north shore of Lake Superior forty-eight hours after the break occurred. On a second train were the deputy adjutant-general, Brigadier A. E. Nash, from Ottawa, and the deputy commissioner of the Ontario Provincial Police, Herbert McCready of Toronto. The three men conferred briefly at the tiny station at Heron Bay, then went directly to nearby Angler to have a firsthand look at Camp X and the tunnel that led from it.

A short time later, an obviously harried Stethem told a reporter what they found. He described the tunnel, indicated where it was, mentioned its size and estimated how long it probably took the prisoners to dig it. He flatly refused, however, to be drawn into a discussion as to whether negligence on the part of the guards contributed to the success of the break. "The tunnel should have been spotted . . . but the break came too soon," was all he told the press.[1]

Privately, however, he was more willing to cast blame. In a letter stamped "Secret" that he sent to the British War Office on June 3 that year, he wrote: "The wall boards were constructed right to the ground, and, although instructions had been issued that some were to be removed as soon as the snow melted, this had not been done. It would appear that there had been a great lack of supervision by the camp authorities. . . ."[2]

In a letter to a friend on April 28, 1941, Stethem said, in part:

> I am afraid the breakout at the western camp was due entirely to negligence on the part of those responsible for the custody of the prisoners. They have been given all kinds of suggestions and advice and the regulations are very explicit, but, if regulations and instructions are ignored, then escapes will occur. . . . Many of the guards are, undoubtedly, beyond the age of usefulness. . . . The trap doors were not discovered because dust had been swept over them, and the area under the floors had not been examined for the storage of earth. Prisoners were in the possession of knapsacks, and table knives had not been checked.[3]

To a senior Veterans Guard officer in Toronto, he wrote:

> Had those responsible for the custody of these prisoners paid any attention to the instructions issued from this office, the escapes would not have occurred. . . . The security of the prisoners must necessarily depend on the alertness of the individual compound policeman or sentry and the constant surveillance of the camp staff.

Unfortunately, the Department of National Defence has sole
control of the appointments to these camp staffs, and, in some cases,
many of the guards have outlived their usefulness as sentries.[4]

He was equally blunt in another letter to a man in Walkerville,
Ontario:

The escape from the western camp was really quite inexcusable.
While the ground is, unfortunately, very soft sand and makes digging
quite easy, it was quite evident that the camp staff . . . were
apparently asleep on the job.[5]

This train of thought was echoed by several newspapers in their
coverage of the escape. The Toronto *Telegram* was most incensed,
as is obvious from the lead editorial written a few hours after the
Germans got out:

News of the mass escape by twenty-eight German prisoners of war
from the camp at Schreiber [*sic*] is intimation that spring has
reached the northern forests and that conditions are suitable for
travelling again. It is also intimation that the custody of enemy
prisoners in Canada is still subject to the same careless, slovenly,
inept and happy-go-lucky stupidity that has marked it from the start.
The force in Canada which had this charge has had an elementary
job of little difficulty, and has discharged it atrociously without,
apparently, any serious concern on the part of the Government in
Ottawa.

In the past the Government has declared that there is nothing to
be perturbed about in the escape of prisoners. It has said that they
always have escaped and always will. This, however, is true only
where the custodians have been careless or venal, and where the
authority above has lacked capacity to make the security of prisoners
sure.

This part of the job of the Department of National Defence has
been marked with shoddy inefficiency. The force in charge might be
entrusted with the guarding of Old Men's Homes, but as guardians
of husky and inventive Germans they have too frequently proved
their incapacity.[6]

The Kingston *Whig-Standard*, in an editorial on April 26, 1941,
was just as critical. The paper said, in part:

There have been too many escapes of prisoners of war. . . . What is wrong with the system of guarding the men? What is the flaw that makes escapes possible? We do not know the exact answers to these questions, but we do know that it . . . must be obvious to all citizens that whatever inefficiency there is (and there certainly is inefficiency of some kind when many escapes occur) is to be found right within the internment camp boundaries. It is very difficult indeed to draw any other conclusions than that some of the guards employed must be congenitally incapable of performing the duties to which they have been assigned, or that various camp commandants are permitting slackness and negligence or have failed to work out suitable methods for keeping a close check on all that goes on in the camps under their command.

When prisoners get the opportunity to dig tunnels all over the place, not only one tunnel through which a number escape, but an entire series of partly finished tunnels, it is difficult to convince us that the guards have been doing their jobs conscientiously. After all, what have the guards to do aside from keeping alert to prevent escapes?

But the authorities at Angler had no time to respond to what the press was saying about the escape. Their first priority was rounding up the fugitives.

The raw overnight wind had whipped the new snow into crusty drifts, and underneath, the water-soaked old snow became so mushy it made search work extremely taxing. Men became exhausted after floundering for a few hundred metres through the bush. With every step they took, they sank to their knees and became soaked to the skin in the process. And once wet, they stayed wet: there wasn't time for the luxury of changing into dry clothes.

The men had taken some provisions with them, but because it was so hard to move about, they didn't try to carry too much. As it was, their stores often got as wet as the pack in which they were wrapped. And slogging through knee-deep snow would have been difficult enough in itself; but the searchers also had to climb over fallen trees, through dense underbrush, over ice-coated rocks and up and down the treacherous slopes and ravines that traverse that forbidding land. In some places, a false step meant a painful fall of ten or fifteen metres or more.

But the Canadians had two things going for them. They knew that travel was just as difficult for the Germans, and, certainly more important, they knew exactly where most of the quarry had gone. The snow might have been a curse to walk in, but it was indispensable to the searchers. Every move the fugitives made was imprinted in the snow. Where someone had stopped to rest, urinate or smoke, the signs were there. And slowly, gradually the searchers narrowed the gap between themselves and their quarry.

Just after eight on Saturday morning, the first three prisoners were apprehended.

A railway section man named Mike Gopek had just finished breakfast and had left for work when three men appeared at his home. Their leader, a tall, blond young man who spoke English, shivered on the doorstep and asked Mrs. Gopek if she had any whisky in the house. When she said she did not, the three walked to a second house. From some distance away, Gopek noticed the trio and, armed with only a shovel, walked back to see what was going on. When it became obvious who the strangers were, Gopek simply demanded that they surrender to him. To his astonishment, they did. They were just too cold to argue.

Not long afterward, two more prisoners were apprehended. Mrs. Hugh McDonnell, wife of the station agent at the tiny hamlet of Peninsula, looked out her window and saw two escapees disappearing over a nearby hill. She called to a group of soldiers who happened to be at the station, and they followed the fugitives.

"They ran after the men," she said later, "and inside of five minutes they were back with the two of them. They were both quite young. They didn't make any attempt to get away. They were wearing black sweaters and they both had packsacks. One was glum and 'sneery.' The other was just a boy. They were both wet through from the rain and sleet. A freight train came along right away, and the soldiers took them back to the camp on the train."[6]

The Angler breakout could be contrasted with a similar event that took place after an escape from a camp at Crossville, Tennessee. In the American version, a woman and three Germans were involved, but the end of the story was somewhat different. John Hammond Moore tells the tale in his book, *The Faustball Tunnel.*

Three enlisted men, one of them from the U-162, got away from a work detail and fled into the Tennessee woods. Several days later the trio came to a mountain cabin and started to get water from a pump. An irascible granny appeared in the doorway, aimed a gun

in their direction and told them to "git." Unschooled in the ways of
mountain folk, they scoffed and paid no attention. A few moments
later she drew and fired, killing one of the seamen almost instantly.
When a deputy sheriff informed the old lady that she had killed an
escaped German prisoner of war, she was horror-stricken, burst into
tears, and sobbed that she would never have fired if she had known
the men were Germans.

"Well, ma'am," he asked, puzzled, "what in thunder did you
think you were aiming at?"

"Why," she replied, "I thought they wuz Yankees!"[7]

At about the same time as Mrs. McDonnell noticed the two
strangers near her home, a pair of Canadian soldiers, Sergeant
Ridgway and Lance-Corporal Thomas, saw wood smoke rising
above the trees a short distance inland from the main rail line.
They investigated and found an old cabin, almost covered with
vines and underbrush, with a thin trail of smoke coming from the
chimney.

While Thomas stood to one side, Ridgway approached the door
of the shack. Just in front of it, he called for whoever was in the
building to come out. At first there was no response. Then the
door opened and a POW emerged. He took one look at Ridgway
and started to run toward the bush — or, at least, he left the
guards with the impression that he was *about* to run. In the
resulting confusion, Thomas raised his rifle, took aim and shot
the man's nose off. Three other Germans who were inside immediately stumbled out with their hands in the air. All four, including the injured man, were marched back to camp.

An hour or so later, two more stragglers were brought in, so
that at nightfall on Saturday, eleven of the original twenty-eight
escapees were back in custody. Just after dark, the sleet that
had drenched the area for so long turned to snow — snow driven
by wild, shrieking winds that swept through the pines. But
the weather did not stop the manhunt completely. Only those
searchers who had been out since dawn returned to quarters.
These men were just too cold, wet and exhausted to look for
anyone. Once inside, they showered, ate and fell asleep the
moment they touched a bed.

The next day, Sunday, April 20, 1941, eight more Germans
were accounted for. Unfortunately, that was also the day of
the single most controversial incident in Canada's Internment
Operations.

We are now half a lifetime away from the events of that Sunday morning, but the mere passage of time has not helped to clarify what really happened that day. In some respects, hindsight seems to have obscured matters even more. Men who were at Angler then have grown older; their memories are not as clear. Some who were not present believe sincerely that they *were* there. Yet few who had any direct connection with the drama actually wanted to talk about it. What happened was as unexpected as it was tragic.

Late Saturday afternoon, search parties combing the bush found food caches in three abandoned cabins. Inspecting the packages, they determined that the food was definitely taken from Camp X and presumably had been deposited by someone who might have cause to return for it. For this reason, the searchers removed the caches from two cabins but left the third supply undisturbed. They agreed that the last cabin would be kept under surveillance all night in case the POWs came back to it. When they did, they would be recaptured.

Like so many schemes of its nature, the plan looked simple and foolproof. But like all manmade plans, the idea was only as good as the human beings who would put it into operation.

Once the scheme was decided upon, officials at search head-quarters ordered the surveillance party enlarged in case several POWs showed up and additional help was needed to effect a capture. Accordingly, an Ojibway Indian guide named Pete Moses led a six-member detachment of the Algonquin Regiment under Sergeant Davies back through the bush to the cabin. It was long after dark when the men took up positions a few yards from the structure, but from the various vantage points, all sides of the building were discernible, and any approach to it would be noticed immediately. Then the watchers settled in for a long, cold wait.

The hours dragged by; the temperature dropped considerably and snow fell almost continuously. At times the outline of the cabin was virtually obliterated in the gloom. The only sound was the wind and the creaking of sleet-covered pine boughs. Each of the watchers huddled close to the ground with a rock, tree trunk or snowdrift behind him as protection from the bitter wind. With each hour, the numbing cold became more intense and the men began to question the wisdom of what they were doing. Finally, at four-thirty in the morning, Davies could take it no longer.

The sergeant conferred with his men and told them he wanted the stakeout retained at the cabin, but that he and another soldier, Private Saunders, were going to move elsewhere.

The previous afternoon, an Indian tracker had told Davies about another old shack some distance away. Because no one had shown up at the cabin they had been watching, Davies began to wonder if perhaps they had been guarding the wrong building. He repositioned his men, then set out with Saunders through the storm to find this second cabin.

Walking was not easy. The two floundered over rocks, sank above their knees in drifts, and tripped on downed branches and scrub underbrush. Most of the time they couldn't see where they were going and had to keep one hand in front of their faces to protect their eyes from branches that were whipping to and fro in the wind. Eventually, they decided that there had to be an easier route to where they were going.

The only roads through the area were the usual crude logging trails, but these were difficult to locate in the darkness. It was then that the men thought of the highway. During the previous summer, construction crews had moved into the country north of Lake Superior, felling trees and blasting granite as they pushed the long-awaited Trans-Canada Highway westward. The great road was far from finished, but at least a rudimentary swath had been cut through the bush. Davies and Saunders headed toward it.

Once they got there, travel was easier and they made better time. There were still a lot of stumps and sinkholes around, but the dense underbrush was gone. Unfortunately, they also realized, the cover of the bush was also gone. By now the first faint glow of morning could be seen in the eastern sky, and with every minute that passed, the chances of being seen were greater.

The men trudged on in silence. Up ahead, in a rock cut, a few pieces of construction equipment lay to one side, in readiness for work once summer came. On the opposite side of the work area stood an old lean-to, built to shelter the horses used in the road work. The lean-to was open at the front, and because it was so exposed the two men did not intend to give it much notice. They decided, however, to take the precaution of checking out the structure before they moved on.

Davies had his flashlight with him and approached the building. Saunders stood back, his rifle at the ready. There was no sound. As the beam of light flashed inside the lean-to, Davies realized with a start of fear that there were several men sleeping inside. He was not sure how many, but thought he saw at least eight or ten.

We shall never really know what happened next. One fact is certain: the Canadians would kill two men and wound two others in the next few seconds. Whether their actions were justified is still shrouded in mystery. Even the summary of the findings of a court of inquiry into the incident is inconclusive. This secret report, buried in the Public Archives in Ottawa for years, has only recently become declassified. It tells one side of the story:

> Sgt. Davies and Pte. Saunders backed away so as to command as far as possible the open front of the lean-to. Sgt. Davies then gave the order to the prisoners to surrender and to come out with their hands up. Some time elapsed and nothing occurred. Davies and Saunders became apprehensive as dense bushes surrounded the lean-to on three sides and they feared there might be an escape through a rear exit. They heard some sounds of movement. Sgt. Davies gave further orders to come out and surrender. One prisoner of war rushed out and almost knocked Pte. Saunders over. Sgt. Davies then became apprehensive and gave an order to shoot. Both fired several rounds into the lean-to. . . . They both thought, from the sounds of the rush of one prisoner, that all would attempt to do the same. They had been informed that the prisoners were carrying formidable knives and were dangerous and determined. They were both satisfied there was no intention to surrender on the part of the prisoners and that it was necessary to shoot if they were to be apprehended.[8]

When they heard the sound of rifle fire, the four men who had been guarding the cache made their way to the rock cut. When they got there they took custody of Erwin Genssler, the prisoner who had started to run and, on orders from Davies, surrounded the lean-to.

By this time, Davies thought it best that someone should go for help. But when he canvassed his men, he found that none of them knew the country well enough to make the journey back to camp in the darkness. After some discussion, he decided to go himself and take one man with him.

After their sergeant had left, three of the remaining soldiers watched both ends of the shack while Pte. Saunders went to the front and looked inside. Instead of the eight or ten POWs he expected to find there, he saw only four, all of whom were wounded.

Saunders was then joined by his colleagues, as well as Genssler, and together they gave as much first aid to the injured as was possible under the circumstances. As they did so, they knew that at least two of the Germans were dying.

It took Davies about an hour to reach Angler. When he arrived, he was somewhat excited and reported that seven men had been hurt, although he had never actually looked into the lean-to after the shooting. However, as soon as his news was relayed, a carrying party set out for the rock cut.

The trek was somewhat easier than it had been for Davies, mainly because it was made in the early dawn. At the scene of the shooting, the wounded were given first aid and placed on dogsleds.

It was eight-thirty when the grim cortege got back to Camp X, and the two most seriously injured men, Herbert Loeffelmeier and Alfred Miethling, were already dead. In the hours that had elapsed between the shooting and their arrival back in camp, both had bled to death.

The other two wounded were given immediate medical attention and one of them, Kurt Rochel, who had been shot in the arm, foot, chest and groin, was operated on in the camp hospital. Doctor J. G. Barrie and two assistants performed the surgery there, but later Rochel had to be moved to Kingston, Ontario, for two more operations. The doctors saved his life, but as a result of his injuries, the German would be unable to ever father children. The other POW shot at the time was Hans Hauck, who sustained a leg wound.

Almost from the moment they happened, the shootings of the escaped prisoners were a subject of controversy. And even today, in many of the interviews I conducted with former POWs, the subject was raised. Suspicion still exists, even though the Canadian authorities at the time did their best, if not to stifle criticism, then at least to lend the investigation of the incident an aura of absolute fairness and impartiality.

As soon as the manhunt was over, Internment headquarters, backed by Ottawa officialdom, launched an intensive inquiry into both the events that led up to the escape and the circumstances surrounding the shootings. The investigative body, under the leadership of Brigadier-General the Honourable J. F. L. Embury — a reserve member of the Canadian Army and in civilian life a Saskatchewan judge — convened at Camp X on April 28, 1941. Matters dealing with the escape were examined first. Then the court turned to the question of the shootings and, in particular, the incident on the Trans-Canada Highway rock cut.

Major Charles Lindsey was the first witness. He told the court how the escape came about in the first place; then he went on to explain what his orders had been insofar as they affected capture. The order to shoot was, according to Lindsey, only to be carried out if a prisoner refused to surrender or attempted to escape a second time. And even then, searchers had been instructed to fire low, so as to stop any escapee but not to kill him. (Years later, Horst Liebeck told me that Charles Lindsey certainly never gave any order to shoot to kill. "He was not that kind of man," Liebeck added.) In addition, Lindsey pointed out that he had ordered all members of search parties to give "reasonable opportunity" to surrender before there was *any* shooting.

The commanding officer went on to explain why he thought so many prisoners had in fact been fired upon. In the first incident of wounding at the log cabin, where the prisoner's nose had been shot off, the POWs had received instructions to come out with their hands up. Lindsey calmly relayed this information to the court, but explained that one escapee had ignored the order. The CO said that the man barged out of the cabin, almost knocked Sergeant Ridgway over, and then attempted to run. It was at that point that Lance-Corporal Thomas shot the man in the face. No one questioned Lindsey as to how a man who was running away could be shot in the face from behind. Furthermore, no one seemed to think it pertinent to inquire why the man was shot in the head when the searchers had been ordered to fire low.

In a later statement filed with the Swiss Consul-General's Office, the wounded German told his side of the story to the camp spokesman. The report states, in part:

> . . . He discovered Canadian soldiers through a very narrow slit in the door, which he had left open very slightly for the purpose of sighting any pursuers. With him were several other POWs. He shouted to his comrades that they were being encircled and seeing no possibility of escape, he opened the door and walked out "hands up." He had hardly done so when he felt a bullet skimming his face, fired from a distance of about six metres, and immediately fell on the ground where he was left lying. After the other POWs were rounded up, the effect of the wound wore off and to the astonishment of the Canadian soldiers, he got up since they were firmly under the impression that he had been killed. No first aid was given to him until one of his comrades managed to stop the flow of blood and as he was marched away with the others, he was told that it was too bad that he had not been killed.[9]

The man was not correct in his statement that the cabin was "being encircled" as only the two Canadian soldiers were anywhere near the site. But whether his version of the shooting is what really happened will probably never be known.

The shooting on the highway right-of-way caused a great deal more furore. Sergeant Davies had given the order to fire on the prisoners, based on his assumption that there were eight or ten men inside the lean-to. He believed that he and Private Saunders were about to be assaulted by them and the only way to prevent such an attack was to shoot. The wounded, however, stated that as they started to obey the order to surrender, they were cut down by rifle fire. This claim seems supported by the fact that no one at the inquiry disputed that all of the dead and injured were found *inside* the lean-to.

A description of this shooting from the German point of view was also filed with the Swiss authorities. The pertinent section is as follows:

> Upon being surrounded by five or six of the Canadian soldiers, they were ordered to get up from the ground and as they did they were shot at without further preliminaries. They immediately fell flat again but as the rifles were fired from a distance of about three to five metres, most of the bullets found their mark, one man being hit by six bullets, two by five and one by two, while Genssler escaped being hit due to the fact that he feinted death from the very beginning of the shooting and to a major extent simply through sheer luck in not being in the path of the bullets fired.[10]

There were, of course, only two Canadian soldiers present, not the five or six mentioned here.

A second statement on the same incident concerns a German who was one of sixteen in the carrying party ordered to the rock cut after Davies ran back to Camp X for help.

> He was the first to enter the shack in question and found four of his comrades in a heap on the ground in pools of blood, and ascertained that two of them had been killed, one very badly wounded and another wounded. Previous to that, no first aid had been given to the two wounded men. He was told by Rochel that they were shot at without any warning from a distance of a few metres and that no attempt whatever was made to give any first aid previous to his arrival.[11]

Years later reporter Peter Desbarats did a series of interviews in Germany with some of the men involved in the "great escape" from Angler. One of those he tracked down was Kurt Rochel. The former Luftwaffe ace, with seventeen kills and a Knight's Cross to his name, still had vivid memories of April 19-20, 1941. He told Desbarats how he and the four POWs with him intended to walk to Thunder Bay and make their way south from there to the United States. However, because they underestimated the severity of the weather in Northern Ontario, they had had to seek refuge in the highway lean-to while they waited out the blizzard that raked the area that Saturday night. They were sound asleep when Davies and Saunders arrived.

As reported by Desbarats: "Rochel insisted he had not been given a chance to surrender before the guard opened fire." Then the German added: "'I am not complaining about the shooting. After all, we were at war. But the deaths of Miethling and Loeffelmeier were unnecessary and tragic. They were both in their early twenties. They were good men.'"[12]

In its summation to the inquiry, the court described the table knives carried by the prisoners as "formidable"; the supposed threat of these knives, coupled with the misinformation about the number of Germans in the lean-to, led the court to exonerate Saunders and Davies of all blame in the shootings. The report concludes:

> The Court finds from the evidence submitted and inspection of the scene of the shooting, that Sgt. Davies and Pte. Saunders were fully satisfied that to stop and apprehend the Prisoners of War, it was necessary to shoot. This Court is satisfied that their actions in doing so were fully justified and that their conclusion was a proper one under the circumstances. . . . The Court desires to place on record its approval of the conduct of these soldiers and the efficient way in which they performed an exceedingly difficult and trying duty.[13]

What passed for justice had been done.

While the shooting incidents connected with the Angler escape tended to overshadow all other aspects of that manhunt, the search for the rest of the missing prisoners continued.

On Monday, April 21, three more escapees were picked up. By that time search authorities were becoming decidedly more reticent in their comments concerning the conduct of the search. Newspaper reporters who pressed for details about what was going on found themselves getting nowhere. This was particularly true for representatives of papers that had printed stories questioning the way the manhunt was being carried out, and for those who had filed dispatches faulting Camp X security prior to the break. Toronto *Telegram* and Toronto *Star* reporters seem to have been subjected to the most stringent restrictions. Douglas MacFarlane of the *Star* was actually arrested as he stepped from a train at the camp, and Scott Young of the *Telegram* had his notes confiscated and a story he was writing burned in a camp stove by a member of the Veterans Guard.

On Tuesday, April 22, the search was stepped up.

Three tracking dogs were brought in and immediately put to work looking for the last four escapees. Several more Indian guides were hired and attached to patrols fanning out from Camp X headquarters. At nine that morning, an RCMP amphibian plane arrived from Thunder Bay to begin searching the rock and tundra from the air. Colonel Stethem himself boarded the machine, which by early afternoon had crisscrossed almost five hundred square kilometres of wilderness inland from Lake Superior. On the lake itself, a tug borrowed from the Ontario Paper Company was used to check the shoreline for signs of the escapees.

None were found.

While this greatly stepped-up manhunt was in operation, the remains of Herbert Loeffelmeier and Alfred Miethling were interred in the tiny prisoner-of-war cemetery at Angler. Their graves had been dug that morning by fellow POWs and the mounds of sandy soil draped with wreaths and bunting adorned with swastikas. Twenty-five Germans from the compound accompanied the cortege to the cemetery, where an honour guard of Canadian soldiers fired a final salute over the graves.

Before the coffins were lowered into the ground, they were opened and both corpses positively identified. Lindsey told reporters later that this action was merely a precaution in case anyone had climbed inside — intending to use burial as a method of escape.

Finally, two hours before dark on Thursday, April 24, the last four prisoners still at large sneaked out of the bush and hid in a railway boxcar on a siding at Heron Bay. They were still there five hours later when the Mounties checked the car. In six days of freedom, the four were captured less than fifteen kilometres from where their odyssey began.

NINE

Peter Krug: Escape to Texas

The soccer game at Bowmanville on the afternoon of April 16, 1942, was one of the most exciting the inmates had ever played. The participants were the finest athletes in the camp, and the teams were evenly balanced. A huge crowd of POWs watched from the sidelines, as did several guards in nearby towers. The action went from end to end, with one spectacular play after another. Both goalkeepers were superb — stopping shots in a manner usually seen only in great professional matches.

The sun shone in a cloudless sky and a refreshing breeze blew in from Lake Ontario, two kilometres to the south. The manicured lawn of Camp 30 was lush and green, a tribute to the POW groundskeepers, who knew and loved soccer and believed it should be played under the best possible conditions. Even the goal posts had been repainted for this match.

The cheering was as deafening as it was divided. When one team had the ball, their supporters seemed ecstatic. When control of the play passed to the opposition, an equally vociferous roar went up from a second mob of fans. In the towers the guards watched intently, and some made small wagers on the outcome. Once, when the ball went sailing over the fence out of the compound, a helpful guard climbed down and retrieved it. Both groups of supporters applauded his throw-in. The Canadian blushed and waved. He seemed glad to be part of the action.

Shortly after the game started, two men dressed in coveralls and caps and carrying paint, paintbrushes and a ladder strode around the corner of one of the buildings in the compound. They walked to the perimeter fence, propped their ladder against it and proceeded to paint the fence posts. Occasionally they glanced over at the game, but for the most part, they seemed intent on their task. The prisoners paid little attention to them, and the guards gave them only a passing glance. Once or twice, when the roar of the crowd was especially loud, the painters stopped their work and looked over at the playing field.

The two would paint the inside of a post, then climb over the fence and do the outer side. After they had completed three posts in this manner, they paused for a smoke — one sitting on the ground; the other leaning against the fence. When they finished the cigarettes, they returned to their task. By two o'clock the painting was finished.

On the field, the score was tied and the action even more exciting than it had been. A corner kick was called on the inner side of the pitch. All spectators, prisoners and guards alike, watched keenly. The referee blew his whistle and the ball arched up and in for a goal. The crowd went wild.

Everyone forgot about the painters.

While the teams had been lining up for the corner kick, the two workmen finished painting the outside of the post they had reached, took down their ladder, put the lid on the paint can, and walked away.

The "painters" were Peter Krug and Erich Boehle, both officers in Hitler's Luftwaffe. They had just escaped from Bowmanville.

Almost from the moment the two reached the final fence post, those at the soccer match knew the break would succeed. The game, of course, had only been a cover for the escape: a means of distracting the guards while the resourceful Krug and Boehle painted their way to freedom. Prisoners who were there that day recall that while they actually watched the game and cheered harder than they had ever done before, they also saw the "painters" go through their charade. "We had to act interested in the game," says one, "but it was damned hard not to glance over as our guys went out of the camp. They were so calm about the whole thing, I could hardly believe what was happening." Another former prisoner said he couldn't believe how cool the escapees were. "They should have been on the stage," he remarked. "It was like a play."

Years later, Peter Krug recalled his feelings during the escape.

"I was nervous all that morning. I had breakfast and tried to eat some lunch, but I was just too excited to be hungry. When it was time to go, our friends came around and wished us luck and so forth. We shook hands, promised to look each other up when we got back to Germany. Climbing over the fence to paint the first post was hard, but going over the last time was the worst. We were both scared as we walked away, but the hardest part then was to keep from running. We knew that if we were too eager, it would be all over. We would be shot."

At the time of the escape, Peter Krug was only twenty-one, Erich Boehle twenty-seven. Boehle had been in Bowmanville well over a year, while Krug had been there about five months. The two were drawn together by their shared obsession: escape. Boehle had got away once before but had been recaptured after eight hours of freedom. Krug's earlier escape plans of jumping from the train with von Werra at Smiths Falls had never materialized. In their separate ways, both were eager to make this breakout work.

About a month before their plan came to fruition, they discussed the idea with the German camp leader who, along with other members of the Bowmanville escape committee, gave permission to proceed with the necessary preparations. Two weeks before the date of the proposed break, the committee again reviewed the scheme, suggested one or two minor improvements, and granted final approval. From then on, the two officers worked out the last little details of their idea.

Both men knew it would be impossible to simply walk up to the fence and climb over it. If they did, the most inept guard in the place would sound the alarm. For that reason, it was obvious that not only a diversion would be needed, but some kind of a disguise as well. The diversion was not a problem; it could be staged on ten minutes' notice. A suitable disguise, however, was not quite so easy.

Several possibilities were suggested and rejected. Some were too obvious; others too elaborate. Finally, the decision to dress as Canadian painters was made. Earlier that spring, maintenance personnel had been in the compound, repairing eavestroughs and retouching the brickwork on the outside of building 2. The people who did the work were unknown to the POWs and, it was thought, to most of the guards as well. A couple of the strangers had worn coveralls and had carried identity discs. Neither the coveralls nor the discs would be too hard to make.

Some means of identification would be necessary once the escapees were outside. They expected that travel in wartime

Canada would not be easy and that new names backed up by forged citizenship papers would be essential. Boehle decided to be Pilot Officer A. Hille of the Fifth Squadron of the Free Norwegian Air Force. He also carried a certificate attesting to his Norwegian military service and a letter stating that he was on leave in Toronto. The letter was purportedly signed by his commanding officer, a Major Brownes. Krug's name was to be Jean Ette, a Frenchman and former deckhand from the S.S. *Normandie*, a liner that had burned and capsized a few weeks earlier in New York harbour. Krug's story was that Ette had fled the United States because he feared internment and had come to Canada because he had been offered a job in Windsor, Ontario.

Krug had chosen his *Normandie* cover deliberately. He had read about the sinking in the Canadian papers available in Camp 30, and the story excited him. He felt that it was the kind of flamboyant background a daring escapee ought to have. The Associated Press account of the disaster of February 10, 1942, gives an indication of the story's obvious appeal:

> Like a great wounded monster but, somehow, majestic still, the fire-seared and water-logged former French liner *Normandie* succumbed to the surging tide today and toppled to ignominious rest on Hudson River mud.
>
> Ravaged by flames, a gaping hole cut in her hull in a vain attempt to counteract pressure of the incoming tide, the $60-million vessel rolled over at 2:45 a.m., E.D.T., and now lies on her port side in forty feet of water alongside her pier.
>
> Touched off by sparks from a welder's torch, flames raged through the naval craft for three and a half hours yesterday before being brought under control by every available piece of land and sea firefighting equipment in Manhattan.
>
> Two hundred and twenty of the twenty-two hundred workmen and naval personnel aboard suffered injuries, and one welder died last night in hospital of a fractured skull received when he jumped from deck to pier.
>
> It was ever so gently and with scarcely a noise that the thirty-thousand-ton ship dipped her fire-blackened superstructure to the water's surface in surrender.
>
> Only the crunch of ice and final belch of smoke and flame — quickly extinguished by fireboats — marked the settling of the sea giant while spotlights from fire equipment on shore and in the river played on her toppling bulk.

In addition to their cover stories, both men garnered all the Canadian money they could — as well as maps and any tidbits of information about southern Ontario that were available in camp. Then they concentrated on how their absence could be covered once they were gone.

This part was easy for the two escapees — and a risky challenge for those staying behind. The men decided to build a pair of life-sized dummies of themselves. With the help of many others in camp, two suits of long underwear were stuffed with newspaper and straw, and pieces of wood inserted down the centre. Then heads of papier mâché were constructed and real hair from the barber shop glued on. A camp artist painted the faces.

The two mannequins were then dressed in extra Luftwaffe uniforms. Shoes were attached to the bottoms of the legs and the hands stuffed in the pants pockets. At a glance, the imitations were quite life-like. These creations were paraded successfully on two occasions the day Krug and Boehle escaped. Roll calls at Bowmanville that spring were at eight in the morning and eight and ten-thirty at night, and the dummies were used at both evening checks. The POWs lined up in rows of five, making it comparatively easy for the assembled Germans to support the dummies in their midst. A prisoner simply positioned himself on either side of a straw man and carried it out with a backward glance. In the shadows of dusk, the ruse worked. Both evening counts were certified correct. The prisoners went back to quarters and gloated over their success.

For their part, Boehle and Krug had a quiet afternoon. Once they were outside the POW compound, they carried their ladder and paint into a forested area not far from the camp. There they hid the props under some brush and heaps of dead leaves; then they set out for the CPR station on the western outskirts of Bowmanville. A hundred metres or so from the building, the two ducked into a clump of hawthorn bushes and settled down to wait for darkness.

The hours passed slowly. Train after train stopped at the station, but the escapees had no intention of risking their freedom by hitching a ride in daylight. Instead, they talked softly about the escape and mentally rehearsed their plans for the night ahead. They decided to stay together as long as possible without taking needless risks.

Shortly after nine-thirty, a long freight pulled in from the east. After several boxcars that had been sitting on a siding were coupled to the train, Krug and Boehle sneaked out of their hiding place, raced along the trackside ditch, and climbed up between two cars. They did not try to climb into any car in case they were seen. Ten minutes later they were on their way to Toronto.

The first part of the ride was the worst. The two pilots stood on the bumper at the end of a car and held onto the steel ladder running up the end of the carriage. Their positions were precarious even when the train was moving slowly. However, once it picked up speed, the lurching from side to side, the jerking motion of the cars and the flying cinders from the railbed made the perch a nightmare. Engine smoke and soot swirled in their faces and the constant clamour from the wheels was deafening. Then, just as they had endured about all they could stand, a series of lights flashed by and the train slowed down. A couple of kilometres farther on, it stopped.

Because they now knew they *had* to ride somewhere else, the Germans immediately set out in opposite directions to look for an open car. Boehle found one, but no sooner had he climbed into it than two railway workers came along and closed it. When Krug saw this happen, he scrambled up on a flatcar and hid behind some wooden freight cases. A few seconds later, a whistle sounded and the train lurched forward. Soon the lights of Oshawa were far behind.

An hour later, the train stopped in Toronto.

As soon as he thought no one was around, Krug hopped down from his perch and went looking for his partner. He walked up and down beside the tracks, calling Boehle's name outside car after car. He tried the sliding doors of a dozen cars. None of them opened easily, and some would not budge at all. At each, he tapped on the outside walls and in a loud whisper kept repeating his friend's name. Once or twice he thought he heard a muffled answer, but finally realized he was imagining things. Somehow, in the confusion of boarding the train at Oshawa, Boehle had apparently vanished.

Finally, tired, covered with grime and afraid that at any minute he would be discovered, Krug stumbled across the massive rail yards and made his way to Union Station, the largest and busiest rail terminus in Canada.

As for Erich Boehle, when the car in which he found himself remained motionless, the flyer jerked the door open and climbed outside. When he couldn't find Krug, he simply boarded another train.

Entrance to the Fort Henry tunnel through which nineteen POWs escaped in August 1943. The men had discovered the original drainage system of the nineteenth-century fort from historical floor plans.

Canadian authorities examine the exit to the tunnel at Fort Henry.

The Veterans Guard acted as the security force in Canadian POW camps. Composed chiefly of First World War veterans, the Guard offered an opportunity to older men to serve their country. Major Fred Chapple, centre front.

Standing between two veteran guards is the dummy used to impersonate Peter Krug during his escape from Bowmanville.

Peter Krug enters a Detroit courtroom to attend the trial of Nazi sympa-
thizer Max Stephan on a charge of treason. After he was transferred to
the Gravenhurst camp, Krug escaped again, but this time he was free
for less than twenty-four hours.

Nazi funeral in a western Canadian POW camp.

Camp X at Angler, Ontario, from which twenty-eight men escaped in April 1941. The 150-foot-long tunnel was begun under this building and ran out under the fence.

Horst Liebeck, who jumped a train near Angler and travelled to Alberta before he was caught, lives today in Unionville, Ontario.

The corpses of the Angler escapees who were killed by the Canadian authorities were returned to the camp by dogsled for burial.

courtesy Walter Woehr

Funeral of one of the victims of Nazi slayings at Medicine Hat.

courtesy *Calgary Herald*

Adolf Kratz, Werner Schwalb and Johannes Wittinger were tried for the murder of August Plaszek. Schwalb was sentenced to hang; Kratz received life imprisonment (he was later returned to Germany after contracting tuberculosis); Wittinger was acquitted.

Gestapo chief Bruno Perzenowski (right) was hanged, along with three other men, for the murder of prisoner Karl Lehmann at the Medicine Hat camp.

courtesy Horst Braun

Homeward bound: at Longlac, Ontario, German POWs await the arrival of the train that was the first step of their long journey back to Germany. In spite of their incarceration, many prisoners cherished their memories of Canada and returned to settle here in the postwar years.

At exactly 10:15 the next day Erich Boehle was recaptured on a downtown street in Niagara Falls, New York. Lieutenant Morton Wagner, the American police officer who arrested the German, allowed him to have a shower and then called the RCMP detachment across the river. Boehle never told his captors how he arrived in the United States. But then, he really didn't have to. His soot-covered clothes gave him away.

Two hours before Boehle was arrested in Niagara Falls, the dummies he and Krug had used in the escape were discovered by the veteran guards at Bowmanville. The RCMP Intelligence Branch in Toronto was informed and the Mounties entered the manhunt. A flat, unemotional, rather detached report compiled by RCMP Sergeant R. W. Irvine describes the police involvement in the matter. The submission by Irvine makes reference to the discovery of the dummies, but also reveals that Bowmanville guards had no idea how their prisoners had actually escaped:

ROYAL CANADIAN MOUNTED POLICE
Intelligence Branch, Toronto
April 21, 1942
Peter KRUG and Erich BOEHLE,
Escaped German Prisoners of War,
Bowmanville, Ontario.
17-4-42

1. With reference to the escape of the two above prisoners of war, this a.m. the writer left Toronto for Bowmanville with three constables and police car code No. 3816 and one private car.
2. Upon arrival at the Internment Camp, Lieut. Col. R. O. Bull was at once contacted and the correct names and descriptions of the escapees were received. This information was duly telephoned to our Headquarters at Toronto for distribution to other points.
3. As soon as the names and descriptions of the escaped prisoners was learned, two police cars (including Cobourg Detachment car) were immediately sent out to patrol the surrounding district. In the meantime the writer accompanied Col. Bull on an inspection tour of the barbed wire entanglement but no cut wires or other means of escape were noticed. By this time the Colonel and other camp authorities were at a complete loss as to the manner in which the prisoners had escaped from the camp.
4. At first it was believed that the two men had escaped by crawling through the two water pipes which led from inside the camp to a point outside where they emptied into a small creek some

fifty yards outside the barbed wire, but from the result of several tests made by members of the camp guard, Colonel Bull is satisfied that no persons of normal build could manage to force himself through 100 yards of piping some distance underground.

5.   The writer and one constable then continued the patrol of the district until about 8.30 p.m. when upon reporting to the camp it was learned that one of the prisoners, Erich BOEHLE, had been captured at Niagara Falls, N.Y. The writer then contacted Insp. Bullard at Toronto and was instructed to send the two police cars back to their detachments while the writer and one constable would continue the patrol for some hours longer.

6.   At this time upon further interview with Col. Bull, it was ascertained that the two prisoners had been aided in their escape by means of two dummies. These had been constructed of paper maché. They were made life size and were dressed in German Airforce Officer's uniform. The face and features were almost perfect, while hair had been used for eyebrows and the lips appeared to have been coloured with regular lipstick. The frames had been built by means of stuffing paper into a suit of underwear so tightly that the dummy would stand without bending. The dummies were complete from boots to Officer's peak cap. One of the dummies was seen by the writer.

7.   The dummies were used in the following manner. Apparently during roll call which is at 8 a.m.; 8 p.m.; and 10.30 p.m. daily, the prisoners are paraded in lines of fives and a count is made instead of calling names. It was during the 8 a.m. count of April 17th when one of the inspecting sergeants happened to notice the dummies which were propped up in the centre of two lines of five prisoners and supported by the men on each side. When the fake was discovered, it took some time before it was learned which prisoners were actually missing. It will be noted from this that the actual time of the escape was not known, as it was possible for the dummies to be used during the two previous counts of the night before.

8.   The patrol of this camp was continued this day until 7.00 p.m. when the writer returned to Toronto.

Two days later, Irvine again visited Camp 30 and talked to Colonel Bull. Even then, camp authorities were no closer to learning how Boehle and Krug got out. Years later, in interviews with former veteran guards who were at Bowmanville during or shortly after the escape, I was left with the impression that some of them never did find out how the "painters" got away.

Reporters of the time appear to have been unwilling to let the facts get in the way of a good story. Unlike the authorities, newsmen had no trouble inventing escape methods for Krug and Boehle. An item by the Canadian Press on April 18, 1942, carried this fanciful news:

> Erich Boehle, a Nazi airman, was back behind the barbed wire of an internment camp here today after a brief period of freedom in which he reached Niagara Falls, N.Y. before being captured. His companion in the escape, Peter Krug, is still at large.
>
> Boehle, a blond, thick-set Air Force lieutenant, was captured in Niagara Falls, carrying forged papers of a Royal Norwegian Air Force officer.
>
> The pair cut their way through several layers of wire fencing surrounding the camp, formerly a boys' school.

One wonders what the prisoners thought of that story.

During the Second World War, Toronto's Union Station was the hub of Canada's rail system. Every day, thousands and thousands of people walked into its great hall and from there passed into or left the largest English-speaking city in Canada. There were businessmen, ordinary travellers, immigrants, famous personalities and, of course, trainloads of soldiers destined for battlefields in countries they had never seen and in some cases never wanted to see.

But Peter Krug was unique.

He was not a businessman, an ordinary traveller or an immigrant. He was unknown and wanted to remain unknown. He *was* a soldier, but an enemy soldier, a representative of the forces that the troops he saw in Union Station were going to Europe to kill. As soon as he entered the building, the fact that he was an alien in an alien land weighed on him. Yet he felt he had to come to Toronto in order to go elsewhere. But first he had to wash off the grime of the railway, eat some of the chocolate and dried apricots he carried with him, and somehow find a place to rest.

The men's washrooms in the station were a dozen paces from the main entrance to the building at the west end of the great hall. Standing in front of them were two police officers, neither of whom looked too friendly. As soon as the German saw them, he suddenly became absorbed in the magazines at a station newsstand. Then, as the woman who ran the business came to ask if he wanted something, the policemen moved elsewhere. The POW shot into the lavatory.

In a toilet cubicle, he peeled off the soot-encrusted coveralls and stuffed them in a trash can. He realized then that the grey civilian suit he had on underneath was badly in need of pressing.

So far, no one had taken any particular notice of him, so he assumed he must not look too much out of the ordinary. In order to get accustomed to dealing with Canadians who were not his jailers, he decided to approach someone and try to talk to him. He returned to the great hall, checked to make sure the police were not close by, stopped a middle-aged man, and asked for the time. The man simply pointed to a large clock in the middle of the room and hurried away. Krug doubted if the stranger even saw him.

By now it was almost midnight.

Krug walked to a lower-level departure area of the building where, to his relief, he saw several people stretched out on benches trying to sleep. Back in a corner and behind a bank of lockers, as far from the main concourse as possible, he found a place to himself. In five minutes, he was sound asleep.

At seven the next morning, George Billings, a railway employee who worked in Union Station, was making his rounds, ordering tramps and panhandlers to leave the premises. When he shook Peter Krug awake, the pilot got up and left the building. A couple of hours later, however, Billings noticed the same man back inside. This time he stopped the stranger and asked for his registration card, and demanded to know what he was doing there.

Krug told Billings that he didn't have such a card, but did produce a couple of letters identifying himself as Jean Ette, lately of the French liner *Normandie*. Both letters were on official-looking stationery. The first was in French, from the mayor's office in Montreal, explaining that because Krug was not a Canadian, he did not have a registration card. The second was purportedly from a Windsor firm, F. R. Larkin and Company, offering Krug a position with them as an interpreter.

Krug explained that he wanted to go to Windsor so that he could start work with the Larkin company, but that he did not have the money to get there. He was in the station, he said, hoping that he would be able to locate someone who might help him with the fare.

Billings was impressed by the story — impressed enough to take Krug to see Lance-Corporal A. J. Pearse, a military police-man who happened to be in the station. Though Pearse talked to the POW, he neglected to ask for any identification. If he had challenged the German at the time, Krug's freedom probably would have ended right there. Instead, Pearse accepted the man's story and decided to help him.

The policeman phoned a priest he knew, Reverend Father M.J. McGrath, at the Catholic Adjustment Bureau, a charitable agency in downtown Toronto. The policeman related Krug's story to McGrath and asked if the "Frenchman" might be given some assistance to get to Windsor. Father McGrath readily agreed. This was not surprising. Father Michael McGrath had spent a lifetime helping the poor in Toronto. When he died in May 1980, a colleague described him as "a very fine priest with values and principles that came right from the Gospel. He never said very much, but sometimes you would just discover that he was helping poor kids go to camp. At other times I'd see somebody come into Mass who had a few dollars and give five dollars to Father McGrath. Later in the Mass he would give it to a woman whose husband had died or who had no money."[1] Krug was fortunate to find such a benefactor.

Half an hour after he left Union Station, the German showed up at the Adjustment Bureau's offices and introduced himself to Father McGrath. The priest asked for identification and was shown the two letters. Because both seemed to be in order, and because the stranger's story was quite convincing, McGrath wrote out a requisition for a bus ticket and gave the German cash to buy a couple of meals. The POW expressed his thanks, walked to the terminal, and climbed aboard the 1:15 bus for Windsor.

The journey was a quiet one. Krug kept to himself, not wanting to do or say anything that might attract notice. He sat alone near the back and took special care to bury himself in a magazine when some soldiers boarded in London, where the Greyhound coach had stopped for dinner. The men were busy conversing among themselves, however, and none paid any attention to those around them. Shortly after, it was dark and Krug felt safer. He allowed himself to sleep.

The bus rumbled on through the night. From time to time stops were made along the route, at Thamesville, Chatham, Tilbury and Belle River. A few passengers left the bus at Chatham, and it was there that Krug was given a momentary scare. For some reason, the driver thought that the German should have been getting off, and walked back to check his passenger's ticket.

Krug immediately imagined all kinds of difficulties, but none more worrisome than the possibility that there were police inside the Chatham depot waiting for him. His fears soon vanished, however, when the driver glanced at the ticket, muttered, "Sorry, Mac," and returned to the front.

After that, Krug couldn't sleep.

In the morning, a whole new set of obstacles awaited him in Windsor. To the German, even this small Canadian city was alien and frightening. The idea of entering the massive skyscraper jungle of Detroit, which he could see across the river, was terrifying. To Krug, Detroit's towers seemed to hang over downtown Windsor like vultures waiting for their prey to die. He strolled to the foot of Ouellette Avenue, then turned right on Riverside Drive in order to get a good look at the city he hoped to reach.

In front of him, the Detroit River was wide — much wider than the Main or the Rhine back home. But like them, it was busy. Small motor launches, lake freighters and even a canoe or two plied its waters. Gaudy tugs chugged to and fro, hauling barges piled high with oil drums. And, just passing under a huge expansion bridge on his left, he saw a police launch. So the river was patrolled!

Until now, the POW had given little thought to this possibility. He knew there would be policemen in Windsor and Detroit; apparently he would have to be on his guard and if at all possible avoid them on the river as well. The thought was chilling.

Krug did not have a map of Windsor with him, and he was unable to tell for sure whether the river narrowed at some point, making access to the United States easier. He didn't dare ask anyone for help, because he feared his identity might be questioned. Instead, he started to walk westward along the shore, pretending he was sightseeing; doing his best to look like a tourist. After a couple of kilometres, when it became obvious the river was getting even wider, he retraced his steps and began hunting for a boat.

Shortly after noon he found one. Tied up beside a weather-beaten fishing shack was an old grey flat-bottomed rowboat. The craft looked seaworthy, and mercifully didn't seem to have any registration markings that might draw attention to it. A single rope from the bow anchored the vessel to a rusty metal piling. Krug looked at his find, exulted in his good fortune and decided to stay where he was for the rest of the day. He would continue his journey after dark.

From early afternoon until almost ten that night, the German hid out in a thick stand of bushes at the water's edge, a few hundred metres upriver from where the boat was tied. No one came near him, but the hours dragged. From time to time he tried to nap, but the unevenness of the ground in his hiding place, coupled with the knowledge that at any minute he might be discovered, made his rest fitful. Once when he did fall asleep, the sudden scream of a fire siren a block away awakened him instantly. He almost stopped breathing. After he regained his composure, he ate a few dried apricots he had brought from Bowmanville, and then sat awaiting nightfall.

By nine-thirty, the great river looked like a black pool, reflecting the brilliance of a million lights. On Peter Krug, and on so many others who came from the blacked-out cities of Europe to North America, the lights made a memorable impression that has lasted long after the memories of people and events were forgotten. In her book *The War Brides*, Joyce Hibbert quotes a young Englishwoman, newly arrived in Montreal from the blackouts of Britain:

> But another great thrill was to come. We walked out of the hotel to have a look at Montreal, and there before us was fairyland. All the lights were on. Shop windows were lit up. Neon signs were flashing. And car headlights shone brightly. We hadn't seen lights at night for five and a half years, and it seemed incredibly beautiful. I shall never forget it.[2]

Krug stood on the Windsor shore, almost in a trance, gazing both longingly and anxiously at the lights, feeling less than confident about the journey he knew he must make. An occasional ship still passed in front of him, but to Krug the time had come. He judged that it would get no darker, and that the waterway was as quiet as it would probably get. He checked to make sure no one was around, then crept out of the thicket and walked down the shore to the boat. It wasn't until the tie rope was actually in his hands that he realized there were no oars!

It took a minute for the impact of the discovery to register. Krug climbed into the boat and dropped to his hands and knees and felt around on the bottom. Then, cursing his luck, he jumped back on shore and frantically searched the boathouse. He looked for almost five minutes and knew he was out of luck.

He retied the boat and started to hunt along the shore for some kind of a makeshift paddle. There was nothing for two hundred metres in either direction, so he returned to the shack and, as carefully and as quietly as he could, pried a long slim board from one side. It wasn't a paddle but it would have to do. He laid it in the rowboat, untied the vessel and pushed off.

The first part of the journey was easy. The old boat drifted along, the makeshift paddle was reasonably effective, and the river traffic was sparse. The German watched the land of his confinement recede into the gloom. He had been happy in Canada — happy as one could be in prison — but he was happier now, escaping, running to America, taking one more step on the journey he hoped would eventually lead to the fatherland.

A quarter of the way across the river, his progress was slowed temporarily by a large lake boat. When the vessel passed, he turned into the swell, rode out the waves, and went on.

He was almost in midstream when something far more serious happened. Emerging from the darkness on his right was the big police launch he had seen earlier in the day! It was moving slowly toward him, as if looking for something. On its bow he could see a large spotlight, its beam directed at the Detroit shoreline.

Krug quickly pulled in his makeshift paddle and flattened himself on the bottom of his rowboat. He lay there, unmoving, ears straining, hoping and praying he wouldn't be seen. The launch bore down on him, its powerful engines rumbling in that throaty growl common to large cabin cruisers. Nearer and nearer. The German could hear men talking above the static from a police-band radio. He froze, fearing that at any second he would find himself swimming for his life.

Then, unbelievably, incredibly, the launch passed him by. Its speed never slackened; its direction remained the same. He guessed he was less than fifty metres from it at the closest point. But he had not been seen!

He lay on the bottom until the outline of the police boat was well downriver and its lights had merged with the blaze of neon beyond it. Then he scrambled upright, grabbed the old board and dug in. As he did so, he heard a loud crack.

The paddle, his only paddle, had snapped in two!

At first Krug did nothing — he was too stunned to react. Then he started silently cursing his luck, staring at the short chunk of wood in his hands. Of all the times for this to happen! Here he was, in the dark, in the middle of one of the busiest rivers in North America, without the proper means to move, totally at the mercy of the current and in the path of any large ship using the waterway. The escape that had been a success in Bowmanville seemed to be a failure a couple of days later. There wasn't even a sign of the rest of his broken paddle. It had floated away in the darkness.

Krug sat there for a few minutes, feeling exhausted and totally defeated. He was tempted to lie down in the boat, to let himself fall asleep, to drift with the stress. But whatever attraction the idea might have had, he knew it was foolish. If he was not alert, any freighter coming to Detroit could sail right over his rowboat and not realize anything had happened.

He again checked his bearings and, using one hand and the stump of wood now little longer than a ping-pong bat, slowly eased his little craft forward. Progress was painfully slow, but with each dip of the "oar" he was nearer his goal. His confidence returned and he allowed himself to think of what lay beyond the shore up ahead.

Then he saw the police launch returning.

Again he lay down in the rowboat and again he prayed for luck. The cruiser came on, a bit faster this time, its searchlight now scanning the Windsor waterfront. Krug stayed out of sight, remained quiet, and again went undiscovered. When the cruiser had melted into the murk, he returned to his task.

After what seemed like hours, he touched bottom. It was one in the morning, Saturday, April 18, 1942 — Peter Krug's twenty-second birthday. He clambered up the riverbank, took one last look over at Windsor, then walked into downtown Detroit. As he did so, he thought back to his friends at Bowmanville. He knew they would all be asleep now, asleep on the iron beds and under the grey blankets used in the camp barracks. He wondered what his colleagues would think of him now; whether the escape committee would approve of what he had done.

He wondered also about Colonel Bull, the rather aloof Canadian who ran the camp. Though he had never talked to Bull, the man's reputation for fairness and blunt, firm decision-making was known by every POW at Camp 30. But how would Bull react to the escape, particularly when at least one of the men was still at large after two days? Krug could imagine the red-faced CO haranguing the guards, telling them to "wake up, smarten up, tighten up!" The colonel might be a bluff, strong administrator, but the prisoners respected the man. In other surroundings, they would probably have liked him.

As he came from the large city of Munich, Krug was less intimidated by Detroit than many of his co-prisoners in Bowmanville would have been. Nevertheless, he found himself getting a sore neck from looking at the immense buildings, their towers touching the clouds. The traffic was much the same as in Munich; so was the noise, the bustle and the dusty grittiness of the busy streets. Unlike Detroit's citizens today, the weekend revellers of 1942 were not afraid to come to their city's core in the wee hours of the morning.

For a while, Krug wandered aimlessly, looked into store windows, and started to form some first impressions of America, or — he kept telling himself — America at war. But after a couple of hours, the excitement and strain of the day exhausted him. On a deserted side street he noticed a vegetable market with several large baskets in the darkened doorway. He went to the nearest of these containers, sat down in it and drifted off to sleep.

"Go away, go away, go away," were the first words Krug heard the following morning. He jumped to his feet and found a short, swarthy man in a white apron screaming at him from the now open door of the market. "What are you doing here?" the voice continued.

Krug stared uncomprehendingly at the man, wondering for a moment what he *was* doing there. But soon the memories of the night before came flooding back, and he turned on his heel, and without a word disappeared down the street.

Krug spent the morning of his birthday looking for German sympathizers in Detroit, whose names and addresses he had seen and memorized from gift packages of socks sent into Bowmanville. There was no one at home at the first two locations, but at the third, a dark-haired, plain, tall woman by the name of Margareta Bertelmann opened the door. She stared at Krug for a few seconds, then asked him what he wanted. He told her who he was, showed her a German military epaulet as proof, and asked if he might come inside. Somewhat reluctantly, she invited him to do so.

Mrs. Bertelmann was extremely nervous while Krug was in her home. She made him a cup of coffee and offered him cheese and sardines for breakfast. Then she went to the phone and called a friend, a German-born Detroit restaurateur named Max Stephan. He was a pudgy, ebullient braggart who had a habit of assuring his dining clientele that the Axis forces would win the war. He arrived at the Bertelmann home half an hour after he was called.

Stephan and Krug talked for a few minutes, then both left for the former's restaurant on East Jefferson Avenue. Once there, the

POW was told to go for a walk, but to return later in the day. When he did come back, a beaming Stephan introduced him to a number of German sympathizers who lived in various parts of Detroit. To them, young Krug was a celebrity, a link with home and with the magnificent armies that had marched so triumphantly across the face of Europe.

Stephan and the others toasted the flyer, accepted him as one of them and hung on every word he said. They asked him about the war, about Europe and about his capture. They wanted to know what it was like to fly against the British, how he had felt when he was shot down, and what the POW camps he had been in were like. They marvelled at his stories of Franz von Werra's bravery, and they chortled over the brilliance of Krug's escape. Some of them had been to places he described, but hearing about Munich, Berlin and even Toronto from a hero — and to them, Krug was a hero — gave these cities an aura of glamour that Detroit could never match. They treated him to a grand meal, several drinks, presents and later, in the company of Stephan, a night on the town. It was a birthday celebration Peter Krug would never forget.

Finally, late in the evening — using the alias Peter Mueller, which Stephan gave him — Krug checked into the Field, a hotel not far from the restaurant. The next morning, Stephan handed the flyer $75 and a bus ticket to Chicago.

In the days that followed, the young escapee crisscrossed much of the eastern United States. He was in so many towns and cities and met so many German-American fifth columnists that years later he had trouble recalling either the sequence of events or many of the people he had met en route. His first stop was Chicago, then back to Gary, Indiana, then Harrisburg, Philadelphia, New York, Pittsburgh, Columbus, Nashville and finally Texarkana, Dallas and San Antonio. He met kindly shopkeepers, public employees, Bund officials and at least two beautiful girls who were impressed by this French seaman from the liner *Normandie*. The second woman invited him to her home in Memphis, but he declined the offer.

It was midafternoon, Friday, May 1, 1942, when Krug stepped off a Greyhound bus in downtown San Antonio, Texas. He went to the Nueces Hotel, registered as Jean Ette of Brooklyn, New York, left his belongings in his room, and walked downtown to do some sightseeing. The city made him uneasy, although he was never really sure why. But because he couldn't shake his sense of danger, he stopped at a pawnshop and bought a .32-calibre Hopkins and Allen revolver and a box of cartridges. The gun was thirteen dollars.

The German returned to his hotel and asked the proprietor to waken him at seven the next morning. This request was his downfall.

The hotel owner was suspicious of Krug because he was so quiet and kept to himself, but particularly because of his accent. The owner thought the man was German, but was sure when he dug out a "Wanted" poster with his guest's picture on it.

A short time later FBI agents were at the hotel.

The following Sunday, May 3, 1942, the San Antonio *Express* carried the story. The use of descriptive adjectives such as "arrogant" and "haughty" reflect the influence of propaganda on Americans' perceptions of the Germans. The paper said, in part:

> The vigilance of the proprietor of a small San Antonio hotel Friday night ended the bid for freedom and a return to his native Germany for twenty-two-year-old Hans Peter Krug, a flight Lieutenant in Adolf Hitler's famed Luftwaffe, after a three-thousand-mile flight over the United States since his escape from a Canadian concentration [*sic*] camp with a fellow officer sixteen days ago.
>
> The arrogant young Nazi pilot was taken into custody by two officers of the Federal Bureau of Investigation after the hotel manager noted a striking resemblance in the hotel guest and a picture of Krug, supplied earlier by the FBI.
>
> The hotel manager, whose identity was withheld by the FBI, notified the officers and tried to admit them to Krug's room with a pass key. However, the suspect had cautiously fastened the latch chain before retiring. He refused to admit the officers, but, apparently, realizing escape was impossible, finally relented.
>
> He offered no resistance and refused to admit his identity through approximately two hours of grilling. He was taken into custody at 11:55 p.m. and M. W. Acers, special agent in charge of the FBI here, said he finally admitted that he was the escaped flyer at 1:30 a.m.
>
> The haughty youth demanded that his position as an officer in the German Luftwaffe be remembered and that he be treated accordingly, Acers said.
>
> He demanded this despite the fact that he was an escapee, that he had traveled in disguise over much of the eastern part of the nation, and that he apparently could have given valuable information to the enemy if his escape had been completed.

As he was being fingerprinted, he drew himself stiffly to attention. "You must remember my position as an officer!" he declared.

He balked when he was to be photographed. The officers explained that the pictures they had of him were not good.

"It is good for me that the picture is bad," he said slyly.

Krug, son of a civil engineer, possibly would have been in Mexico in another day or so if he had not been captured. He apparently planned to swim the Rio Grande, for his papers — forged in the name of a carpenter purportedly from the fire-gutted French liner *Normandie* — would not have put him by border officials, Acers said.

Too, he apparently expected to live out in the open in escaping into Mexico, for in his two bags were tinned foods and chocolate bars to last him several days.

Also found in his bag was a United States defense map detailing his escape route — from Detroit, where he was aided by a man now under arrest, to Chicago, then New York, Harrisburg, Pa., Louisville, Nashville, Texarkana, Tex., Dallas, and then Brownwood, Tex.

A homemade knife, candles, matches, two German officer's epaulets, and several articles of clothing were in the bags.

A .32-caliber pistol bought for $13, officers said, at a pawnshop here, was found under an American-made hat on a bureau in his hotel room.

When officers entered his room, he was told to sit on the bed. One officer questioned him, while the others searched the room.

During this questioning, Krug apparently slipped a note into his mouth, for later in a police car en route to FBI headquarters, an officer caught him trying to kick the note, wet with saliva, under the seat.

Nature of the note — turned over to experts — was not revealed, but the speculation was that it contained information about his subsequent plans.

Krug was dressed in khaki-like trousers and a blue shirt. He appeared at the hotel at 3:15 p.m. Friday, registering as "Jean Etti [*sic*], Brooklyn, N.Y."

The manager noticed that Krug spoke with a thick German accent, especially when he called from his room to be awakened at 7 a.m. Having been supplied with a "wanted card" by the FBI, the manager later thought that the guest, who was quiet and kept to himself, resembled Krug.

The manager finally called the FBI at 10:52 p.m. Two agents and City Detectives Otto Leichman and G. E. Robinson went to the hotel to investigate, later making the arrest.

Krug remained in custody in San Antonio for three days, then was returned under armed guard to the Canadian border and finally to Bowmanville. In early July of the same year, he was back in Detroit, but this time in the company of Major Fred Chapple of the Veterans Guard of Canada. The flyer was there as a witness in the treason trial of Max Stephan, fighting for his life because he had helped the POW from Canada.

The trial of Max Stephan became a circus. Day after day, newspapers in Detroit and elsewhere covered the proceedings. Banner headlines trumpeted the news to readers who devoured every detail. Front-page photographs of Stephan, Peter Krug, Judge A. J. Tuttle, Margareta Bertelmann, Fred Chapple and others illustrated the stories. And when none of the principals was handy, the papers printed photos of POW camps, the bus depot from which Krug left Detroit, the view across to Windsor, and even the crowds who showed up each day at court.

Each of the main figures involved were hounded by the press as they entered and left the courtroom. Stories describing what they wore, how they looked, who they were with and what they said were flogged in the streets by paperboys who hardly knew where Canada was, let alone what treason might be.

But the star performer was Peter Krug. The trial had been underway for some time before the Luftwaffe officer was called to testify. The Detroit *Evening Times* of Wednesday, July 1, 1942, described his entry into court.

> The doors of Federal Court swing open to admit an enemy
> Luftwaffe Oberleutnant, Hans Peter Krug.
>
> He is arriving to testify at the trial before Judge Arthur J. Tuttle in which Max Stephan, German restaurateur, is charged with treason for aiding Krug in his flight from a Canadian internment camp, where he is a prisoner of war.
>
> Every eye turns to those doors, and the seconds preceding the enemy's appearance are silent, expectant.
>
> The German heels click on the marble floors in the corridor.
>
> Through the door steps a slight, boyish-looking officer. He is twenty-two. He's dark-haired and his brown eyes are bright.
>
> His blue Nazi uniform has scarlet markings of rank, one insignia bears a small swastika. He removes his officer's cap, places in it his gloves and hands them to FBI Chief John Bugas as if Bugas were his valet.
>
> He carries a book to the witness chair where he sits with

daguerreotype stiffness. The book, which he places on a small table before him, is an English-German dictionary to help if he is at a loss for the right word.

But he is never at a loss for the right word. Luftwaffe Oberleutnant Krug is never at a loss at all.

Just once does he almost reach for his dictionary.

It is when Stephan's counsel, Verne C. Amberson, uses the word "access." In haste Amberson pronounces it "axis."

Krug is startled until reassured by an interpreter.

Many times during the hours he is testifying, Krug's fingers trace the sharp creases down the legs of his trousers. He pulls his officer's tunic into place and arranges his sleeves to preserve their immaculate appearance at all times.

His answers are quick, terse. Numerous questions he refuses to answer because his replies would reveal military information.

The trial continued, and at the end of it, Stephan was convicted of treason against the United States and sentenced to be hanged. However, less than twenty-four hours before the sentence was to be carried out, President Franklin D. Roosevelt commuted it to life imprisonment. Roosevelt did not state publicly the reason for the commutation, although it may have partially stemmed from Stephan's anguished letter to him shortly before the hanging was to take place. The letter itself is a rather rambling, semi-coherent plea for mercy. Its conclusion seems to point to the fact that Stephan felt his trial had not been fair, even though a careful reading of the transcript indicates that the fat restaurateur was grasping at straws. "I never was a member of any Nazi Society," wrote Stephan. He then continued, in part:

> In the 15 years I have been in this country, I have never sent a letter to Germany, not even to my relatives or communicated with anyone. My connections with Germany were entirely cut off. December 17th, 1941 I bought $100 worth of War Bonds.
>
> I really did not look for mercy. All I wanted was truth and justice, but the truth did not come out, so that I have to ask for mercy. . . . I am not a traitor.[3]

As for Peter Krug, he had been returned to Bowmanville, where he served twenty-eight days' detention for his escape. The slap on the wrist seems to have had little effect, because the pilot again got out of Gravenhurst, not long after he and several

Bowmanville officers had been transferred there. This time, however, he was caught after less than twenty-four hours of freedom. In both instances, camp security was tightened, but in the long run, no real improvement occurred. No camp could be made escape-proof.

TEN

Nazi Murder at Medicine Hat

During the prewar years, when Adolf Hitler and his henchmen were gaining a stranglehold on Germany, many who opposed him fled the country. Some crossed into France, joined the renowned French Foreign Legion, and subsequently were posted to such places as Algeria, Tunisia and Morocco.

Not long after the outbreak of war in North Africa, the Germans under Rommel overran some French territories in the area. There many of the same men who had fled Germany earlier found themselves considered German nationals once again, and were pressed into battle in the service of Germany.

Later, following the Axis defeat by the Allies in North Africa, these legionnaires were rounded up once more and tossed into POW camps run by the British. In due course, the North African internment centres were phased out, and many of the prisoners were shipped to Medicine Hat, Alberta.

In July of 1943, the population of Camp 132 at Medicine Hat stood at slightly under five thousand. A hard core of the prisoners were ardent Nazis who not only ran the camp, but also exerted an iron control over those who dared profess more liberal political sympathies. This fanatical inner circle wielded power far in excess of their number, and they did so by threats, beatings, torture — and cold-blooded murder.

During June and early July, the handful of ex-legionnaires at Medicine Hat developed the habit of meeting by themselves in an open area by the side of a camp soccer field. There they sat,

167

smoked, reminisced about their homeland, and told stories of shared experiences in the service of France. These get-togethers were no more than casual affairs that grew out of a mutual affinity.

The Gestapo and Nazi element within Camp 132, however, always looked upon the legionnaires with disdain. At times they went so far as to blame this group for the German defeats in Africa. They claimed that the legionnaires had not fought as well as they should have, with the result that the Axis had been forced into premature capitulation.

It was little wonder then that the legionnaire gatherings by the soccer field were regarded with suspicion. Rumours spread that the participants were Communists, with strong anti-Nazi views, bent on spreading defeatism throughout the camp. The Nazi fanatics took it upon themselves to launch an investigation into the matter.

A series of kangaroo courts were held in an office in a camp building. One by one the legionnaires were taken to "court" and questioned; their answers were recorded. Unknown to the suspects, three or four eavesdroppers sitting behind a screen at the back of the room also heard every word that was said. The men listening were the goons who punished anyone who seemed to have anti-Nazi leanings. The legionnaires were doomed from the outset.

At first they were simply terrorized. Notes were left in their bunks, death's heads drawn on their pillows, excrement placed in their food. Then they were isolated, forbidden to talk with or approach anyone else; put off by themselves at meals, ordered to wash or shower when no one else was in the living quarters, warned not to participate in or even watch any sports events. If they still seemed unrepentant, they were wakened in the middle of the night; their testicles were squeezed or touched with bare electrical wires, and pins were forced under their fingernails.

Most of the legionnaires had received such treatment themselves or knew someone who had been similarly chastised, so they were particularly terrified of the "court" system.

On the afternoon of June 22, four legionnaires were to be questioned in hut Z, at one end of barrack block A. The first was a prisoner by the name of Weidhauer. During his interrogation, four inquisitors confronted him, while three others were concealed behind the screen. This session lasted for over an hour, but at the end of it, Weidhauer was still maintaining that he had done nothing wrong. Because the court was unable to break the man, they sent him back to his hut and ordered him to remain there.

The next man to appear was Christian Schulz. He, too, was grilled for close to an hour, but his testimony was not satisfactory to the court. They threatened him, bullied and screamed at him, then told him he would be held for further investigation in an adjoining hut.

He never got there.

Because of the way the hearing had gone, Schulz knew he could expect more questioning, and in all probability beatings and torture as well. He decided an escape attempt, with all its risks, was preferable to that prospect. As he was hustled out the door of hut Z, his chance came.

He broke away from his escort and ran for protection to the warning wire or guard wire along the outside camp fence near guard tower 7. On duty there was Private R. H. Back of the Veterans Guard. Back later told the RCMP about the incident:

I was on sentry duty from 5 p.m. till 7 p.m. in tower number 7, which is about a hundred yards west of the west recreation hall. At 5:20 p.m. I saw a man come running from the hut across the road south of the hall toward my tower. He was followed by two other POWs. He was waving a white handkerchief and shouting in German and ducked under the guard wire. The other two also ducked under the wire, but I raised my rifle and they backed out. I immediately phoned my guard room and told them a POW was asking for protection. At first there were only the two POWs chasing this man, but they were quickly joined by others and the first two were lost in the crowd. In about ten minutes the guard room phoned back and asked what the matter was. At this time I said there were about two hundred POWs getting turbulent and throwing stones at the escapee. It must have been another five or ten minutes before the scouts came down to the escapee and before they arrived I fired a shot over the crowd as it looked as if they might make a rush. The scouts took the escapee around inside the fence to the main entrance and there were about a thousand POWs shouting and swearing. After they got around near the guard house they were hidden from my sight by buildings but as near as I could see after the crowd following the escapee around, they dispersed.[1]

Back was wrong about the dispersal.

Once the mob realized they could not get their hands on

Schulz, they turned their attention to a third legionnaire, a short, mild-mannered, balding man named August Plaszek. Shortly before Schulz made his break, the forty-one-year-old Plaszek had been in his hut listening to a fellow prisoner play the harmonica. When the music stopped, Plaszek left to go to dinner. He got as far as hut Z, where he was ordered inside and told to wait, because someone wanted to ask him some questions.

He was still waiting when the mob came for him.

Four men raced up the steps into hut Z, grabbed Plaszek, and pushed the little man to the door. As he was forced through it, Adolf Kratz, as rabid a Nazi as his namesake in Berlin, picked up a huge rock in both hands and smashed it down on the legionnaire's head. Plaszek slithered down the steps to the ground. Then several others hit and kicked him, and Kratz slashed the victim's face with his own dinner knife.

Once again Private Back called the guard room, and again they were slow in answering his plea. In a later statement, he described what he saw:

> POWs started to gather around the north end of the hut facing the south side of the recreation hall. I realized something was brewing and in about five minutes there were about fifty milling around. In just a minute, they went half way across the road toward the hall. Then they halted and the main body divided and I saw four men dragging another man — two on each side — backward into the recreation hall. I phoned my guard room again and reported what I had seen. It must have been another ten minutes, and when no action had been taken I phoned again. All the Vet's Guard knew pretty well what is going to happen when they see a POW dragged by other prisoners and I felt the man would be dead because of the delay. In another four or five minutes I saw the staff car drive in near the west hall. There was a large crowd there then. The car was in for two or three minutes and then drove out. Before the car arrived it seemed that everyone around the building went in to view something and after the car left they went in, in twos and threes. About five minutes after the car left, a man I took to be one of the leaders called these men together and spoke to them and they all dispersed orderly.[2]

Obviously, Back could only report what he could see from his vantage point.

When the mob reached the recreation hall, several closest to

Plaszek went inside; the doors were closed and the windows covered. Close to eight hundred remained in the area outside. Taunts of "swine," "traitor" and worse were hurled at the half-conscious victim. The terrified Plaszek pleaded for his freedom and asked his tormentors what he had done. His question was answered by a chorus of epithets.

The recreation hall was thirty-five metres long and forty wide, and its main entrance had sliding double doors on one side. Inside, the hall was divided into eight bays, separated by heavy wooden roof supports, five metres apart. On the third support, a horizontal beam three metres from the floor, supporting a punching bag, stuck out from the wall.

Plaszek was dragged, kicking, screaming and crying, over to this beam. Someone produced a light rope from the sports hut near the recreation hall. Adolf Kratz and another prisoner, Werner Schwalb, wound the cord around Plaszek's neck and tossed the rope over the beam, between the punching bag and the wall. The legionnaire clawed vainly at the rope and tried to pull it off, but by this time he was so weak that his effort was pointless. He was hauled upward, but just as his feet cleared the floor the rope broke and he fell.

Schwalb grabbed more rope, lashed it twice around Plaszek's neck, and, with the help of Kratz and others, got the legionnaire into the air. When the condemned man's feet were about a foot off the floor, Kratz grabbed Plaszek and jerked him downward. This caused the victim's features to constrict, his body to twitch, and his tongue to protrude. He took only a couple of minutes to die. Gradually, the baying of the mob ceased. They had done what they came to do.

The sliding doors of the building were thrown open and the crowd that had been standing outside surged forward. They surrounded the corpse and someone even kicked it. One prisoner removed Plaszek's shoes and disappeared with them. Pale and shaking, Max Nolte, the German camp doctor, pushed through the crowd, touched the body, and ordered it cut down.

One man swung up onto the crossbeam and started to cut the rope. The knife was dull and the man had to use a sawing motion. Finally the rope parted and the corpse fell like a sack. Several men in the crowd laughed. One prisoner complained because a good rope had been ruined.

For some time the corpse lay in a bloody heap on the floor. Then Dr. Nolte placed a shirt over the face and left the building.

Just then a Veterans Guard staff car pulled up to the door.

Four Canadian soldiers viewed the body, then asked for its removal. They also ordered assistant camp leader Richard Elstermann — the leader was ill — to clear the hall and secure it. The German complied. He also posted a notice in the camp, telling everyone to calm down, be quiet, and be of good order. Copies of the notice were placed in all barracks.

Plaszek's body was taken to the Patison Funeral Home in Medicine Hat, where an autopsy the next day gave strangulation as the cause of death.

Within hours of the murder, an investigation under RCMP Corporal A. R. Bull was begun into the cause. And though Bull could not know it at the outset, this killing and another related incident soon afterward would involve the most taxing and time-consuming investigative work imaginable. Nor could the policeman know that the day he came to Camp 132 to look into the cause of the first murder, he was becoming involved in what he would later cite as the most frustrating assignment of his career.

Bull began his investigation by visiting the scene of the crime, attending the autopsy, and interviewing witnesses. Here he met a brick wall. Canadian officials, of course, came forward quite readily to give statements as to their actions during the disturbance and before and after the murder. But even though Bull spent several hours obtaining information from the authorities, he knew the hard evidence had to come from inside the wire. Unfortunately, those inside the compound lived in a society that was close to a miniature police state. Medicine Hat camp housed a segment of inmates whose blind obedience to the Fuehrer and routine use of Gestapo terror tactics would have done Heinrich Himmler proud.

From Christian Schulz, the prisoner who ran from his captors and remained outside the compound, Bull obtained much of his initial information concerning the situation in the camp. Schulz was a willing witness whose fear of the Gestapo was eased somewhat, now that he was beyond their control. Then in the days following the murder, a number of other prisoners, including legionnaires who had been threatened with death, asked for and were granted protective custody. Their stories were checked and all worthwhile information recorded.

But much of what they had to say was hearsay evidence. None of them had seen the killing; they naturally avoided the areas where the Nazis congregated. They had heard accounts of what had taken place, however, and almost all had picked up some of the names that were mentioned in connection with the murder. But to Bull, having a few names at his disposal was a long way from proving that the men named were the ones who had hanged Plaszek.

During the period immediately after the murder, a military court of inquiry was held into the incident, but it was unproductive. The RCMP investigation continued as usual.

One by one, witnesses and suspected witnesses to the killing were brought out of the compound and interrogated. However, because of the fear instilled by the dreaded Gestapo, the questioning was often futile. Several men whom Bull believed knew worthwhile information kept silent because they were too afraid to talk. They knew that if they told Bull anything, they would be beaten up once they went back inside. Most simply stated that they were in another part of the camp the day the hanging took place; they knew no one who had participated, and they heard the name of no one who was involved. And even some of those who were granted protective custody refused to say much because they were afraid of reprisals against relatives back in Germany.

In September 1943, the RCMP placed an undercover man, Constable G. G. Krause, at the camp in the guise of a Veterans Guard officer. Krause, who was fluent in German, tried to engage prisoners in conversation, but soon found that each time he did, another POW moved in to hear what was said. The prisoners were intensely suspicious of each other. The veteran guards, on the other hand, were largely indifferent. A month after the murder, they rarely mentioned it. To them, one dead German was of little consequence.

All mail entering and leaving the camp was screened more carefully than usual. There were some veiled references to the killing in letters, but nothing of real value to Bull.

He decided to try another approach. Several of the POWs who seemed to know more than they were telling were transferred out of Medicine Hat to the Lethbridge compound. From there, they were placed on various farms throughout the district in order to remove them completely from Gestapo influence. The farmers were not told what was going on, but little by little the news leaked out. Eventually, most did know and all cooperated in the matter. As time went on, the POW farm workers gradually became less reticent under police questioning — which was often done right on the farms where the prisoners worked.

Gradually Bull was able to piece the story together. This involved a great deal of travelling here and there across Alberta and, in some instances, to camps in other provinces. It was known that several prisoners participated in the killing, but the actions of three in particular eventually came in for most scrutiny. On October 15, 1945, the three — Werner Schwalb, Adolf Kratz and Johannes Wittinger — were arrested and formally charged with the murder of POW No. 042024, August Plaszek.

A preliminary hearing was held at Medicine Hat a month later, and on February 25, 1946, the three appeared before Chief Justice W. R. Howson of the Supreme Court of Alberta to face the murder charge. The same day the defence petitioned the crown to grant the accused separate trials. The request was granted. Schwalb's trial began the next day, Kratz's two weeks later and Wittinger's on June 17. Evidence against all three was roughly similar.

Schwalb was positively identified by other POWs as one of those who helped drag Plaszek into the recreation hall. He was seen standing in the hall with blood on his hands. Immediately after the killing, another prisoner saw him in the same condition outside the hall. When he was asked what he had done, he told the questioner to go into the hall and see for himself. A few minutes later, Schwalb was seen going into one of the huts nearby and attempting to wash his bloody hands and clothes. In an adjoining room, several prisoners were discussing the murder. Schwalb could overhear them, and at one point in their conversation he called through to them: "It was *I* who asked for the rope."

Some time after the murder, another prisoner identified Schwalb as the man who said he had been unable to sleep because he had participated in the Plaszek killing.

The evidence against Kratz took into account his appearance on the steps of the hut before Plaszek was dragged away. POWs in the crowd outside remembered seeing Kratz smash the legionnaire's head with the rock. Two prisoners heard Kratz say, just after the murder: "Well, I have helped hang one of those swine." A minute or so later he repeated the same words to another man and added: "It was my duty. All the swine should be hanged." Two men who shared quarters with Kratz had seen him enter their hut and start to eat a boiled egg. As he did so, he remarked: "This egg will taste as good again since I helped hang a traitor."

Several POWs reported seeing Johannes Wittinger helping to drag Plaszek toward the recreation hall. A few minutes after the killing, Wittinger was seen with blood on his hands. At the time he said to another prisoner: "Now I have beaten one to death with a stone and afterward took him to the west hall and hung him." The next day another prisoner reportedly said to Wittinger: "You have killed a family man." The accused replied: "Hold your tongue. I have . . . instructions to do that."

In all, twenty-nine witnesses gave evidence for the crown. No hard evidence was offered by the defence, although several times the defence counsel did question the actions of some who testified.

The crown was represented by W. D. Gow, K.C., the agent for the Alberta attorney general at Medicine Hat. L. S. Turcotte, a Lethbridge barrister, conducted the defence, having been appointed by the federal minister of justice in accordance with the terms of the Geneva Convention. The authorities in Alberta and in Ottawa intended to do everything in their power to ensure the trial was absolutely fair in every respect.

The language barrier not only had made the investigation of the murder particularly difficult, but it also lengthened the proceedings before the court. Interpreters were present throughout the trials, and the judge exercised very great care to ensure that all the proceedings were fully understood by the three accused.

On February 5, 1946, Schwalb was convicted and sentenced to be hanged on June 26, 1946. The jury made no recommendation and had no trouble reaching a verdict. A Medicine Hat teenager named Joyce Reesor skipped school that day to watch the proceedings in court. Later on, she had to do a written assignment to compensate for her truancy. The essay that she turned in to her teachers gives us a glimpse of what it was like to be in court at the close of the trial. It reads, in part:

> Entirely unique in Judicial history of Canada, are the trials of three German Prisoners-of-War which are being conducted at Medicine Hat.
>
> I consider myself fortunate for, after spending four hours in that courtroom I learned more of Canadian justice and court procedure, than any classroom or text-book could teach me in a month.
>
> The crowded court-room was hushed as the six man jury filed in and the Sheriff called the roll. It was all so overwhelming that I, who find it difficult to sit still for even a short time, sat enthralled for almost four hours as Chief Justice W. R. Howson elaborated to the jury, the facts of the case, and the law as written in the Criminal Code of Canada. I was particularly proud of our democracy when

the Judge, speaking slowly and deliberately, stressed over and over again that if there was the slightest fragment of a reasonable doubt as to the man's innocence, a verdict of "not guilty" must be the final conclusion.

The jury however, after . . . careful deliberation, returned to a breathless court room.

Even the ticking of the clock seemed exaggerated as the elected foreman of the jury rose, and delivered the verdict: — "We find the accused guilty of murder."

The silence was electric. The low monotone of the interpreter could be heard as he translated into German the dreaded statement. What could Schwalb be thinking? The Judge spoke solemnly, but for the first time that afternoon I tried to exclude his words from my thoughts. I could not see the face of the prisoner — what emotion was betrayed there when his interpreter translated into his own tongue:

"And you shall be hanged by the neck until you are dead — and may the Lord have mercy on your soul."

Sergeant Werner Schwalb stepped from the prisoner's box, a mask of arrogance covered his face, and after a forced smile at his interpreter, he walked haughtily from the court room.

Canadian justice had been dealt — a life for a life — and the drama in the Medicine Hat court room came to a close.

Morbid curiosity did not draw my attention to the trial of Werner Schwalb. I honestly wanted to witness the procedure, and I believe my education gained, rather than suffered, when I skipped an afternoon of school to see history made.[3]

Schwalb's hanging took place on schedule. In the Kratz trial, however, the jury was out for several hours before they returned to the court, claiming they were unable to agree. At this point, they asked if they could add a recommendation. Mr. Justice Howson allowed them to do so and they retired a second time. Finally, they came back with a guilty verdict, but with a strong recommendation for mercy.

In his book *Behind Canadian Barbed Wire*, David J. Carter attempts to explain the plea for mercy. In his view, defence lawyer Turcotte's summation, coupled with a charge from Howson, seems to have been enough to convince the jury that some clemency was in order.

L. S. Turcotte claimed that of the twenty-nine witnesses called, only two had in any way testified seeing Kratz take any part in the incident. He claimed conflicting evidence was given by a number of the witnesses. He claimed no one had testified that Kratz had entered the hall where the murder was committed. . . . Turcotte reminded the jury [that they had] three choices in their decision — acquittal, manslaughter or murder. He urged them to bring in a verdict of acquittal.

Chief Justice Howson warned the jury that their decision must be unanimous and that every benefit of the doubt be given in favour of the accused in considering the evidence. "You are not concerned with the guilt of any others. You are only concerned with the guilt or innocence of the young man who is the accused. He is the only one you must pass judgment on. The action of the mob which participated in the murder of Plaszek could best be described as a lynching."[4]

So, whatever the reason for it, the recommendation had an effect. The sentence of hanging that Howson originally imposed was subsequently commuted to life in the federal penitentiary at Prince Albert, Saskatchewan. Kratz later contracted tuberculosis and was sent back to Germany.

The six-member jury in the Wittinger trial reached a consensus much more rapidly. They only took two hours of deliberation before finding the prisoner not guilty. The case against the man was dismissed.

One of the men on the jury later explained why the "not guilty" verdict was brought in — and then how it was received both within the courtroom, and later, outside it.

We just went over the evidence very carefully and I remember on the first ballot it was unanimous, not guilty. As far as we were concerned they could not place this man at the scene of the hanging. Before we went into the jury room the judge had said, "You are not sentencing the man, you are asked if he is guilty or not guilty. The Crown passes sentence." He said that to take the pressure off our conscience if it was going to bother anybody.

We came out and I could see the POW standing at attention looking over at us. He was very pale. When the verdict was interpreted it didn't sink in. The face was sort of blank. It seemed like an eternity. Man, the light on that man's face, I'll never forget it! Of course, undoubtedly he thought that everyone else had been condemned to die, he was the last one, automatically he figured he would die. He just couldn't believe it, the tears and smiles of joy.

Unforgettable! I was very happy to be on the jury that could bring in "not guilty" as the verdict.

We were later criticized by various people around town as being Nazi sympathizers![5]

During the period when the Plaszek hanging was being investigated, a second murder took place at Medicine Hat. This time, the victim had not been in the French Foreign Legion, but the seeds of hatred that resulted in the killing had also been sown a continent away from the camp on the Canadian prairie.

Before being sent to Canada, several Roman Catholics who were incarcerated in the POW camp outside of Oldham, England, invited a local German-speaking priest to come and say mass for them and give those who wished to do so the opportunity of going to confession. Max Schoellnhammer, the ski trooper who had been captured in Narvik, was also in Oldham at the time.

"A makeshift confessional and an altar had been built in the theatre we had there," he remembers. "Then most of the Catholics, and there were quite a few of them, started lining up to confess to the priest.

"The guys telling their sins didn't realize it, of course, but the confessional had been built in such a way that it had a false back. Someone could approach it from the rear, where he would not be seen, and would be able to hear everything that was said inside. And that was what happened. Each one of those confessions was heard by the priest, and secretly by the Gestapo as well. They controlled everything that happened in the camp, and they knew everything that happened. What they got from the confessional helped them keep the men in line later.

"One of my friends in Oldham was a guy by the name of Perzenowski. He was one of those who had hidden behind the confessional, although I did not know it at the time. I didn't even realize that he was Gestapo until later. He seemed so friendly, although he was always asking you questions, about what you thought and so on. He often asked me what others were saying, too. I told him to ask them."

Several former prisoners believe that one of the men who went to confession that day was Dr. Karl Lehmann, a thirty-eight-year-old former professor of languages at the University of Erlangen in Germany. Lehmann had been captured at Tunisia and sent to Oldham; there he attracted the attention of the Gestapo, principally because of his disavowal of Nazi doctrine and his habit of expressing his beliefs aloud. Even while he was at Oldham, he began to tell anyone who would listen that Germany would lose the war. Understandably, such opinions did not sit well with the Nazi hard-liners in camp, and as a result, Lehmann often found himself in trouble.

In 1942, he, Perzenowski and hundreds of others were shipped to Canada. After a period of time in various camps, many of them were transferred to Medicine Hat. Lehmann continued to speak out against the Nazis and often was accused of being a Communist because of his views. Whether he was a Communist is debatable; for one thing, he probably went to confession in Oldham. It's more likely he was labelled a Communist because that was a catch-all term used by the Gestapo for those who disagreed with them.

At any rate, for a short while after the Plaszek murder, the Gestapo enforcers in Camp 132 maintained a fairly low profile, continuing to gather evidence to further cement their case against Lehmann and others like him. It was about this time that Schoellnhammer began to suspect just what kind of man this Perzenowski was.

"I knew him very well," says Schoellnhammer. "I played on the same hockey team with him, and we often walked around the camp together. Eventually I realized what a staunch Nazi he was — but I still did not think of him as a fanatic. He was my friend, so perhaps I was blind to his faults. He flew in Spain in 1936. He had been decorated with the Iron Cross, First Class, and he had been shot down in Wales on April 14, 1941. He was a good listener and a fine all-round athlete. I was good in sports and he liked me for that reason, I suppose. But when I found out that he was a Nazi number one, I stayed quiet because I didn't care for that stuff. I never knew what he really thought.

"At Medicine Hat, ten or fifteen men were in my sleeping area. One of them was a man from Sudetenland, that border area in Czechoslovakia that Germany occupied. He was a little man with bow legs who was a baker like me. One day he asked me if I would like to walk around the camp. The camp was large — thirty-two hundred metres or so around. We walked around the fence for more than an hour. This man told me he was from Czechoslovakia and did not think much of Hitler, Goering, Goebbels or any of the rest of them. In a bush camp he had tried to escape to the Canadians, but had been turned back into the camp again. Then, he said, he had been moved to Medicine Hat.

He told me he was against Germany's war effort. He was very open with me.

"Two days later I was called to the office to a court the Nazis had set up. Perzenowski was there. There was also another guy there from the Luftwaffe. The camp leader was there, as well as another guy from the Afrika Korps. Their first question was: 'You were seen talking to so and so two days ago. What did you talk about, Schoellnhammer?' Right away, I knew what they wanted. They were all Gestapo. I was afraid. I didn't dare say what we talked about. 'Oh,' I said, 'he is a baker and so am I. We talked about sports and so on. We were both in the bush camps.' If I had told them what we really said, that guy would have been executed. Maybe me, too. Finally they stopped questioning me and let me go. I felt better when I got out of there. I was sweating, I'll tell you that.

"Perhaps I picked the wrong guys for friends. I also knew Adolf Kratz, and I remember him bragging to me about the Plaszek killing and about the fact that he helped. Many people saw that murder and Kratz told many more. He always seemed a bit crazy to me.

"In any of the camps, if you didn't agree with Germany's war effort, you didn't dare speak out. You *never* could speak out. It was just too dangerous to do so. There were too many people who were always listening."

Another prisoner who was at Medicine Hat at the time told the Toronto *Star* recently that he, too, feared for his life in Camp 132. In an interview published on March 15, 1981, Max Weidauer commented on the laxity of Canadian authorities at Medicine Hat. "They allowed us to maintain our own discipline in the camps, and that meant . . . a Gestapo man in every hut."

Weidauer, who spoke English at the time he was a prisoner, had often translated Canadian newspapers to fellow POWs. It was this practice that got him into trouble. The Gestapo goons called him to a kangaroo court and asked for an explanation of his actions.

"I thought, my God, if I can get out of this I'll be lucky," recalls Weidauer. "They asked me if I made remarks that for Germany the war was already lost. I told them that with the Russians in the war, it would be more difficult for Germany to win."

Weidauer, who had won the Iron Cross, First and Second Class, in North Africa, was let go, but he also recalled: "The days and weeks following Plaszek's death, I could not sleep. I thought they would come and get me."

In Medicine Hat, one of the most ardent Gestapo types was Walter Wolf, an Unteroffizier who loved to brag about his role in Jew-baiting and murder in Mannheim before the war. Wolf had a habit of ingratiating himself into the company and then into the friendship of his fellow prisoners. Under this guise of friendship, he managed to get men to say incriminating things, which he remembered and recorded for later use. Eventually, most men who knew Wolf were guarded in what they said to him. But not Karl Lehmann.

The professor continued to speak his mind, even though he had been threatened time and time again. Because he knew several languages, including English, he read the Canadian papers and was able to decide for himself which way the war was going. And, unfortunately for his own safety, he told others — including Walter Wolf.

Wolf built up his case against Lehmann, but for some time seemed unable to decide when to act on it. Ironically, it was the Canadians who ultimately brought the matter to a head. Because of the widespread evidence of Gestapo activities in Medicine Hat, Internment headquarters in Ottawa decided to remove many of the more ardent Nazis from the camp and move them to Neys, where they felt their influence might be more contained. Neys was smaller, 650 as opposed to 10,000, so there they would be preaching to the converted. Not surprisingly, Wolf and Perzenowski were among those scheduled for transfer. The move was set for September 11, 1944.

As soon as the departure date was known, Wolf decided that the time had come to make his move. He met with Perzenowski, and together they drafted four others to assist: Max Voigt, Heinz Reihme, Willi Mueller and Heinrich Busch. The group worked out a plan. Its goal: the elimination of Karl Lehmann. Later on it was determined that Voigt and Reihme were little more than bystanders to what followed, while Busch and Mueller offered their enthusiastic support. The group sat down to work out a plan.

Lehmann had been teaching English, French and Russian to his fellow prisoners at Medicine Hat. Most of this instruction was done in ZD6, a long, single-storey frame building in the northeast corner of the camp. Lehmann's classroom contained benches, tables and a couple of blackboards. It was heated by gas, and overhead gas pipes ran the length of the room.

Late in the afternoon of September 10, Wolf sent Lehmann a message ordering him to report to ZD6 between the two meal shifts that evening, so that he could sign language proficiency papers for those of his students who were being transferred to Neys. Lehmann received the information and reported as directed in good faith. He went alone, because most of his friends were either eating at the time or waiting to go to dinner.

The plotters were waiting in ZD6. They had gone to Lehmann's classroom earlier in order to look over the scene and make a few last-minute preparations. They placed a portable blackboard in front of one window and draped blankets over the lower half of the others. One of the men brought a rope.

Lehmann arrived on schedule. Perzenowksi met him just outside the door. The two men talked for a minute, then both stepped inside. Perzenowski told the professor to sit down. Then, like a pack of wolves moving in for the kill, the others in the room surrounded Lehmann. They called him a traitor and swore at him. Willi Mueller, the boxing instructor at the camp, repeatedly smashed his fist into Lehmann's face, quickly reducing it to a bloody pulp. Then the boxer slammed his fist into the victim's stomach, knocking him, doubled over, onto the floor. Perzenowski knelt down, forced a gag back into the professor's mouth, and asked for the rope.

Busch and Mueller wound it around Lehmann's neck and, with direction from Perzenowski and help from Wolf, looped it over one of the gas pipes.

The rope broke.

They doubled the cord and lashed it up again, and this time it held. Lehmann was hauled into the air. By the time the spasms ceased in his writhing body, the murderers had cleaned themselves up and were ready to go to dinner.

Doctor Lehmann's body was not found until eight the next morning — after all the murderers had departed by train for Neys. The camp spokesman informed the Canadians of the death, and the body was removed from the camp. A subsequent autopsy gave the cause of death as "asphyxia as the result of hanging."

The investigation of the Lehmann murder proceeded along the same lines as the Plaszek inquiry. This time, however, the only witnesses to the crime, apart from those who had committed it, were Max Voigt and Heinz Reihme — and they were not talking. Corporal Bull was the officer in charge.

At first, the RCMP ran into the same brick wall they had faced when investigating the earlier killing. Little by little, however, bits of information came out — but never easily. For example, each time Bull or one of his men wished to interview a particular POW, the Canadian commanding officer had to issue a written order for that individual to be released for questioning. This order was given to the camp leader, who insisted that twelve hours' lead time was necessary to locate a man. This ruse was more than just a delaying action. It gave the Gestapo time to properly indoctrinate each POW before interrogation. By the time a prisoner was questioned, he was so afraid of a beating or of reprisals against his family in Germany that he generally said little. He then had to give a complete account of what he did say to his Nazi bosses as soon as he returned to the enclosure.

The investigation soon spread beyond Medicine Hat to Neys, Angler, Lethbridge and a number of bush camps in northern Ontario. The interviews at Neys gradually became the most significant, but again it was not until the end of the war that real progress was made. By that time, though most of the prime suspects were known, the police still had to compile the necessary proof in order to obtain convictions. Occasionally they were aided in strange ways.

Late in the afternoon of Tuesday, June 19, 1945, the commanding officer at Neys received an anonymous letter from a prisoner there. Its contents are interesting:

> In giving you this news my feelings are not guided by any revengefulness. It isn't possible for me anymore to hand the guilty ones over to a Court of Justice after the collapse of Germany. It was my solemn will to do this. May now the enemy be the judge: These people have not deserved a better fate on account of justice. They have made life hell for their co-prisoners behind the wires. They talk despotic so that one has to take for granted that they intended to satisfy their perverse feelings. I do not wish that those men should be allowed to still carry their "mask" for the sorrow of others.
>
> During the three years of my prisonship, I have not experienced the least unpleasantness on the part of the Canadians guards. But these types of human beings which I will name, have made life hell for us during this long time. They were always those who passed themselves off as 150% moralists. Do not try and search for me because you will not guess who wrote you these lines.

The letter was a long, well-documented indictment of Walter Wolf and of his actions as a prisoner of war. The writer alleged that Wolf ordered men beaten, often in the middle of the night. He could have men isolated, so that no one was allowed near them at meals or at recreation. The beatings were his method of rooting out anti-Nazi sentiment and homosexual activity.

Wolf, the letter said, had informers in every hut. This was one means of retaining his power of life or death over *all* men in the camp. The letter said the senior officers (who were actually NCOs) did what Wolf wanted because they too feared him and the Gestapo. Wolf knew of this fear and used it to his advantage.

The writer alleged Wolf was behind the killings of both Plaszek and Lehmann. In this connection, Wolf had one man beaten because he had spoken out in defence of Plaszek. The beaten man then stayed quiet because he feared for his life. Not a lover of due process, Wolf either burned or ordered others to burn evidence taken at the kangaroo courts, the letter continued.

The allegations also revealed that after the defeat of Germany, Wolf started to see his own behaviour in a different light. He feared for his life in the camp and tried to get himself repatriated early. Wolf once ordered a sick POW to give his name as Wolf during X-rays, in the hope that he could be shipped back on medical grounds.

The letter then ended:

> Please go after these affairs. A great many inmates of this camp will now be able to talk more freely. Please make a white chalk mark plainly visible on the guard building as a sign that you have received this letter.[6]

Whether the chalk mark was made is unknown, as is the identity of the writer. The letter itself told the RCMP little that they did not already know, but it did help reinforce their suspicions. Bull had already talked to Wolf and had made no progress. He decided to try again.

Wolf started to talk and, half boasting, half teasing, admitted his own involvement. Finally, after countless hours of listening, Corporal Bull was able to piece the story together. Wolf was, like Werner Schwalb, a braggart. He loved to have his say, to have an audience, to have someone think him important. But he also had few scruples about loyalty to his friends. He started to name them: Perzenowski, Busch, Mueller, Voigt and Reihme. He also called Lehmann a traitor, a spy within the camp and a collaborator. In Wolf's eyes, the professor had to die, and Wolf felt it had been his duty to kill him.

One facet of his statement was undoubtedly true: Lehmann did assist the Canadians, and in many instances his help was of great value to them. In a letter on October 13, 1944, to Louis St. Laurent, then federal minister of justice and later prime minister, RCMP Commissioner S. T. Wood wrote about Karl Lehmann:

> POW Lehmann was well educated, being a Doctor of Languages, and as such detailed to give instruction in languages to the prisoners. He was anti-Nazi and had on a number of occasions given considerable valuable information to the camp officials regarding the Gestapo activities in the camp.
>
> As a result of information received from this prisoner, the camp officials had issued instruction for a large number of the Gestapo group to be transferred to other camps, and it was evident to the group that they had been informed upon by a fellow prisoner. They had previously had Lehmann under observation as a suspect, and the transfers evidently confirmed their suspicions, with the result that Lehmann was murdered on the night prior to the transfer taking place.
>
> Lehmann knew that he was a suspect, but despite this continued to pass information of value to the camp officials. He was offered protective custody prior to his death but refused to take advantage of the offer.[7]

Whether the professor's actions were those of a traitor is at best debatable. Even though he did give information to the enemy, his courage was silently applauded by what one must imagine was a sizable portion of the prison population, who prided themselves on being loyal German soldiers rather than Gestapo sadists.

Having obtained a statement from Wolf, Corporal Bull turned his attention to Perzenowski, Mueller and Busch; one after the other they too admitted their involvement in the killing. Initially Perzenowski tried to claim responsibility for the whole thing, stating that the others were only acting on his orders. Bull ignored this.

On April 6, 1946, the four POWs were placed under arrest, and individual preliminary hearings were conducted the following month. The trials for murder were held during June and July 1946, before Chief Justice W. R. Howson, the same magistrate who was on the bench in the Plaszek case. Voigt and Reihme testified for the crown. The defence did not offer any evidence. Separate juries were chosen for each case.

All four men were found guilty and were sentenced to hang in Lethbridge during the early morning hours of Wednesday, October 16, 1946.

One of the spectators in the courtroom the day sentence was pronounced on Perzenowski was Constable George Krause, the RCMP officer who had worked undercover in the Medicine Hat camp. He can still remember his reaction to the event.

> Justice Howson pronounced the sentence. As he was reaching his last words, "You shall be taken to the place of execution and there hung by the neck until dead. May the Lord have mercy on your soul" — just as he completed these remarks the school bell nearby commenced to toll. The passing of the death sentence itself creates a very tense and gripping atmosphere and is more than impressive, but with this added ringing of a bell, my thoughts interpreted, "For whom the bell tolls."
>
> I could feel a prickling on my scalp starting at the neck. I looked around and the whole courtroom seemed similarly affected. Every face was white and you could have heard a pin drop in the silence, which lasted a full minute.
>
> That was one of the most gripping experiences of my life.[8]

Bill Westgate was another RCMP officer who still vividly recalls the murders. He was one of the men who cut Lehmann down the morning after the hanging. Later Westgate helped guard the prisoners in the basement of the RCMP barracks in Medicine Hat. "While guarding the prisoners, we became quite attached to them. In fact, Mueller, who was the boxer who had hit Lehmann, used to ask if he could shine my boots. He really put a good shine on them because he didn't want to go into court with a scruffy-looking policeman. He also made me a watch strap.

"Later I was invited . . . to attend the hanging. . . . I visited them in death row, but declined the invitation to attend the hanging. I just couldn't go."[9]

There was very little public reaction to the executions — or to the last of the trials. The day Mueller's hearing began, the only spectators in the court were two newspapermen.

Finally, after the date of execution had been delayed twice because of defence appeals on legal technicalities, the four men were hanged on December 18, 1946, in the yard at the Lethbridge provincial jail.

The case was closed.

ELEVEN

Freedom — and Return to Canada

Today, former prisoners and guards often look back upon their shared experiences in the internment camps in much the same way as the rest of us watch scenes from old war movies. The sound is fuzzy, the picture often grainy and rather blurred, and the actors are all so young. But unlike Hollywood's celluloid fantasies, the Canadian internment operation was real. The camps did exist; the events did take place; and the daring escapes were all part of the history of the time.

But as with an old movie and its happy ending, no one was sorry to see the POW camps close. Least of all, the men who were in them. And even if camp experience was unpleasant at times, the intervening years seem to have eradicated most of the unhappy memories. When former prisoners get together now, they talk of the good times, in the compounds, on farms or in the bush. They laugh about incidents that, when taken out of the context of the situation, seem more ridiculous today than they did when they were happening. They are also able to laugh now about occurrences that were not so welcome when they took place.

For example, when the Battle of Bowmanville was being fought in October 1942, the German officers at Camp 30 seriously wanted to protest the shackling decree issued by Winston Churchill. Years later, those same officers laugh about all the broken handcuffs, the barricaded buildings and the bravado of the Kingston commandos. The violence and rage of the riot are almost forgotten and even though the Gestapo reign of terror at Medicine Hat resulted in tragedy, the men who were there during the war now joke about the petty posturing, the kangaroo courts and the insane utterings of Hitler's brainwashed bully boys on the Canadian prairie.

In Gravenhurst, so the story goes, a cheering band of townspeople approached the POW camp on May 8, 1945 — V-E Day. A prisoner who heard the racket questioned a guard about what was happening. "The war in Europe is over," came the answer. The prisoner is then supposed to have asked: "Who won?" Hidden in the anecdote, according to several men who told the story to me, was the grim reality that many staunch Nazis refused to the end to accept the fallibility of their cause.

The first two weeks of May 1945 were memorable in every POW camp. A few days before Germany's surrender was announced, all Canadian commanding officers were alerted. At the time, one of these was James Stewart, a corporal in Company 5 of the Veterans Guard, who was in charge of one of the northern Ontario bush camps. His diary tells us what he wrote about two specific dates:

> *May 5, 1945* — Received two letters today. One was marked "Secret" and the other "Most Secret." I am not supposed to open it until I receive a telegram from HQ. POWs are to go on as usual with their work.

> *May 9, 1945* — One POW injured cutting wood. Very bad. Had to be sent to hospital. At 1500 [hours] received a telegram stating Germany had surrendered. I called the camp leader and opened the "Most Secret" letter. It was the unconditional surrender of Germany — which the POWs did not care a great deal about.

The next day, the logging went on as if nothing had happened.

Oberleutnant K. H. Boettger of German Panzer Division 15 was at Bowmanville on V-E Day. "Everything was shattered by the news," he recalls. "But after the Canadian commandant had spoken and announced the capitulation, General Ravenstein [Johann von Ravenstein, senior German officer at Bowmanville at the time] spoke to us. He had been through the days of defeat after 1918 so he could understand our feelings. I still know what he said: "I know how you feel. It is the saddest day for a soldier to be told that his arms have failed and that he has been defeated in war. But, my young fellow countrymen, I tell you: it is better that

Germany has lost this war. If we had won, we would have lost ourselves, our souls."

George Fehn was at Monteith when the European war ended. He remembers the kindness of the guards at the time: "The Canadians were very nice about the way they told us the war was over and we were defeated. They got us all together in the mess hall and told us the war was over and that Hitler had shot himself and so forth. We were very quiet. Nobody said anything. Then the Canadian CO got up and said to his own men: 'Gentlemen, leave the boys alone for two days and don't come near them for any reason.' We were always treated so well — never harshly, even at the time of our defeat."

David J. Carter describes the scene at Medicine Hat.

> On that day the German government ceased to exist and a proclamation was required to be read to the prisoners to inform them of their change of status.
>
> All the POWs were assembled in the large sports stadium the POWs had erected on their sports ground, to the immediate west of the present Medicine Hat Exhibition stadium.
>
> Each block was formed up and marched to the stadium where they filed into the tiers of seats marked off for them. The block leaders brought the prisoners to attention and then marched off to the centre of the file to report his block to the Assistant Camp Leader.
>
> The POW band was marching around the facility playing military music. Two minutes before the announced time of the parade the Camp Commandant arrived in his car. Escorted by several officers of the camp staff he mounted his dais.
>
> The German Camp Leader called "Achtung" and every man of the ten thousand prisoners came to attention and stood perfectly still. The Camp Leader saluted, the Camp commandant asked him to stand his men "at ease" and proceeded to read the proclamation.
>
> The prisoners learned they had lost the war and all power was now in the hands of the Allies.
>
> An interpreter read the proclamation.
>
> The parade was brought to attention, salutes exchanged, and the Camp Commandant left in his car.[1]

The Veterans Guard newspaper *P.O.W. WOW* carried this comment a day or so later:

> It was a splendid example of German military discipline: and although many were seen afterward weeping and obviously

distraught with the bitter news they had heard, they certainly behaved like soldiers while the proclamation was read to them. It was an impressive spectacle and will long be remembered by those who were privileged to witness it, as many thousands of them were dressed in their uniforms in Army, Navy and Air Force, as the case might be, and the parade symbolized the end of German might.

In the fall of 1946, a period of limbo when the war was over but the POWs were still in Canada awaiting repatriation, former merchant seaman George Fehn and several of his countrymen were working at a brickyard at Cooksville, Ontario, and living in billets nearby. Life was better than behind the wire at an internment camp, because here there was little regimentation. At Cooksville the men could pretend for a time that they were free, though they all had been told they would have to go back to camp before the time to depart for Germany finally came. In their off-hours and during the evenings the Germans were largely on their own or were able to entertain visitors at concerts, soccer games and so on. It was at one of these games that George Fehn met a girl.

The attraction was not exactly love at first sight, but it was mutual and became more pronounced as the weeks went by. Before long, the couple realized they were in love and they decided to get married. Fehn chuckles as he explains the situation: "Getting the marriage licence was difficult. My future wife went to city hall in Toronto and said that her fiancé was working in Timmins as a painter and was only able to come down south on some weekends. Because the office was closed on the weekend, she asked the people there how I might be able to get the licence.

"They asked her to go and get an affadavit saying I was who I claimed to be, and that I was the man she wanted to marry. They told her to find a lawyer, get the affidavit, and come back for the licence. Then we went together to see a lawyer. An old guy on Spadina Avenue. I told him I was George Fehn, gave him five bucks and got the paper. He couldn't have cared less who I was. He didn't check — just took my word for it. Then my fiancée went down with her father and picked up our licence. Her father was born in Germany and he had come to Canada in 1928. He knew what his daughter was doing.

"Now, we had to find a minister.

"We finally turned up an old Presbyterian cleric who must have been around seventy-five at the time. We selected him because we thought he wouldn't ask any questions, and he didn't. He was a real fuddy-duddy. The marrying was done in his house. My wife's brother was the best man, and her friend was bridesmaid. We had no one else there. The ceremony started. My wife's friend could play the piano and there was an old piano, so she played 'Here Comes the Bride' or something.

"My second name is Dietrich. The poor old guy could never spell it. He kept calling me District. George District Fehn. Finally he opened the Bible and the ring was placed on it. Then he tried to get my name straight and dropped the ring. There we are: all four of us on our hands and knees looking for it. He actually dropped it twice and each time we had to do another search for it. The trouble was, I thought he was doing this on purpose. I thought the RCMP were just waiting outside ready to grab me. All in my imagination, of course.

"At last he finished. I gave him twenty dollars in an envelope and told him: 'Fellow, you did a great job. Goodbye.' Then we got out of there. The date was November 12, 1946. A week later a friend of mine, Heinz Behrendt, did the same thing. A different lawyer and another clergyman were involved this time."

While Fehn and Behrendt got married in Canada to girls who were here, there were several other marriages before the war ended. But most of those new wives never left Germany. In the November 1944 issue of *Canadian Business*, a story on the POWs mentioned that fifteen hundred had married by proxy up to that date. By the time the war was over and the last prisoner left Canadian soil, many more had married in this way.

Two weeks after his marriage, Fehn and all the other POWs at Cooksville were ordered to report back to the camp at Monteith. Everyone was to go back to Germany. Until he was at Monteith a few days, Fehn thought he had a fairly good chance of remaining in Canada, as he had hoped to do for some time.

"I thought that because I was married, they might let me stay here. The marriage was all perfectly legal and they couldn't do anything about it. As well, they said that four hundred guys would be staying behind to clean up the camp and to dismantle a lot of it. A list of the names would be posted.

"When it went up I ran to check to see if my name was on the list. It wasn't. So I went to the commandant. First off he said, 'Who the hell are you?' I said, 'Wait a minute. Let me explain.' So I told him I was married and he just about flipped. 'Jumping Jesus Christ. Goddamned bastard. Christ!' He went on and on.

"Finally he caught his breath and said, 'Keep your goddamned mouth shut and don't ever tell anyone about this. Tomorrow you will be on the list.' I said, 'Thank you. That's all I want to know.' The next morning my name was on the bottom of the list. Then Heinz did the same thing. This time the CO almost had a heart attack. All he could blurt out was: 'I hope there aren't any more.' The next day, Heinz was on the list also," says Fehn.

"The returning veterans got wind of the fact that four hundred of us were supposed to stay behind in Canada to dismantle the camp. They needed jobs, so they protested in Ottawa and their protest was a success. Plans were then reversed and we were sent back to Germany. They ordered a special train for us right to Halifax.

"As soon as I got to Germany, I started to do everything I could to get back to Canada. My wife was still here, of course, and she was pregnant when I left. Finally, on January 29, 1950, I got back to Canada. My son was four years old by this time, but it was the first time I had seen him. I tell you, I was sure glad to be back."

At last it was over. The prisoners were going home.

From barbed-wire compounds, from farms, logging camps and road construction projects they came, some reluctantly.

Many POWs wanted to stay in Canada, but under the terms of the Geneva Convention, and because returning Canadian servicemen needed jobs, they were unable to. Some were not interested in remaining here. These could hardly wait for the train to Halifax. Those who wanted to stay, however, were the subject of a great deal of controversy in Canada. Farmers, logging companies, factory owners and others urged the government to let certain POWs remain in this country. Letters to the editor, newspaper editorials, radio commentators all reflected the view that not *all* prisoners should be sent back to Germany. Those who had "proven themselves" in farms and factories were often mentioned as desirable potential citizens. An editorial in *Saturday Night* magazine on November 30, 1946, is typical of the media of the time.

There is a growing demand that German prisoners of war in
Canada, who have been employed in manual labour in this country
for the last three or four years and are now being shipped back to
Germany, should be given an opportunity to remain in this country
as free men, on probation but with an ultimate prospect of

citizenship, if they elect to do so and if their record is suggestive of good character. The opposition to this demand is extremely vocal, and is based on one or the other of two completely contradictory assumptions. One, that of a resolution passed by the Canadian Legion in convention after a somewhat hasty debate, is that the privilege of admission to freedom in Canada is one which is much too good to be accorded to any man who has ever fought, or served on a ship, for Germany. The other is that the retention of these men in Canada would constitute "slave labour" and would be inhumane and discreditable to Canada.

There is not the slightest basis for either of these assumptions. There is nothing in the fact that a German national fought against Canada and her allies in the last war, which proves of itself that he is unfit for residence, and even for ultimate citizenship, in Canada. If he was an active Nazi, that is another matter; but by the time a POW has been in Canada three years it is easier to tell whether he is an active Nazi or not than if he had been in Germany for the same period and the occupation authorities had just run into him. Even the fact that he doesn't want to go back to Germany is pretty good evidence that he doesn't expect Germany to conquer the world again during his lifetime.

As for "slave labour," there is no proposal that these Germans should remain in Canada in their past capacity of prisoners of war. If they have any grievance about the way they have been treated from the time of their arrival here (or perhaps from the time of the German surrender) up to the present time, which we doubt, that would seem to be an argument in favor of giving them the option of remaining in Canada as free men if they wish to do so; the privilege could act as a sort of compensation for any injustice they might be supposed to have suffered. The terms on which they would be allowed to remain would be closely comparable to those granted to the Anders Poles, which are certainly not slavery or anything approaching it, and are not on the other hand a privilege in payment for past services, since nobody suggests that mere membership in the Anders army should give a right to such privilege. In both cases men would be allowed to "enter" Canada, in one case from the technical foreign land of a POW camp and in the other from the actual foreign land of Italy, and to remain in Canada for two years on condition of engaging in certain restricted occupations at the going rate of wages, after which they would be free agents and capable of acquiring citizenship.

The country is in urgent need of labour of exactly this kind, men who will engage in hard physical tasks which the great majority of Canadians decline to do — and have always declined to do whenever they could get immigrants to do them instead. The Germans, or at least a fair number of the best of them, are actually here in Canada and can be turned into immigrants by the signing of an order-in-council, without a single ship bottom being needed to transport them. They want to stay here (nobody proposes to keep anybody who doesn't want to stay), they will be happier here, and they will be vastly more useful here than in Germany. But to Germany they are being compelled to go.

Being a prisoner of war affected different people in different ways. In general, however, the treatment Canadians received in Germany was less humane than the experience of Germans in this country.

In the *Saturday Night* of May 12, 1945, a Canadian by the name of Charles Badbury described what life had been like for him during five years as a POW in Germany. He pointed out that while living conditions and treatment were never good, he felt that his jailers behaved "correctly." He stated that for him at least, conditions "improved steadily from 1942."

He was less enthusiastic about the food in camp.

> The meat, sugar and jam rations could each be comfortably contained in a matchbox. German rations support life but no more; to run brings a blackout; no one has the mental energy to concentrate on study or organized activities.
>
> To be placed on German rations was the worst punishment a prisoner could receive — but . . . thanks to the magnificent food parcels of the Red Cross, Canadian prisoners were independent of the German ration except for bread and potatoes.

Badbury went on to describe what the fact of incarceration had done to him mentally.

> Five years in a barbed-wire cinder-patch must have some effect, but I believe sincerely [that] . . . depression, consciousness of the barbed wire and the loss of freedom, a period of disillusionment and frustration [are] usually short. Morale recovers, men come to terms with the present and set about recreating their world in miniature within the camp. The long period of boredom, when a man's main problem is his own entertainment, and the tantalizing uncertainty of

the length of his sentence plays havoc with attempts at intelligent planning. The chief difficulty here is to prevent one's occupations losing significance.

Captivity is by no means an unusual condition of humanity. Every man is a prisoner behind wire of his own weaving — his job, his family, his ambitions, greed, incompetence or vanity. Imprisonment by barbed wire is impersonal. It gave us detachment. Because we were in a physical prison we found ourselves mentally free.

Other Canadians had other experiences. Mike Niewolski of Scarborough, Ontario, spent three years and three days in six POW camps in Germany. "He remembers nothing good about those times," said an article in the Toronto *Star* on August 15, 1977, "except the friends one made and lost, usually to starvation or on one of the forced marches the Germans made as the Russians advanced."

Ted Musgrove, also of Scarborough, was captured at Dieppe and spent two years and eleven months in German POW camps. As a reprisal for the shackling of Germans in Canada, Musgrove and his fellow prisoners had their hands in chains for fourteen months. They soon became adept at lock-picking, however, but if caught had to stand for hours with their toes and noses just touching the fence around the compound. If they moved, they were slugged in the back with a rifle butt.

Former German POW Ed Billet was asked what his incarceration in Canada had done to him.

"I was a prisoner of war for five and a half years, " he recalls. "My years in captivity affected me in certain ways. When I was first free, I had real reservations about meeting people in public. I don't know whether you would call it shyness or not. I just didn't seem to fit in. It took me a while to get over this.

"I could not complain about the guards I had. After the war, I came back to Canada to live and I went to see some of them. We became friends and talked of old times when we were together on different sides.

"Before we came here, most POWs thought Canada was all bush, Indians and so on. We didn't know much about the country. It was never covered in school in geography — it was part of America. We knew Canadians were good fighters and good pilots, but we did not know much else about them.

"We were delighted with the beautiful surroundings of the Gravenhurst camp. It was in an ideal location. We had every reason to be happy there. Later, when I escaped in the bush, I discovered the real beauty of Canada. This country is at its best to anybody who is willing to open his eyes to the unlimited opportunity it still offers. This was why I came here to live. Canada is now my country and I love it here."

Many other former POWs feel the same way. They returned to Canada for the freedom and for the opportunity to be found in this land. And though a few harbour occasional nostalgic feelings for Germany, they prefer to remain here. "I love to go back to Germany to visit every couple of years," a former prisoner told me, "but I could never live there now. I came to Canada in 1952, and I guess I have been spoiled by all the space in this country. Germany is so cramped and everyone is so intent on making money; they can't spare a minute to relax. That is not for me."

But there are many for whom family, job and other commitments mean they won't leave Germany. Peter Krug is one of them.

Today the former Luftwaffe escape artist is a prosperous businessman living in Letmathe, West Germany. He travels extensively on the Continent, drives expensive cars, flies his own plane and relaxes beside his swimming pool or at any of a number of ski resorts in the Alps. At the end of a day-long interview at Krug's home during the research for this book, I mentioned that I was returning to Canada in a day or so, and would be landing at Toronto, an hour's drive from Bowmanville, where Krug had done so much time. The German then extended his hand to say goodbye. There were tears in his eyes as he said softly, "I wish I was going with you. Someday I want to come to Canada again."

Colonel K. H. Boettger is another former POW who feels the same way. Boettger, who is again a member of the West German military, harbours many pleasant memories of his years of incarceration. "I was a prisoner from July 1942 until the end of 1946. We were treated excellently at all times. I have been fortunate enough to return to Canada several times in order to see old friends and renew acquaintances."

On one of these visits, Boettger spent time at my home. "You know," he said after a couple of bottles of Canadian beer, "you Canadians are a wonderful people. I love your country."

Tony Kleimaker and Siegfried Bruse, former Luftwaffe and U-boat officers, now operate a large and successful real estate firm in North Bay, Ontario. Both came to Canada for the opportunity this country held out to them.

"I like Canadians," Bruse says. "They made my life as pleasant as possible from the day I came here as a prisoner. Later, when I returned as a landed immigrant, I knew this was my country.

"One day after I returned to Canada in 1952, I walked into a Canadian Tire store in North Bay. The clerk who waited on me said, 'I know you.' I told him that was impossible, as I had just come to Canada. 'I don't care, I know you,' the man repeated. When I insisted that he couldn't know me, he asked what country I came from. As soon as I said Germany, he grabbed my hand and said, 'Welcome to Canada. I was one of your guards when you were a prisoner at Bowmanville.' Then I recognized the man and we grabbed each other. It was such an emotional moment. Gradually we became close friends. A few years later I was at his funeral. I miss that man a lot.

"I came back to Canada for the large, empty spaces. There was also the feeling that you could create something here, that you could achieve what you wished in this land."

Kleimaker feels the same way. "I and a lot of others wanted to stay in Canada when the war was over. We had grown so attached to this country that we had no wish to leave it. I had been working on a farm, along with several others I knew. The farmers were glad of the help and they really tried to convince the authorities to allow us to stay. It was no use, however; we were all sent back. But as soon as I could, I applied to return here."

Horst Braun, the U-boat wireless operator who first saw Canada through the periscope of a sub, echoes Kleimaker's sentiments.

"We were treated so well here," he says now. "Even the train trip to camp was pleasant. The food was good, and the train was actually heated! The whole thing was so utopian after what we had been through. At that time I could not speak English, so I started to learn English as quickly as I could. I did nothing else for nine months, seven days a week, eight hours a day. I really worked, but of course we had time on our hands. I talked to everyone I could who spoke English. The guards were particularly helpful. They taught me all the swear words first, then the local slang, then the right way to say things. The work paid off because right after the war I was hired and made my living working as an interpreter for the occupation forces back home in Germany. So the time was not wasted. I owe that to Canada.

"In camp everything was supplied by the Canadians. They were so good to us. I was busy learning languages and trying to prepare myself for life after the war. Then when I was sent to a bush camp, I appreciated Canada all the more. We wrote letters home, of course, and I received letters. But when the war was over and I was sent back to Germany with everyone else, I was terribly homesick *for Canada!* I couldn't wait to get back here.

"From September 1943 until April 1946 I worked for a timber company in Northern Ontario. There I met a clerk of the company, Moe Whalen, and he became a good friend. Later on, he sponsored my return to Canada after the war. He was one of the Canadians whom I met at the time who made me appreciate what a wonderful country this is."

George Fehn, the first prisoner to get married in Canada, had two very special reasons for wanting to return to Canada as soon as he could after the war. "As soon as I got back to Germany, I started to do everything I could to leave there," he says. "My wife was here and after a while I had a son.

"And I don't think life in the camps hurt me. I worked and studied. The barbed wire was the worst thing, but after a while I gave up pacing around the wire. Gradually more of us became resigned to the whole situation. At first we laughed at the POW uniform. But then we got used to it. After a couple of years the big circle was faded and bleached out. My POW years were great years. We didn't have to work if we didn't want to. We had a great life. The best of food. We missed women, but after a while you even get used to abstinence."

German Red Cross Corporal Leo Hoecker, captured in Normandy, harbours no bitterness about his POW existence in Canada. He remembers the bush camps and the guards there with a special fondness.

"Those veteran guards in the bush camps really treated us well," he says now. "Some of us were interested in hunting, so the veteran guards often used to loan us their rifles and off we'd go. Because we were trusted like that, we always came back. Really, though, there was no place to go anyway, but the trust was the thing that I remember. I loved the bush camps, and I told my wife that after the war. That was why I wanted to get back to Canada. Prison life was okay, I suppose, but the thing I disliked about being locked up was the lock."

Some of the incidents of camp life that former POWs remember were the seeds that later grew into the desire to return to Canada. "We were friendly with most of the guards," recalls Horst Liebeck, the Angler escape expert. "We used to tease our guards by making tiny signs saying such things as: 'By pushing such and such a board, tunnel 9 will collapse.' These signs were very tiny, written in German. We used to laugh at the guards' reactions when something like this was found. They would take the little message very unobtrusively during a hut search. I suppose it was then translated and a search would start — even though they sometimes tried to pretend it wasn't a search. We put up signs like that when there were no tunnels. It was just fun. The guards took it all in stride, because they were pretty good fellows. In Canada we were treated as soldiers and were expected to behave as soldiers. We never forgot that.

"Even after my escape from Angler, Charles Lindsey was very pleasant to me. He said: 'As a sportsman, I must congratulate you. However, as camp commandant, I have to give you twenty-eight days.' Then we shook hands. There were no hard feelings."

And now, four decades after the global bloodletting of the Second World War, thousands of men who came to Canada as prisoners of war still recall their time spent here. While many of them live in Canada, many more have returned to visit. One such group made a nostalgic tour of several eastern and western camp sites in the fall of 1980. The trip was a success, and it was at Gravenhurst, Ontario, that they found a fitting souvenir of those years.

Amid the debris and the weeds where Camp 20 once stood, they located a chunk of rusty barbed wire. They took the wire with them, as a symbol of all their bittersweet memories of another age.

Appendix

Camps in Which Prisoners of War and Internees
Were Held During the Second World War

Camp L	Cove Fields, Quebec
Camp H	Red Rock, Ontario
Camp T	Three Rivers, Quebec
Camp V	Valcartier, Quebec
Camp 10	Chatham, Ontario
Camp 20	Gravenhurst, Ontario
Camp 21	Espanola, Ontario
Camp 22	Mimico (New Toronto), Ontario
Camp 23	Monteith, Ontario
Camp 30	Bowmanville, Ontario
Camp 31	Kingston (Fort Henry), Ontario
Camp 32	Hull, Quebec
Camp 33	Petawawa, Ontario
Camp 40	Farnham, Quebec
Camp 41	Île aux Noix, Quebec
Camp 42	Sherbrooke (Newington), Quebec
Camp 43	Montreal (Île Ste-Hélène), Quebec
Camp 44	Grande Ligne, Quebec
Camp 45	Sorel, Quebec
Camp 70	Fredericton, New Brunswick
Camp 100	Neys, Ontario
Camp 101	Angler, Ontario
Camp 130	Kanaskis, Alberta; later Seebe, Alberta
Camp 132	Medicine Hat, Alberta
Camp 133	Ozada, Alberta; later Lethbridge, Alberta
Camp 135	Wainwright, Alberta

This list is a facsimile of that in the files of the Director of Internment Operations, Public Archives of Canada. It is by no means a complete list of all the prisoner-of-war camps in Canada during the Second World War. In addition to these compounds, several other centres were used from time to time as bases for logging, farming and manufacturing operations.

Camps were designated by letter or number, or both. Often the camp name or camp number or camp letter — or even all three — were used by the Internment Service in official communications or by the media when specific camps were mentioned.

The size and type of compound varied, as did the class of prisoner. For example, Camp 10 at Chatham, Ontario, had a rated capacity of 325. The internees were housed in tents and worked in area farms. Camp 20 at Gravenhurst, Ontario, was a converted sanatorium, housing up to 400 officers and a few other ranks. Bowmanville was a school, Espanola a factory, Hull a jail, and Lethbridge several barracks. The camp at Lethbridge could hold 12,500 men, the huts at Angler 650, the fort at Kingston 600.

POW Daily Routine: Medicine Hat Camp

As of April 1, 1943	Weekdays	Sundays
Reveille	0603 hours	0700 hours
Breakfast	0700	0730
Work Parties	0830	
Commandant's Inspection	1000	
Dinner	1200	
Work Parties	1330	
Supper	1700	
Lights Out	2200	

Rations for Combatant POW

Beef, five ounces twice weekly
Mutton, six ounces once weekly
Fresh pork cuts, six ounces once weekly
Sweet pickled ham, six ounces once a month
Fish, five ounces of fresh, frozen or canned, once weekly
Eggs, one daily or one-half ounce of dry egg powder daily

Butter, one-half ounce daily
Cheese, one-quarter ounce daily
Milk, evaporated or whole, three and three-quarter ounces daily
Bread and biscuits, ten ounces daily
Flour, eight ounces once a week
Baking powder, one-half ounce a week
Fresh vegetables, eight ounces five times a week, or six ounces of
    canned vegetables, or one and one-half ounces of dehydrated
    vegetables five times a week
Split peas, two ounces once a week
Beans, two ounces once a week
Sugar, white or brown, three-quarter ounces daily
Boiled oats, or cracked wheat, one ounce daily
Macaroni or spaghetti, two ounces twice a week
Barley, one ounce once a week
Cornstarch, one-half ounce twice a week
Jam, one-half ounce daily
Canned pumpkin, three and one-half ounces a week, or half an ounce
    of dried apples once a week
Tomato juice, six ounces once a week
Canned tomatoes, six ounces twice a week
Prunes, two ounces once a week
Tea, three-sixteenths of an ounce daily
Coffee, one-quarter of an ounce daily
Salt, one-half ounce daily
Pepper, one-tenth ounce weekly
Vinegar, one ounce weekly

(Reprinted from *Behind Canadian Barbed Wire*, by David J. Carter.)

Notes

Chapter Two

1. George Creasy, preface to *The Golden Horseshoe*, by Terence Robertson, p. ix.
2. Eric Koch, *Deemed Suspect*, pp. 60-62.
3. Ibid., p. 56.
4. R. H. Roy, letter to the author, October 8, 1976.
5. Toronto *Globe and Mail*, July 5, 1943.
6. Kingston *Whig-Standard*, January 24, 1941.

Chapter Three

1. Eric Koch, *Deemed Suspect*, p. 119.
2. Ibid., p. 118.
3. Lita-Rose Betcherman, *The Swastika and the Maple Leaf*, p. 114.
4. *P.O.W. WOW*, November 24, 1945.
5. W. A. Higgins, "Prisoners of War, Canada's Unwelcome Guests," *Saturday Night*, September 21, 1940, p. 22.
6. Barry Broadfoot, *Six War Years 1939-1945*, p. 127.
7. Ibid., pp. 61-62

Chapter Four

1. Public Archives of Canada, Files of the Director of Internment Operations, 1939-1945. All subsequent references to Public Archives are to the same files.

2. Ibid.
3. W. A. B. Douglas and Brereton Greenhous, *Out of the Shadows*, p. 217.
4. Public Archives.
5. Jerome Davis, "In Canadian Prison Camps," *The Christian Century*, August 19, 1942, pp. 1002-1003.
6. Public Archives.
7. David J. Carter, *Behind Canadian Barbed Wire*, p. 184.
8. Eric Koch, *Deemed Suspect*, p. 157.
9. Public Archives.
10. Ibid.
11. *Time*, October 24, 1942.
12. Toronto *Star*, February 25, 1979.
13. Public Archives.
14. Public Archives.

Chapter Five

1. Kingston *Whig-Standard*, January 24, 1941.
2. Kendal Burt and James Leasor, *The One That Got Away*, p. 213.

Chapter Seven

1. Peter Desbarats, "They Tunnelled to Freedom in Wartime Canada," *Weekend Magazine* 5, 1964, p. 6.

Chapter Eight

1. The Toronto *Telegram*, April 23, 1941.
2. Public Archives.
3. Public Archives.
4. Public Archives.
5. Public Archives.
6. The Toronto *Telegram*, April 21, 1941.
7. John Hammond Moore, *The Faustball Tunnel*, p. 65.
8. Public Archives.
9. Public Archives.
10. Public Archives.
11. Public Archives.

12. Peter Desbarats, "They Tunnelled to Freedom in Wartime Canada," *Weekend Magazine* 6, 1964, p. 12.
13. Public Archives.

Chapter Nine

1. The *Catholic Register*, May 24, 1980.
2. Joyce Hibbert, ed., *The War Brides*, pp. 64-65.
3. Max Stephan, from a letter to U.S. President Franklin D. Roosevelt, copy given to the author by Peter Krug.

Chapter Ten

1. Information supplied by RCMP.
2. Ibid.
3. David J. Carter, *Behind Canadian Barbed Wire*, pp. 8-9.
4. Ibid., pp. 246-247.
5. Ibid., p. 251.
6. Information supplied by RCMP.
7. Ibid.
8. David J. Carter, *Behind Canadian Barbed Wire*, pp. 265-266.
9. Ibid., p. 269.

Chapter Eleven

1. David J. Carter, *Behind Canadian Barbed Wire*, p. 227.

Bibliography

Adachi, Ken, *The Enemy That Never Was*. Toronto: McClelland and Stewart, 1976.

Bailey, George, *Germans*. New York: Avon, 1972.

Betcherman, Lita-Rose, *The Swastika and the Maple Leaf: Fascist Movements in Canada in the Thirties*. Toronto: Fitzhenry and Whiteside, 1975.

Brickhill, Paul, *The Great Escape*. London: Faber, 1951.

Broadfoot, Barry, *Six War Years 1939-1945*. Toronto: Doubleday Canada Limited, 1974.

Broadfoot, Barry, *Years of Sorrow, Years of Shame*. Toronto: Doubleday Canada Limited, 1977.

Burt, Kendal, and James Leasor, *The One That Got Away*, London: Collins, 1956.

Carter, David J., *Behind Canadian Barbed Wire*. Calgary: Tumbleweed Press, 1980.

Douglas, W. A. B., and Brereton Greenhous, *Out of the Shadows*. Toronto: Oxford University Press, 1977.

Gansberg, Judith M., *Stalag: U.S.A.* New York: Thomas Y. Crowell, 1977.

Graham, Burton, *Escape from the Nazis*. Secaucus, N.J.: Castle Books, 1975.

Hibbert, Joyce, ed., *The War Brides*. Scarborough, Ont.: Signet, 1980.

Koch, Eric, *Deemed Suspect*. Toronto: Methuen, 1980.

Manchester, William, *The Arms of Krupp*. New York: Little, Brown, 1968.

Moore, John Hammond, *The Faustball Tunnel*. New York: Random House, 1978.

Nakano, Takeo Ujo, and Leatrice Nakano, *Within the Barbed Wire Fence*. Toronto: University of Toronto Press, 1980.

Robertson, Terence, *The Golden Horseshoe*. London: Evans Brothers, 1955.

Robertson, Terence, *The Shame and the Glory: Dieppe*. Toronto: McClelland and Stewart, 1962.

Shelley, Sidney, *Bowmanville Break*. New York: Delacorte Press, 1968.

Stacey, C.P., *Six Years of War*, vol. 1. Ottawa: Queen's Printer, 1966.

Stalmann, Reinhart, *Die Ausbrecherkönige von Kanada*. Hamburg: Verlag de Sternbücher, 1958.

Von der Porten, Edward P., *The German Navy in World War II*. New York: Thomas Y. Crowell, 1969.